Literature and National Identity

Literature and National Identity

Nineteenth-Century
Russian Critical Essays

Translated and edited by
PAUL DEBRECZENY and JESSE ZELDIN
Introduction by
PAUL DEBRECZENY

UNIVERSITY OF NEBRASKA PRESS · LINCOLN

The quotations from Gogol's *Dead Souls*, translated by Helen Michailoff, copyright © 1964 by Washington Square Press, are reprinted by permission of the publisher. The quotations from Tolstoy's *War and Peace*, translated by Rosemary Edmonds, are reprinted by permission of Penguin Books Ltd.

Publishers on the Plains

UNP

International Standard Book Number 0–8032–0748–4

Library of Congress Catalog Card Number 77–109598

Manufactured in the United States of America

CONTENTS

INTRODUCTION

In his poem on the death of Napoleon (1821) Pushkin wrote that Napoleon had "revealed the lofty destiny of the Russian people." Indeed in Russia, as elsewhere in Europe, national self-awareness was growing considerably during and after the Napoleonic Wars—a period marked also by the growth of the romantic movement in philosophy and literature. For young Russians the search for a national self-image was made painful by the evident contrast between Russia's military might and social backwardness, sources of both pride and shame. A need for social and political change was recognized by many, but the crushing of the Decembrist uprising in 1825 put an end, at least for the time being, to all progressive strivings. This made the building of a national self-image even more difficult for writers and intellectuals.

Poets and critics affiliated with the Decembrist movement attempted to chart the destiny of the nation in their works. A. A. Bestuzhev-Marlinsky, for instance, published surveys of Russian literature in the *Polar Star* [Poliarnaia zvezda] in 1823, 1824, and 1825, placing the literary output of the day in the perspective of national history and contrasting it with general European developments in a manner that was to become characteristic of V. G. Belinsky's essays a decade later. Prior to 1825, however, the preoccupation with national destiny was not so widespread as it became later; most critics contented themselves with analyzing the literary works at hand rather than striving to expound their own historicophilosophical systems.

The change that occurred after 1825 was connected with an upsurge of interest in German idealist philosophy. Professors D. M. Vellansky, M. G. Pavlov, A. I. Galich, and I. I. Davydov had already lectured on Schelling, and the group known as the "Lovers of Wisdom" had already been formed before the uprising, but views of the nation's destiny on the broad scale of spiritual development came into focus only in the second half of the twenties. Avenues to practical social or political action had been closed, and those concerned with the fate of the nation had to find consolation in the idea that eventual progress was inevitable since it was part of the unfolding of the Spirit in human history. As Vladimir Solovev was to explain later, the idea that the nation had a purpose and a destiny implied that it was like a living organism capable of growth. Nationalism, historicism, and organicism—attributes of romantic philosophy—became integral components of Russian social and philosophical thought. Russian thinkers began to ask: how old was this living being, the Russian nation; what marks had its past imprinted on it; in what way did it differ from other nations? Since a direct expression of social or philosophical ideas was difficult because of the censorship, the search for national identity had to be carried out largely on the pages of literary works and, even more so, on the pages of literary criticism. Beginning with the second half of the twenties, the majority of the critics were more anxious to convey their own ideology to the reader than to analyze the artistic merits of the literary works reviewed. One of the first manifestations of this new state of affairs in literary criticism was Kireevsky's essay on Pushkin's poetry.

Ivan Vasilevich Kireevsky (1806–56), one of the founders of the Slavophile movement, was born in Moscow of a gentry family. His father died when he was six years old, and his mother remarried when he was eleven—two events that may have contributed to the sense of emotional insecurity which plagued Kireevsky all through his life. He received the usual education of people of his class, and in 1824 took a position as a clerk in the Moscow Archives of the Ministry of Foreign Affairs. Here he found himself in the company of young men of his own background who were interested in philosophy and literature and whom Pushkin was to call the "Young Men of the Archives." He also became one of the "Lovers of Wisdom." His ambition at this time was to devote himself to literature and philosophy, and in 1827 he enthusiastically participated in establishing a new journal, *The Moscow Messenger* [Moskovsky vestnik], which was to become a forum for the philosophically inclined young men of Moscow. It was in this journal that he published his essay "On the Nature of Pushkin's Poetry."

Kireevsky's literary career was interrupted by an affair of the heart: he fell in love with a distant cousin, Natalia Arbeneva, and proposed marriage to her, but was rejected. On the verge of a nervous breakdown, he sought distraction in travel and set out for Germany early in 1830. He attended university lectures, mainly on philosophy and theology, in Berlin and Munich, made the acquaintance of Schelling and Hegel, and was generally well received; yet his letters of the time are as full of passionate xenophobia as those of Dostoevsky were to be some years later.

After his return to Russia, Kireevsky established his own literary journal, *The European* [Evropeets], and published his essay "The Nineteenth Century" in its first issue (1832). This essay incurred the disapproval of the authorities and the journal was prohibited after the second issue. Like so many others in the annals of Russian history, Kireevsky, under the all-pervading political and intellectual pressure of the regime, became more and more conservative. Even as late as 1848 he was opposed to the emancipation of the serfs and cautioned his friends against a struggle for the abolition of censorship—an unusual stance for a Slavophile. At least partially under the influence of Natalia Arbeneva, whose hand he had finally won in 1834, he also underwent a religious conversion and became a devout Orthodox.

In his later years Kireevsky made several attempts to participate in public life, but without success. His Slavophile philosophy—which, together with A. S. Khomiakov's philosophical work, gave the initial impetus to the movement—was elaborated largely in the course of drawing-room debates; its most coherent expression in print is his essay "On the Nature of European Civilization and its Relationship to the Civilization of Russia," published in the *Moscow Miscellany* [Moskovsky sbornik] in 1852. He died one year after the death of Nicholas I—just as Slavophile periodicals came into being and new opportunities were opening up for him.

Kireevsky's essay on Pushkin's poetry (1828), as an early work, does not reflect the Slavophile image of Russia in full, but several thoughts expressed in it point in that direction. The idea of Pushkin's threefold development, that is, his arrival at a purely Russian phase after two phases of foreign influence, hints at the emergence of an independent Russian self-awareness. The assertion that Russia is not ripe for the appearance of Childe Harolds, since she has not yet reached the age of disillusionment, has its roots in Slavophile organicism. The rejection of Onegin and Aleko as heroes alien to the Russian spirit establishes a tradition to be followed by Apollon Grigorev and Nikolai Strakhov. The sympathetic acceptance of Tatiana is a point of view to be taken up by Dostoevsky in his Pushkin speech of 1880. In general, a remarkable fact about Kireevsky's essay is that it is one of the main sources of Dostoevsky's famous speech, although there is a notable difference between them. Kireevsky, defining the Russian character in connection with Pushkin's third phase, stresses magnanimity and impulsiveness, features which were no doubt integral parts of the national self-image and were to be incarnated in such fictional characters as Taras Bulba and Dmitry Karamazov. Dostoevsky, on the other hand, sees the third phase of Pushkin's development as an expression of Russian humility and universality— a feature Dostoevsky derived from Slavophilism. The absence of this latter feature from Kireevsky's definition is a sign that he had not yet reached the full Slavophile concept of Russianness at the time he wrote the essay.

The essay reveals Kireevsky's critical insight in several instances. He sees the old Finn's story as an ironic commentary on the central love intrigue in *Ruslan and Liudmila;* he emphasizes the structural importance of the atmosphere both in *Ruslan* and in *The Fountain at Bakhchisarai;* he points out obvious incongruities in *The Gypsies*, and so forth. But the basic thesis of the essay, the purpose for which he wrote it, has little in common with Pushkin's art. In order to illustrate Kireevsky's definition of the Russian character, one has to turn to later fictional heroes. His definition grew, not from his analysis of Pushkin, but from his own historical and philosophical searchings.

The search for national identity, of which Kireevsky's essay represents only the beginning, was conducted along several routes. Belinsky, who was not far from the incipient Slavophiles during the 1830s, eventually came to view Russian identity as an ideal of the future, to be reached by radical reforms. At the opposite end of the spectrum stood N. I. Grech, F. V. Bulgarin, O. I. Senkovsky, and other men of official nationality who, while offering little in the way of original ideas, insisted on a government-regulated patriotism in their critical reviews. A place between Slavophilism and official nationality was occupied by Shevyrev.

Stepan Petrovich Shevyrev (1806–64), also of the gentry, received his education at a preparatory school attached to Moscow University. Of the same age as Kireevsky, he moved in the same circles: he was also one of the "Young Men of the Archives," and he became literary editor of *The Moscow Messenger*. In 1829 he went abroad and stayed, mostly in Italy, for three years. He wrote a dissertation on Dante, and in 1834 was appointed lecturer at Moscow University. Several "firsts" at that university are to his credit: he was the first to give a course in the history of the Russian language, the first to occupy a chair of Russian literature (before his time there had been a chair only in general literature), and the first to publish, in four volumes between 1845 and 1860, a comprehensive history of Russian literature. He combined his academic work with prolific political and journalistic activity, publishing numerous reviews, mainly in *The Muscovite* [Moskvitianin], which he edited with his close friend M. P. Pogodin between 1841 and 1856. He found time for more travel—a close acquaintance with the West was what inspired a search for national identity in many cases—and through his marriage to Sofiia Zelenskaia, an adopted daughter of Prince B. V. Golitsyn, he became attached to the highest social circles in Moscow. Both his academic and journalistic activities were hampered by a pomposity and petty vanity which set him against his colleagues at the university and alienated several potential contributors to *The Muscovite*. His university career came to an abrupt end in 1857 when, during a scholarly meeting, he literally came to blows with a Count Bobrinsky who had made critical remarks about conditions in Russia. Dismissed from his professorial chair, he went abroad and died in Paris.

Shevyrev's review of *Dead Souls* (1842) was written at the height of his career, and it displays most of his strengths and weaknesses. His insistence (following Gogol's own words) that the novel is populated by swindlers and fools because they were chosen by Chichikov, a swindler himself, was a valid defense of Gogol's work against attacks in the press of official nationality. The idea that the tone of the novel shifts from gaiety to sadness both in the presentation of the characters and in style is as brilliant an observation on the structure of *Dead Souls* as has ever been made. On the other hand, Shevyrev's nationalistic concern makes him introduce some ideas which verge on the ludicrous. His description of Chichikov as an "acquirer" bent on acquiring worldly goods, with the suggestion that business enterprise inevitably involves dishonesty, betrays a Slavophile-inspired romantic anticapitalism. It is not at all clear from his discussion why Selifan, any more than Petrushka, is a true representative of the simple Russian people with its admirable qualities. And the idea that Gogol combines the qualities of Dante and Shakespeare, the plastic beauty of the South and the introspection of the North, is, to say the least, bold; it springs from a Russian adaptation of Schellingian historiosophy, demonstrated, for instance, in Kireevsky's "The Nineteenth Century," which presents Russian culture as the crowning achievement of the dialectical historical process of development.

The most interesting aspect of the essay is, however, Shevyrev's view of what direction Gogol's future development should take. He had grown close to Gogol in Rome just prior to the publication of the novel, and could rely not only on the evidence of the novel itself, but also on the privately expressed opinions of its author. Aware that Gogol intended to write two companion volumes to the novel in a positive vein, that is, glorifying rather than ridiculing Russian life, Shevyrev underplays the significance of Gogol's humor; he even suggests that it impedes the development of the writer's creative imagination. He does not condemn the picture of Russian life as seen in the first volume, but, in search of a glorified national image, encourages Gogol to move on to new horizons. To be sure, this was what Gogol most wanted to hear, but it was what he least needed to hear, for his talent lay in a humorous, sometimes grotesque, at all times complex and heterogeneous representation of life. Gogol could not produce the idealized image of Russia he longed for, and history proved Shevyrev's predictions wrong. The search for national identity, pervading most of the literary criticism of the time, was extremely harmful to Gogol: his talent might have been appreciated for what it was, and he might not have been urged in the wrong direction, without the influence of nationalistic and ideological concerns.

When Gogol published his *Selected Passages from Correspondence with Friends* (1847), a volume revealing his conservative and nationalistic inclinations, Belinsky received it with amazement and considered it as something of an anachronistic oddity. In fact, however, the social and psychological forces of nationalism, at play in the 1830s and early 1840s, had by no means run their course, and from the perspective of Dostoevsky's mature work—from the vantage point of the 1860s and 1870s—Gogol's volume was to seem no oddity at all. While Belinsky's followers—N. G. Chernyshevsky, N. A. Dobroliubov, D. I. Pisarev, and others—continued to approach literature from the point of view of social and political progress, insistence on Russian tradition and separateness was carried on by a new generation of Slavophile-oriented critics. One of the critics who reviewed Gogol's *Selected Passages* favorably was Grigorev.

Apollon Aleksandrovich Grigorev (1822–64) has been considered by many as one of the most brilliant, although at times erratic, Russian literary critics of the last century, second only to Belinsky. The son of a civil servant by a former serf, a woman of powerful character and intellect, he was brought up in Zamoskvoreche, a suburb of Moscow inhabited mostly by merchants which he described colorfully in his autobiographical work *My Literary and Moral Wanderings*. After graduating from Moscow University, he worked for a while at the university library, but in 1843 he abruptly left his parents' house and moved to St. Petersburg in order to attempt a literary career. Here he contributed critical reviews and poetry to several periodicals, having meanwhile a brief courtship with atheism and socialism. But, since literary work did not prove to be lucrative, Grigorev got deeper and deeper into debt, and finally his father had to rescue him from his creditors. Around this time he underwent a stormy conversion to nationalism and Orthodoxy; a contemporary describes how he threw himself on his knees, after a long night of drinking and singing Russian songs, and begged his friends to receive him into the fold of patriots.

Back in Moscow, he worked for several local newspapers until he found a more stable position with *The Muscovite* in 1850. In the hands of Pogodin and Shevyrev, the journal was losing popular support, and in an attempt to revitalize it, Pogodin invited several young men, among them A. N. Ostrovsky and A. F. Pisemsky, to participate in editing it. As a party to the "young editorship" of the journal, Grigorev came into his own as a critic. But even during these years—the early fifties which he described as the happiest period of his life—he was by no means free of trouble. Pogodin proved to be a tight-fisted editor, and Grigorev's financial affairs went from bad to worse. The young editors were in the habit of combining writing with pub-crawling and Grigorev became a confirmed alcoholic, a condition aggravated by his unhappy marriage to Lidiia Korsh.

After *The Muscovite* collapsed in 1856, Grigorev went from journal to journal, writing brilliant reviews but quarreling with every editor, not over pay—he was willing to work for very little so long as he could say what he wished—but usually over literary policy. Wherever he published, he applied a consistent method—what he called "organic criticism"—and expounded a consistent theory—that of *pochvennichestvo*, Grigorev's coinage derived from the Russian word for soil. At last, after 1861, he found a haven in Dostoevsky's journals, first in *Time* [Vremia] where he published his major essays on Tolstoy, and subsequently in *Epoch* [Epokha]. But by this time he was too far gone in alcoholism, had incurred tremendous debts, and was too irritable to coexist peacefully even with the sympathetic Dostoevsky, who shared his literary views. After abortive attempts at editing another journal and at becoming a teacher, he came back to *Epoch*, but in 1864 he was put in debtors' prison. Eventually a philanthropic lady paid his debts for him, but he died four days after his release.

By 1859, when he wrote his review of Turgenev's *A Nest of the Gentry*, Grigorev's literary views had been fully formed; indeed, it was in this same year that he published his methodological essay, "A Few Words on the Precepts and Terms of Organic Criticism," in no. 5 of *Russian Word* [Russkoe slovo]. Although he repeatedly insists on a difference between the Slavophiles and himself, his basic view of Russian society—that its westernized upper crust had split off from the soil-bound mass of the nation since the time of Peter I—derives from the historical writings of Khomiakov, Ivan Kireevsky, and Konstantin Aksakov. He concurs with Kireevsky's assertion that Pushkin, in some of his works, incarnated the spirit of the whole nation; but in the post-Pushkinian period he sees a constant struggle against the false glitter of morally deficient foreign ideals as well as against their corollary—an altogether negative naturalism, devoid of any ideals. Biased though Grigorev's argument may be and however meandering its course, the reader is rewarded by a lively presentation of all the literary currents of the middle of the century which influenced Turgenev.

Of these currents, Grigorev finds the heritage of M. Iu. Lermontov most harmful. His opinion of Pechorin recalls Shevyrev's review of *A Hero of Our Time* (*The Muscovite*, no. 2 [1841]). The older critic commented that Pechorin was a symptom of a western disease which some Russians only imagined they had and that the disillusionment and moral indifference of the hero were a mere shadow cast on Russia by the West, *un mirage de l'occident*. Shevyrev could easily dismiss Lermontov's hero on this basis. Grigorev, on the other hand, although he accepts Shevyrev's view of the hero's western origin, cannot dispose of him so easily; he is haunted by Pechorin's evil attraction and sees a powerful corrupting influence in him. The passages in Grigorev's essay discussing the difficulty of ridding Russia of this dangerous type are among the best he wrote, for here he ventures into social psychology and discovers what modern critics would call myths people live by. He comes to an understanding of the social role of literary images, of their powerful effect on the formation of patterns of behavior. What he calls "organic criticism" is just such an integrated approach to literature and society, although not without a touch of intuitive irrationalism.

Shevyrev did not reject Gogol's humor, although the writer's positive ideals were dearer to him. Grigorev, on the other hand, can accept only the positive ideals in Gogol—those expressed in *Selected Passages*—while viewing his humorous writings as a largely negative influence on Russian letters. The difference between the two critics' respective attitudes to Gogol springs from different perspectives in time: in 1842 Shevyrev could not yet see what new trends Gogol would give rise to, while the younger critic, from the vantage point of the 1850s, regards Gogol as the initiator, albeit unwitting, of the new school of naturalism. In Grigorev's opinion, this so-called *naturalnaia shkola* and the later heirs of its tradition emerged out of a necessity to measure the false attraction of alien ideals against bare reality. Naturalism, just like the false ideals it sought to debunk, fell outside the mainstream of Russian national life and only hindered Turgenev in his search for a positive Russian hero.

Although Grigorev, like the other two critics so far discussed, is striving to convey his own cherished theories, his argument is not unrelated to the objective fact of Turgenev's work. For instance, the incongruity Grigorev observes between the love plot and the hero's pathetic end in *Rudin* is a structural flaw several critics pointed out, both at the time of the novel's publication and later. Further, noting that Turgenev was unable to fill the large canvas of *A Nest of the Gentry* with characters, Grigorev perceives the genuine difficulties Turgenev encountered in creating the novel form—difficulties the writer was to overcome only in his *Fathers and Sons*. Also perceptive are Grigorev's observations that Turgenev had an ambivalent attitude to Rudin and that he cast about for features of various types in order to mold the character of Lavretsky (hence the "incompleteness"). Grigorev was searching for a positive hero, and so was Turgenev; only Grigorev did not guess correctly in which direction Turgenev's search was to continue. Neither Insarov nor Bazarov were to be meek types, reconciled to the Russian "soil"; and had he lived to read *Smoke*, Grigorev would have been scandalized.

Nikolai Nikolaevich Strakhov (1828–96) followed closely in the steps of Grigorev. He lost his father, a priest and a teacher at a theological seminary, at an early age, and was brought up by an uncle, the rector of another seminary. Although he guarded his family's religious tradition all through his life, Strakhov did not pursue a priestly career: he studied mathematics and natural sciences at the University of St. Petersburg and subsequently at a teachers' training college. Having graduated from the training college in 1851, he became a high school science teacher. In 1857 he completed a master's thesis in zoology which was found acceptable by the thesis committee at the University of St. Petersburg yet failed to earn him the degree because, shy and reticent as he was, he was unable to defend it at the required public debate. Barred from a university career by this failure, he continued teaching at a St. Petersburg high school until 1861, when Apollon Grigorev, whom he had befriended several years before, persuaded him to join the staff of *Time*. Working in close association with Grigorev and the Dostoevsky brothers, he became a publicist and a literary critic. One of his best efforts during this period was a review of Turgenev's *Fathers and Sons* (*Time*, no. 4 [1862]).

Strakhov's scientific training left its mark on his critical and journalistic work: his approach was always objective, calm, and logical, with an appreciation of his opponents' views. This approach inadvertently caused harm to *Time* in 1863, when he published an article on the Polish uprising. Strakhov's attitude to the Polish question was nationalistic enough, but in the first half of his article he outlined the Polish point of view in order to be able to refute it in full in the second half; since only the first half appeared in print as the first installment, the authorities mistook Strakhov's intentions and prohibited the journal.

Strakhov was once more associated with Grigorev and Dostoevsky on the staff of *Epoch*. After this journal was discontinued in 1865, he supported himself by translating, among others, Kuno Fischer, Hippolyte Taine, and Claude Bernard. He also tried his hand at editing literary journals, among them *The Dawn* [Zaria] in which his review of *War and Peace* was published for the first time. All of his editorial ventures met with failure for one reason or another. Finally, in 1873 he took a job with the St. Petersburg Public Library and held it for the next ten years. A retiring, quiet person, he never married and lived almost a monastic life in his modest apartment overcrowded with books. The last ten years of his life were the happiest, for his reputation grew among the younger generation and he was able to collect and republish the more important of his critical and journalistic work.

Strakhov's review of *War and Peace* (1869–70) is a conscious effort to continue Grigorev's critical work. Quoting Grigorev extensively, he devotes a great deal of attention to the harmful appeal of Pechorin's type and to the destruction of this type in the works of naturalism. He begins, seemingly, where Grigorev left off; but in fact his view of Russian naturalism—by this time defined as realism—differs slightly from the view held by the older critic. Grigorev was fascinated by what he regarded as the Lermontovian and Gogolian trends in Russian literature and spent most of his time analyzing them, but his argument implied that the new Russian hero would emerge when these trends would at last be overcome. Strakhov, on the other hand, sees the emergence of the national hero as a logical outcome of the naturalistic trend. The difference, once more, is due to different chronological perspectives. In 1859 and 1862, when Grigorev wrote about Turgenev and Tolstoy respectively, a full-blooded incarnation of the national ideal was still only a dream. For its fulfilment, he looked wistfully to Turgenev, Ostrovsky, Tolstoy, and—rather absurdly—even to I. A. Goncharov. But in the years immediately following Grigorev's death, the epic of Russian life—*War and Peace*—was born, and it altered the whole process of literary development which had led up to it. Strakhov could now perceive that Kutuzov had to appear as a counterpart to Napoleon, that is, the positive national ideal had to emerge as a result of a minute, negative, naturalistic dissection of the alien ideal. What is more, naturalistic analysis in Strakhov's view not only served to create the alien counterpart against which the Russian character stood out in bold relief, but was the very medium through which the Russian character itself came to light. Tolstoy applied the Gogolian method of exposing the banality of man, but with such thoroughness that it revealed the heroism as well.

Strakhov's review of *War and Peace* is the culmination of nineteenth-century Russian critical efforts at outlining national identity. It is fitting that the search for a Russian self-image should end with a novel about the Napoleonic Wars—the very period that engendered the search. Strakhov as a critic had an easy task to perform. His predecessors had had to voice their ideas vaguely tangentially to, or even despite, the literary works reviewed; he had the good fortune to have a novel in front of him which contained his ideas. What he emphasizes in *War and Peace*—the sanctity of the Russian family cherished by the Slavophiles, the subjugation of passions by moral principles dear to Orthodoxy, life's superiority to reason expressed in *Notes from Underground* as well as in Slavophile philosophical essays, the victory of Russian humility and simplicity over foreign "cleverness" and false heroism, and so forth—is all there in the novel; he does not have to invent it. In fact, Tolstoy, his protestations to the contrary notwithstanding, had acquired the same ideas as Strakhov;

what had originally appeared as a trend of criticism only, had now penetrated fiction.

The fifth essay included in the present volume is also an example of almost complete agreement between writer and critic. Its author, Vladimir Sergeevich Solovev (1853–1900), is more famous for his philosophical writing than for his literary criticism, and he belongs in the present volume only for the first half of his career, since in the second half he shed the nationalistic colors of his thinking. Son of the noted Russian historian Sergei Solovev, he was brought up in Moscow, where his father was teaching. From early youth he displayed mystical inclinations: at age nine he saw a vision of a beautiful lady in the chapel of Moscow University. In his teens he became a passionate enemy of God, but in 1872 he had an erotic adventure— with him usually a prelude to spiritual experiences—saw another vision, and was converted back to Orthodoxy. He had at first studied natural sciences at Moscow University, but after his conversion switched to literature and philosophy. After graduating in 1873, he spent a year attending lectures at the Moscow Theological Seminary, and in 1874 defended his master's thesis on "The Crisis of Western Philosophy." He was given a lectureship in philosophy at Moscow University, but he did not lecture very long before he decided to go to London to do research in the library of the British Museum. Here the beautiful lady, whom he also called his Eternal Companion, appeared to him again with the command that he should travel to Egypt for another meeting in the desert. After eventually returning to Moscow, he resumed lecturing at Moscow University in 1876, but resigned from his post the same year because of political tensions at the university. For the next few years he had an informal association with the University of St. Petersburg and also held a part-time government position. In 1880 he defended his doctoral dissertation "A Critique of Abstract Principles."

During the seventies Solovev was strongly under the influence of Slavophilism. This influence is apparent in his *Lectures on Godman-hood* (1878), which is also famous as the first formulation of the doctrine of Sophia as the divine wisdom—a doctrine he derived from his mystical experiences. The Slavophile influence is even more apparent in his lecture "Three Forces" (1877), in which he establishes

—after the fashion of Khomiakov's Cushite versus Iranian principles —two spiritual forces currently at play in the world. The first of these is the Moslem East which glorifies an inhuman god, while the second is Western civilization based on the aggrandizement of godless man. The future of mankind, Solovev claims, will bring a synthesis of these two forces which will create a humanized god. In the process of this synthesis, a third force—Orthodoxy deposited primarily in the Russian people—will emerge on a world-wide scale.

In 1881, after the assassination of Alexander II, Solovev urged the new emperor, both in a public lecture and in a private letter, to show his Christian forgiveness to the assassins. This brought him into conflict with the authorities; he resigned his government post and was barred from public appearances, except for a few more lectures. He worked for several Slavophile periodicals in 1883, but soon left them, disillusioned with Slavophilism. For the next seventeen years he disappeared from public life, to reappear again only in the year of his death. Immersed in writing his major philosophical works, he was oblivious to the material conditions of his life; he traveled abroad, lived sometimes in Moscow, sometimes in St. Petersburg, and sometimes on the country estates of his friends. His theological teaching turned more and more toward ecumenicism, and he accused the Slavophiles of glorifying the very faults of the Russian people which separate it from the rest of mankind. In his last years he became a pessimist, no longer believing in the kingdom of God on Earth but expecting the coming of the Antichrist. His contributions to literary criticism after 1883 were some perceptive essays on the poetry of Pushkin, F. I. Tiutchev, A. K. Tolstoy, A. N. Maikov, A. A. Fet, and Ia. P. Polonsky.

Solovev's first Dostoevsky discourse (1881) was written just at the time he was beginning to re-examine his views on nationalism, and it shows the tension between his old beliefs and new ideas. Much like Strakhov and Tolstoy, Solovev is basically in accord with Dostoevsky, or at least with the ideas Dostoevsky drew on. In Dostoevsky another Russian writer had emerged capable of incarnating a Slavophile-inspired national self-image in his fiction, and the critic's role was simply to formulate the ideas inherent in the works examined. Dostoevsky, who had been a personal friend of Solovev, would no doubt have approved of the critic's account of his career: his early attraction to social reforms, his encounter with the faith of the simple people in Siberia, his attempt to present an extreme example of nihilism in Raskolnikov, his prophesies about the revolutionary movement in *The Devils*, and so forth. Further, Solovev's view of critical realism as a trend preparing the ground for the art of the future is similar to Strakhov's view of naturalism; and his claim that the West had degraded art to an agent of pleasure—a claim to be made by Tolstoy even more eloquently in his *What Is Art?*—is Slavophile inspired. Finally, the contrast he shows between Russian religious "socialism" and the materialistic socialism of the West corresponds closely to Dostoevsky's own ideas.

A slight departure from Dostoevsky's thought is the attempt to divorce Russian Orthodoxy from nationality. Dostoevsky's faith, Solovev argues, is correct not because it happens to be the faith of the Russian people, but because of its absolute truth. Guidance for the future should be sought in the church rather than in the nation. This slight shift in emphasis—only slight since Dostoevsky himself had also emphasized the church—is a sign of the new direction Solovev's thought is taking. Yet he fails to assert (as he will later) that by church he means a universal, reunited Christian Church, and without such an assertion he can only be interpreted as referring to the Russian Orthodox Church. If such is the case—if it is the Russian Orthodox Church that will guide the whole of mankind to truth—then Solovev has not abandoned Dostoevsky's Russian messianism.

The essays by Strakhov and Solovev complete a cycle. As a result of an abstract inquiry by a few thinkers, a particular Russian self-image emerged. Its presence, eventually both in criticism and major fiction, suggests that it was part of the public consciousness, at least in certain segments of the Russian population. The search for this self-image had begun as a reaction to a political situation in which the greatness and power of Russia sharply contrasted with its social backwardness. This basic contradiction also showed in the self-image that eventually emerged. Kireevsky's emphasis on the broadness and impulsiveness of the Russian character, for instance, had its negative aspect: not only did it imply the admirable quality of a capacity for powerful emotions, but it also served as justification for the absence of certain other qualities. Among these were industry, perseverance, and moderation in the conduct of everyday affairs—all the "German" qualities Goncharov was to incarnate in the character of Stolz. The absence of these qualities from the Russian self-image made Nicholas Berdiaev write in his Dostoevsky study—a century after Kireevsky's first formulation—that Russia was incapable of middle-class culture; she could only produce saints or criminals. Other nations deserved respect for achievements earned through hard labor; Russians deserved it for their broad nature. This theory was obviously a face-saving device invented under circumstances unfavorable to social and economic progress.

Another aspect of the Russian self-image as seen in the present volume is simplicity, humility, meekness. The same contradiction is inherent in this aspect. According to both Pogodin and the Slavophile historians, Russia was the only European state established by invitation to a ruler rather than by conquest. Ever since Prince Riurik's time the Russian nation lived by a Christian social ideal and did not interfere with the politics of its rulers, did not demand rights for the individual, did not seek formalized legal institutions. The Decembrists, the members of the Petrashevsky circle who marched to Siberia with Dostoevsky, and other individual rebels had acted against their Russian nature, and were justly brought back in line by their rulers. They had not realized that they would have been greater in humility than in political rebellion. This theory, once more, was a glorification of defeat, an attempt at self-respect under circumstances which would otherwise have induced despair. It was the theory which created a national hero out of a Prince Myshkin.

But the most striking contradiction is between Russian humility and the historical mission of the Russian people. All signs, as read by the Slavophiles and their followers, indicated that the young organism of Russia was destined for world leadership. This leadership was to be a leadership in humility. In the Napoleonic War, as depicted by Tolstoy and interpreted by Strakhov, humble simplicity won over foreign sophistication and pretentiousness. The Russian ideal of Christian love, according to Dostoevsky's messianism, was to establish the brotherhood of man on Earth. Yet the universal love that was to emerge was to be of a Russian kind, and a material force

—Russia's military might—was barely concealed below the surface of this striving for universality. It was not by accident that Dostoevsky, at the same time that he was urging his fellow men to humble themselves, was advocating the taking of Constantinople by force. This contradiction, inherent in the particular kind of Russian consciousness we are dealing with, was what made both Tolstoy and Solovev turn away from patriotism in the 1880s.

Only one of the five critics represented in this volume belonged to the Slavophile movement proper, yet the national self-image that emerges on these pages is, on the whole, Slavophile inspired. The Slavophile view of Russia was, of course, only one particular view, which existed alongside other views. We have mentioned the other powerful trend in nineteenth-century Russian intellectual history—the political radicalism that originated with Belinsky—and it is obvious that this trend came to entirely different conclusions about the nature of Russia. Slavophilism itself did not exist in its original form for long: from the 1860s on it grew into chauvinism and Pan-Slavism at one extreme, and contributed to the ideology of populism at the other. Yet the national self-image that emerged from its original theory had such a wide appeal that few writers or critics escaped its effect. It is for this reason that the present volume is offered as a study in the intellectual background of nineteenth-century Russian literature.

PAUL DEBRECZENY

TRANSLATORS' NOTE

For transliterating Russian names and words the Library of Congress system has been used, with three simplifications: diacritical marks have been omitted, soft and hard signs have not been indicated, and the *-yi* and *-ii* adjectival endings have been replaced by *-y*.

All notes not designated "Author's note" have been supplied by the translators. Russian titles occurring in the authors' notes have been translated in order to provide a complete rendering of the original in English; those occurring in the translators' notes, on the other hand, have been transliterated for the sake of exact reference.

Literature and National Identity

Ivan Kireevsky

ON THE NATURE OF PUSHKIN'S POETRY

"Nechto o kharaktere poezii Pushkina," originally published in Moskovsky vestnik 8 (1828): 6, under the pseudonym "9.11." The full text of the original is given in translation.

Accounting for the pleasure works of art give us is both an indispensable requirement of, and one of the highest gratifications for, the educated mind: why then has so little been said about Pushkin? Why have his best works been left unexamined,[1] and why do we hear, instead of analysis and judgment, only fatuous exclamations: "Pushkin is a poet! Pushkin is a real poet! *Onegin* is a superb poem! *The Gypsies* is a masterly work," and so forth? Why has no one so far ventured to define the over-all nature of his poetry, to appraise its merits and faults, and to determine what rank our poet has succeeded in acquiring among the leading poets of his time? Such silence is all the more incomprehensible since the last thing our public can be reproached for is indifference. But, some may say, who has the authority to speak about Pushkin?

In a country where an enlightened public has found authentic spokesmen in literary matters, a few legislators of public opinion have the power to pronounce final judgment on any novel phenomenon in the world of letters. But in our country, no one's voice is superfluous; any man's opinion, if conscientiously formed and based

[1] All that has so far been said in *Son of the Fatherland, Ladies' Journal, Messenger of Europe*, and *Moscow Telegraph* about *Ruslan and Liudmila, The Prisoner of the Caucasus, The Fountain at Bakhchisarai*, and *Onegin* has been limited to mere notices about the appearance of these poems in print, or else has had as its main subject some other topic, such as romantic poetry, and so forth. Pushkin's narrative poems themselves have not yet been properly analyzed. (Author's note.)

on pure conviction, has the right to universal attention. I will go further: in our time each thinking person, not only can, but positively must express his views before the public—unless, of course, outside circumstances prevent it. For only our concerted effort can achieve what all well-meaning people have desired for so long and, nevertheless, we still do not have: to wit, public opinion—which is both a result and condition of national culture and therefore of national welfare. Also, public pronouncements are useful simply because they have been made: if just, for their justness, if unjust, for eliciting objections.

When speaking about Pushkin, however, it is difficult to express one's opinion resolutely; it is difficult to bring the diversity of his works into focus and to find a general criterion for the nature of his poetry, which has taken on so many different shapes. For, excepting the beauty and originality of their poetic language, what traces of common origin do we find in *Ruslan and Liudmila, The Prisoner of the Caucasus, Onegin, The Gypsies*, and so forth? Not only is each of these narrative poems different from the others in its plot development and in its manner of narration (*la manière*), but some of them differ in their very nature, reflecting diverse views of the world by the poet, so much so that in translation it would be easy to take them for works, not of one, but of several authors. The light humor—a child of gaiety and wit—which in *Ruslan and Liudmila* dresses all objects in sparkling colors, is no longer to be encountered in the poet's other works. In *Onegin*, its place is taken by scathing mockery—an echo of a skepticism of the heart. Good-natured gaiety has here changed into a dismal coldness which regards all objects through the dark veil of doubt, conveys its observations through caricature, and creates only in order to revel in the imminent destruction of its creature. In *The Prisoner of the Caucasus*, on the other hand, we find neither the trust in fate which vivified *Ruslan*, nor the contempt for human beings that we remark in *Onegin*. Here we see a soul embittered by treason and loss, yet one that has still not betrayed itself, nor lost the freshness of its former sensations; one still faithful to its sacred inclinations. It is a soul maimed but not conquered by fate; the outcome of the struggle is still a question of the future. In the narrative poem *The Gypsies*, the nature of the poetry is again unique, different from

Pushkin's other narrative poems, and the same can be said about almost every one of his major works.

Yet after a careful perusal of Pushkin's works, from *Ruslan and Liudmila* to chapter five of *Onegin*,[2] we find that his poetry—with all its meandering course—has had three periods of development, each of which differs sharply from the others. We shall attempt to define the distinctive feature and content of each of these, and then draw broad conclusions about Pushkin's poetry in general.

If it is permitted to divide poetry, like painting, into schools—according to the temper, tone, and finish common to the spirit of different nations' artistic creations—then I would call the first period of Pushkin's poetry, that including *Ruslan* and some minor lyrics, the period of the *Italian-French school*. The sweetness of Parny, the ingenuous, light wit, the delicacy, the purity of form, which are all characteristic of French poetry in general, have here been united with the splendor, lively exuberance, and freedom of Ariosto. Let us stay a while with that work of our poet which brought about the first acquaintance of the Russian public with its future favorite.

While in his subsequent works Pushkin was to endow almost all the creatures of his imagination with the individuality of his own character and way of thinking, here he often appears a *poet inventor*. He does not seek to convey to us his own special view of the world, of fate, life, and man; he simply creates for us a new fate, a new life, a new individual world, and populates it with beings that are new and disparate, belonging exclusively to his creative imagination. This is the reason why no other poem of his has the same completeness and congruity which we remark in *Ruslan*. This is why each canto, each scene, each digression has its own distinctive, full existence; why each part is woven into the pattern of the whole creation so indispensably that nothing could be added or subtracted without utter loss of harmony. This is why Chernomor, Naina, the Head, the Finn, Rogdai, Farlaf, Ratmir, Liudmila—in short, each character (except, perhaps, the hero of the poem himself) is endowed with particular, sharply outlined, and at the same time profound features. This is why the author, correlating the parts with the whole, carefully avoids

[2] Only five chapters had been published at the time Kireevsky was writing his review; the full text of the novel in verse did not appear in print until 1833.

anything pathetic which might stir up the reader's soul. For strong feelings are incompatible with the comically miraculous; they agree only with the majestically marvelous. Charm alone can lure us into the realm of magic; and if in the midst of enchanting impossibility something affects us in all seriousness, making us revert to ourselves, then good-bye to our faith in the improbable! Miraculous specters are scattered to the winds and the whole world of the fantastic collapses, disappears, the way a motley dream is interrupted when something among its concoctions reminds us of reality. The Finn's story, if it had a different ending, would destroy the effect of the whole poem, just as one episode—the account of the main hero's misfortunes, admittedly one of the best episodes—shakes the soul too forcefully in Wieland's *Oberon*, thereby destroying the enchantment of the whole and depriving it of its chief merit. In the Finn's case, the unexpectedness of the *dénouement*, the repulsiveness of the old witch, and the Finn's ludicrous predicament momentarily turn the whole earlier picture of unhappy love into caricature and so masterfully connect the episode with the tone of the whole poem that the episode becomes an indispensable component part. In general one can say that even if an exacting criticism should find weak, uneven passages in *Ruslan and Liudmila*, still it will detect nothing superfluous or irrelevant in it. Chivalry, love, sorcery, feasts, war, mermaids—all the poetry of an enchanted world—were here combined in one creation, and despite the motley parts, everything is well-proportioned, harmonious, *congruous*. The introductory stanzas to each canto, borrowed from the singer of Ivan's deeds,[3] maintain the same tone throughout, lending a general air of gaiety and wit to the whole work.

This poem of Pushkin's, in which we meet a minimum of powerful emotional shocks and profound sensations, is nevertheless the most perfect of all his works with regard to the balance of parts, the harmony and completeness of invention, the richness of content, the graceful transitions, the continuity of the dominant tone, and finally the veracity, diversity, and originality of characters. On the other hand, *The Prisoner of the Caucasus*, which satisfies the just demands of art less than Pushkin's other narrative poems, is nonetheless richest

[3] An allusion to M. M. Kheraskov whose *Rossiada* (1778) described the taking of Kazan by Ivan the Terrible.

of all in its power and profundity of feelings. With *The Prisoner of the Caucasus* begins *the second period of Pushkin's poetry* which could be called an *echo of Byron's lyre.*

If in *Ruslan and Liudmila* Pushkin was exclusively a *poet* faithfully and unfalteringly transmitting the impulses of his fancy, in *The Prisoner of the Caucasus* he appears as a *poet-philosopher* who in his poetry tries to depict the doubts of his reason and thus gives all objects the general color of his individual views, often forsaking the objects in order to dwell in the realm of abstract thinking. What he presents, in *The Prisoner, Onegin,* and other works, are no longer sorcerers with their miracles, nor unconquerable heroes or enchanted gardens; rather, his subject is real life and the human being of our time, with his emptiness, insignificance, and dullness. Unlike Goethe, however, he does not seek to elevate his object by revealing both the poetry in ordinary life and a full reflection of all mankind in contemporary man; rather, like Byron, he sees only contradiction in the whole world, only betrayed hope, so that one could call almost every one of his heroes *disillusioned.*

It is not only in his view of life and man that Pushkin concurs with the bard of *The Giaour:* he also resembles him in other aspects of his poetry. The manner of presentation is the same; so is the tone and the form of his poems; there is the same vagueness with regard to the whole and the same detailed explicitness in the parts; the structure is the same; and even the characters in most cases are so similar that at first glance one would take them for immigrant aliens who have journeyed from Byron's world into Pushkin's creations.

Nevertheless, despite such similarity to the British poet, we find in *Onegin,* in *The Gypsies,* in *The Prisoner,* and in other works so much original beauty belonging exclusively to our poet, such guileless freshness of feeling, such veracity of description, such subtlety in observation and naturalness in presentation, such originality in language, and, finally, so much that is purely Russian that even in this period of his poetry he cannot be called a mere imitator. Yet it cannot be assumed that Pushkin concurred with Byron accidentally, that, because they were brought up in the same century and perhaps under similar circumstances, they had to agree in their way of thinking, in the spirit of their poetry, and consequently in its very forms. (For real poets the forms of their works are never fortuitous, they are always merged with the spirit of the whole, like body with soul in the works of the Creator.) I say we cannot allow this opinion because Pushkin, even where he came closest to Byron, still retained a great deal of his own that revealed his innate tendency. It is evident to those who have looked into the souls of both poets that Pushkin did not meet Byron accidentally, but borrowed from him, or more accurately, unwittingly submitted to his influence. Byron's lyre had to reverberate in his epoch, for it was itself the voice of its epoch. One of two antagonistic tendencies of our time gained expression in it. Is it surprising that it did not sound for Pushkin in vain? Only perhaps he yielded too much to its influence. Had he retained more originality, at least in the exterior form of his poems, he would have invested them with even greater excellence.

Byron's influence was manifested first of all in *The Prisoner of the Caucasus*. Here the marks of similarity mentioned above are particularly evident. The structure of the poem demonstrates, however, that this was Pushkin's first attempt in this particular manner: for the descriptions of the Circassians, their way of life, customs, games, and so forth—which fill the first canto—arrest the action to no end, snap the thread of interest, and do not accord with the tone of the poem as a whole. It is one's impression that the poem has not one, but two unblended subject matters, each appearing separately and diverting attention and feeling in two different directions. But by what merits is this important fault redeemed! What poesy pervades all the episodes! What freshness, what power of feeling! What veracity of lively descriptions! No other work by Pushkin offers so many faults and so many beauties.

Just as great—or perhaps an even greater—similarity to Byron appears in *The Fountain at Bakhchisarai*, but here a more skillful execution reveals the greater maturity of the poet. Harem life relates to the subject matter of *The Fountain at Bakhchisarai* as the Circassian way of life relates to that of *The Prisoner of the Caucasus*: both provide a backdrop to the presentation, yet how different is their meaning! Everything that happens among Girei, Maria, and Zarema is so closely united with their environment that the whole tale could be called a scene from harem life. All the digressions and interruptions are tied together by one prevalent feeling; everything strives to produce one principal impression. An apparent irregularity in narration is an invariable criterion of the Byronic manner; but this irregularity is only seeming, for the dissonant presentation of objects reverberates in the soul as a harmonious train of sensations. In order to understand this kind of harmony, one must listen to the inner music of feelings born of the impressions from the described objects. These objects themselves serve only as instruments, as keys striking the cords of the heart.

This spiritual melody is the chief merit of *The Fountain at Bakhchisarai*. How naturally and harmoniously are eastern voluptuousness and sensuality here blended with the strongest outbursts of southern passion! The contrast between the luxurious description of the harem and the gravity of the principal action betrays the author of *Ruslan*. He has descended to earth from the immortal world of enchantment, but he has not lost his sense of enthralling sensuality even in the midst of conflicting passions and misfortunes. His art of poetry in *The Fountain* could be compared with the Oriental peri who, although bereft of paradise, has retained her unearthly beauty: her aspect is thoughtful and grave, but through the affected coldness a strong agitation of her spirit is perceptible. Enveloped in a dense cloud, she flies by us quickly and serenely, like a spirit—like Zarema; and we are enchanted by what we have seen, but even more so by the images our inflamed imagination impulsively supplies in order to complete the unseen. The tone of the whole poem, more than that of any other, approximates the Byronic.

The poem of Pushkin's which is furthest from Byron is *The Robber Brothers*, despite the fact that by its subject matter, episodes, descriptions, and all other elements it must be called a replica of *The Prisoner of Chillon*. It is more a caricature than an imitation of Byron. Bonnivard and his brothers suffered " For the God their foes denied "; and however cruel their torment may be, there is an element of poetry in it which commands our sympathy. On the other hand, Pushkin's detailed description of the sufferings of the captured robbers engenders only revulsion—a feeling similar to what we experience at the sight of the torment of a criminal justly sentenced to death. It can be asserted that there is nothing poetic in this poem beyond the introductory stanzas and the charming versification—which latter is always and everywhere a mark of Pushkin.

This charming versification is seen above all in *The Gypsies*, where the mastery of versecraft has reached its highest degree of perfection and art has assumed the appearance of free casualness. Here it seems that each sound has poured forth from the soul unconstrained, and everything is pure, complete, and free, despite the fact that each line—except perhaps two or three in the whole poem—has received the ultimate in polish.

Does the content, however, have the same merit as the form? We see a nomadic, semibarbaric people which knows no laws, despises luxury and civilization, and loves freedom above all. Yet this people is familiar with sentiments characteristic of the most refined community: the memory of a former love and a nostalgia for the inconstant Mariula fill the old gypsy's whole life. But, while the gypsies experience exclusive, lasting love, they do not recognize jealousy; Aleko's feelings are incomprehensible to them. One might assume that the author wished to represent a golden age, in which people were just without laws, in which passions never trespassed beyond proper limits, in which all was free but nothing disturbed the general harmony, and inner perfection was the result, not of an arduous education, but of the happy innocence of a natural integrity. Such an idea could have great poetic merit. But here, unfortunately, the fair sex destroys all the enchantment, and while the gypsies' love is "*drudgery and anguish*," their wives are like the moon which "serenely strays, / On all creation gently pouring / Her undiscriminating rays."[4] Is this feminine imperfection compatible with the perfection of the tribe? The gypsies either do not form permanent, exclusive attachments, or if they do they are jealous of their inconstant wives; in the latter case revenge and other passions cannot be alien to them. If such is the case, then Aleko cannot seem strange and incomprehensible to them, then European manners differ from theirs only by the advantages of education, and then they represent, not a golden age, but simply a semibarbaric people which is not bound by laws and is poor and wretched, just like the actual gypsies of Bessarabia. And then the whole poem contradicts itself.

[4] Walter Arndt's translation, *Slavic Review* 24, no. 2 (1965): 283.

But maybe we should not judge the gypsies at large by Zemfira's father alone; maybe his character is not the character of his people. Even if he is a unique being, however—whose character would always and under any circumstances be formed in the same way and would, consequently, always constitute an exception among his people—even then the poet's purpose remains obscure. For in a description of gypsies to select the one person in their midst who contradicts their general characteristics, and to present him alone to the reader, leaving others at a hazy distance, amounts to the same thing as emphasizing in the description of a man just those examples of his actions which belie the description.

Aleko's character, the episodes, and all other parts taken by themselves are, however, so rich in poetic beauty that if one could, after having read the poem, forget its subject matter and retain only the memory of the pleasure derived from it, one would be able to call it one of Pushkin's best works. But aesthetic feeling differs from simple pleasure just in this, that it has a greater effect on us in the ensuing moments of remembrance and reflection than at the time of first-exposure enjoyment. Really poetic creations *live* in our imagination; we abandon ourselves to them, develop the undeveloped, tell the untold and, transported to a world of the poet's creation, we live more expansively, more fully and happily than in the old one of reality. So the gypsies' life lures our fancy at first; but it fades away at our first attempt to consign it to our imagination, like the mists of the North Sea which, assuming the aspect of firm land, entice the curious traveler, only to evaporate, warmed by the rays of the sun, before his very eyes.

But there is a quality in *The Gypsies* which redeems in a way the disorder of the subject matter. This quality is the poet's greater originality. The author of "A Review of Literature in 1827"[5] correctly observed that this poem reveals a struggle between Byron's idealism and the Russian poet's nationally oriented paintings. Indeed, take the description of gypsy life separately, regard Zemfira's father, not as a gypsy, but simply as an old man with no reference to his nationality, consider the passage about Ovid: the completeness of creation, developed in all details and inspired by an originality, will

[5] See *Moscow Messenger* 1 (1828). (Author's note.)

prove to you that Pushkin had already sensed the power of his independent talent, free of foreign influences.

All the faults of *The Gypsies* are functions of these two discordant tendencies: one original and one Byronic. Therefore the very imperfection of the poem is a guarantee of the poet's future progress.

A striving for an independent brand of poetry is even more manifest in *Eugene Onegin*, although not in its first chapters where Byron's influence is obvious, nor in the manner of narration which derives from *Don Juan* and *Beppo*, nor even in the character of Onegin himself, which is of the same kind as that of Childe Harold. But the further the poet moves from his main hero, abandoning himself to collateral descriptions, the more independent and national he becomes.

The time of Childe Harolds, thank God, has not yet come for our fatherland: young Russia has not partaken of the life of western states and our people, as a personality, is not getting old under the weight of others' experiences. A brilliant career is still open to Russian activity; all kinds of art, all branches of knowledge still remain to be mastered by our fatherland. Hope is still given to us: what is the disillusioned Childe Harold's business among us?

Let us examine which qualities the British flower transplanted into Russian soil has retained and which it has lost.

The British poet's most cherished vision is an extraordinary, lofty creature. Not a paucity, but a superabundance of inner strength makes this creature unsympathetic to his environment. An immortal idea dwells in his heart day and night, consuming all his being and poisoning all his pleasures. Whatever shape it takes—haughty contempt for mankind, nagging sense of guilt, gloomy despair, or insatiable yearning for oblivion—this idea is all-embracing and everlasting. What is it if not an instinctive, constant striving for the better, a nostalgia for an unattainable perfection? Childe Harold and the ordinary crowd have nothing in common: his torments, his visions, his pleasures are incomprehensible to others; only high mountains and bare crags give him secret responses, audible to himself alone. But just because he is different from ordinary people, he can reflect in himself the spirit of his time and serve as the threshold of the future; for *only dissonance can unite two different consonances.*

On the other hand, Onegin is an entirely ordinary and insignificant being. He is also indifferent to his environment; not despair, however, but an inability to love made him cold. His youth also passed in a whirlpool of amusement and dissipation, but he was not carried away by turbulent passion and an insatiable soul; rather he led a fashionable fop's empty, indifferent life on the parquet floor of the salon. He also quit the world and people; not, however, in order to seek scope for his agitated thoughts in solitude, but because he was equally bored everywhere,

> Because he yawned with equal gloom
> In any style of drawing room.[6]

He does not lead a special inner life which rises above the lives of other people, and he despises mankind merely because he is unable to respect it. There is nothing more common than this breed of people, and there could not be less poetry in such a character.

This is, then, the Childe Harold of our fatherland: praise be to the poet that he did not present us with the real one. For, as we have already said, the time for Childe Harolds has not come to Russia, and we pray to God that it never will.

It seems that Pushkin himself felt the emptiness of his hero and for this reason did not anywhere in the novel try to bring him close to his readers. He gave him no definite physiognomy; he represented, not one person, but a whole class of people in his portrait: Onegin's description may fit a thousand different characters.

The frivolousness of the main hero may be one reason for the frivolity of content of the first five chapters in general; but the manner of narration has also probably contributed. Those who justify it by referring to Byron forget how the form relates to both the subject matter and the main characters in *Beppo* and *Don Juan*.

As far as *Eugene Onegin* in general is concerned, we have no right to judge the plot by its beginning, although we can hardly imagine the possibility of a well-composed, complete, fertile plan emerging after such a beginning. Still, who can discern the limits of possibility for

[6] *Eugene Onegin*, trans. Walter Arndt (New York: E. P. Dutton, 1963), chap. 2, stanza 2.

such poets as Pushkin? It is their prerogative to amaze their critics at all times.

The faults of *Onegin* are in essence the last homage Pushkin paid to the British poet. The narrative's innumerable merits—Lensky, Tatiana, Olga, St. Petersburg, the countryside, the dream, the winter, the letter, and so forth—are our poet's inalienable property. It is in these that he clearly reveals the innate tendency of his genius. These signs of original creation in *The Gypsies* and in *Onegin*, coupled with the one scene we know from *Boris Godunov*,[7] constitute, though they do not exhaust, the third period in the development of his poetry, which could be called the *period of Russo-Pushkinian poetry*.[8] Its essential features are: a pictorial vividness, a certain abandon, a singular pensiveness, and, finally, an ineffable quality, comprehensible only to the Russian heart: for what can you call the feeling with which the melodies of Russian songs are imbued, to which the Russian people most frequently resort, and which can be regarded as the center of its spiritual life?

In this period of Pushkin's development one particularly notices an ability to be absorbed in the environment and in the passing moment. This same ability is the foundation of the Russian character: it is at the very inception of all the virtues and failings of the Russian people. From this ability emanate courage, lightness of heart, intractability of momentary impulses, generosity, intemperance, vehemence, perspicuity, geniality, and so on and so forth.

It hardly seems necessary to enumerate all the merits of *Onegin*, to dissect its characters, situations, and introductory descriptions, in order to prove that Pushkin's later works are superior to the earlier ones. There are things one can feel but cannot prove in less than several tomes of commentary on each page. Tatiana's character is one of the poet's most felicitous creations; we shall not speak about it since it fully reveals itself on its own.

Why is it not so easy to praise the beautiful as it is to find fault?

[7] Kireevsky is referring to the monastery scene which had been published in *Moskovsky vestnik* 1 (1827). Further fragments of the play were printed in 1828 and 1830, but its full text did not appear in print until 1831.

[8] We are not treating Pushkin's minor works which also manifest three stages of development. (Author's note.)

How enthusiastically would we express all the incomparable aesthetic feelings for which we are indebted to the poet and which, like precious stones in a simple necklace, glitter along the weary path of the Russian people's life!

The above-mentioned scene from *Boris Godunov* particularly manifests Pushkin's maturity. The art which in such a narrow frame represents the spirit of the epoch, monastic life, Pimen's character, the state of contemporary affairs, and the beginning of the dramatic action; the special, tragically serene atmosphere that invokes the chronicler's life and presence for us; the new, striking manner in which the poet acquaints us with Grishka; and finally the inimitable, poetic, precise language: all this taken together makes us expect of this tragedy—let us say it boldly—something *magnificent*.

Pushkin was born to be a dramatist. He is too many-sided, too objective[9] to be a lyric poet. One can observe in each of his poetic tales an instinctive urge to endow each separate part with individual life—an urge injurious to the whole in epic creations but necessary and invaluable to the dramatist.

It is reassuring to observe an uninterrupted progress in the poet's development, but it is even more reassuring to see the strong influence he has on his fellow countrymen. Few are selected by fate to enjoy the affection of their contemporaries during their lifetime. Pushkin belongs to their number, which reveals to us still another important quality in the nature of his poetry: a *congruence with his time*.

It is not enough to be a poet in order to be a national poet: it is also necessary to have been raised, as it were, in the midst of the nation's life and to have shared in the fatherland's hopes, aspirations, and passions—in short to live its life and to express it spontaneously while expressing oneself. Such a lucky attainment may be a rare accident: but are beauty, intelligence, insight—all the qualities with which man captivates man—not just as accidental? And are these latter qualities any more substantial than the capacity to reflect a nation's life in oneself?

[9] We are forced to resort to this foreign word for want of an equivalent in our language. (Author's note.)

Stepan Shevyrev

THE ADVENTURES OF
CHICHIKOV, OR DEAD SOULS
A NARRATIVE POEM BY
N. GOGOL

Published under the title "Pokhozhdeniia Chichikova, ili Mertvye dushi. *Poema N. Gogolia*" in Moskvitianin *7–8 (1842), signed S. Shevyrev. The full text of the original is given in translation. This review, together with a review of Lermontov's* Geroi nashego vremeni *in* Moskvitianin *2 (1841), are the best known and most original of Shevyrev's critical essays.*

Strange is the destiny that overtakes a poetic work when it advances fully armed from the artist's brain and passes into readers' possession! The artist now is quiet and, having abandoned his creation as a sacrifice to the mob, has withdrawn into the sanctuary of his soul. Now external trouble begins. A mass of readers picks the living, whole creation apart and enjoys it in crumbs; millions of points of view are visited upon it: each from his own rostrum, on which he was placed by nature, education, and social position, strains to cast a look at the phenomenon which has struck all eyes. Some are spontaneously delighted with it; others spontaneously disapprove of it. There a petty envy crept out of its hole in the shape of a journalist and pointed its rickety and dark microscope at a few grammatical mistakes which had accidentally stolen into the work.[1] Here, from another side, from the narrow ranks of the rag fair of letters, an insolent blusterer darted out in the form of a clamoring pigmy with brazen brow and sweeping

---

[1] Several critics objected to Gogol's language, but Shevyrev's later remark indicates (see below, p. 49, n. 10) that he is alluding to O. I. Senkovsky, who reviewed the novel in *Biblioteka dlia chteniia* 53 (1842).

arm: rejoicing in the opportunity to praise himself with the excuse of praising a talent, he stands before the work, stretches his lean figure over it, strains to cover it with himself, and then swears to you that he has shown it to you accurately, and that without him you would not understand it.[2] Silently does the work rise above the upstart—this uninvited trumpeter of its glory—setting in relief his tininess and intellectual impotence. Having been torn to pieces, it secretly keeps its wholeness and lives the full life the artist gave it. We seldom have a chance to apply aesthetic criticism to contemporary works of Russian literature and touch upon important questions of art when speaking about them. Shall we now let that chance pass by when it is so brilliantly offered to us in the work of an artist who, after such a prolonged silence, has suddenly presented us with the fruit of many years' thought, study, and creative work? Of course not. On the contrary, we will return to *Dead Souls* many times, for it is hardly possible in one time to speak out on all the host of thoughts and questions which this work arouses.

It is a long time since poetic phenomena have produced so strong a reaction in us as *Dead Souls* has produced, but unfortunately we live in a time when a creation which would unite all voices unanimously on its behalf can hardly appear. If a genius of the first rank, if Shakespeare himself should appear anew, would he conquer those minds divided by a strange difference of opinion?

Is it surprising, in view of this, that Gogol's work should be exposed to various interpretations and judgments? We have even noticed that such completely contrary opinions have hardly ever been formed as in the present case; such a phenomenon cannot be without cause—no, it is extraordinarily important and demands an explanation. It was even possible to meet people who combined these extreme contraries within themselves, who wavered between one and another opinion, unable to give a full explanation to their strange vacillation. If such a phenomenon actually occurs in thinking, dispassionate people who are the innocent recipients of impressions, then the cause must of course be in the creation itself. We so assume. Every work of an artist has two sides; on one side it is addressed to the life from

---

[2] The allusion to Belinsky is clear, particularly from the reference to his lean figure. Belinsky reviewed the novel in *Otechestvennye zapiski* 7 (1842).

which it draws its material, its content, but on another side it belongs entirely to its creator, it is the fruit of his artistic spirit, the secret of his internal life. Those who judge can by and large be divided into two groups: these pay attention only to the content and to the connection between the work and life, especially contemporary life; those unconsciously or consciously enjoy the skill of the artist and the question of life does not worry them. It is a long time since we have met a work in which external life and content are presented in such sharp and extreme contrast with the wonderful world of art, in which the positive side of life and the creative strength of fiction appeared in such a striking struggle with each other, a struggle from which only Gogol's talent could emerge with dignity, with the wreath of a victor. Perhaps this is what the character of contemporary poetry should be in general. However that may be, here lies the primary source of that difference of opinion by which the work was met. It is clear that a view of it will be complete only when it embraces both sides—the sides of life and art—and shows their mutual relations in the artist's creation. This is the difficult problem which we now set ourselves and which we will answer according to the measure of our strength and according to an internal, impartial persuasion.

First let us uncover the side of external life and as thoroughly as possible trace those springs which the narrative poem sets in motion.[3] Who is its hero? A swindler, as the author himself expressed it. In our first burst of indignation against Chichikov's behavior we could even call him a scoundrel. But the author profoundly reveals to us the whole secret psychological biography of Chichikov: he takes him from his swaddling clothes, leads him through family, school, and all the possible windings of his life; he clearly reveals his whole development to us, and we are fascinated by the extraordinary gift of understanding which the author reveals in the wonderful anatomy of this character. An internal propensity, the lessons of his father, and circumstances bred a passion for acquisition in Chichikov. Having followed the hero along with the author, we tone down the title of scoundrel and even agree to rename him an *acquirer*. He is apparently the hero of the century. Who does not know that the passion for acquisition is the overruling passion of our time, and who does not

---

[3] Gogol gave his novel the subtitle *poema*.

acquire? Of course, the means for acquisition are various, but when everyone acquires it is impossible for the means not to become corrupted—and in the contemporary world there are probably more bad means of acquiring than good ones. If Chichikov is looked at from this point of view, we will not only accept the invitation of the author to call him an acquirer, we will even be forced to exclaim, following the author: is not some part of Chichikov in each of us? The passion for acquisition is terribly contagious at every step of the complicated ladder of a man's fortunes in contemporary society, at each of which we find perhaps several Chichikovs. In short, when we look at the matter more profoundly and more intently, we finally conclude that Chichikov is in the air, that he inundates all contemporary humanity, that there is a full crop of Chichikovs, that they are bred invisibly, like fungi, that Chichikov is the actual *hero of our time*, and therefore is perhaps the proper hero of a contemporary poem. But of all acquirers, Chichikov is distinguished by an extraordinary poetic gift in the invention of his means of acquisition. What a wonderful, really *inspired*, as the author calls it, idea occurred to his brain! Once having spoken with some secretary and having heard from him that dead souls are counted on the census lists and fit for business, Chichikov plotted to buy a thousand of them, settle them on land near Kherson, announce himself the possessor of this fantastic settlement, and then convert it into cash capital by mortgaging it. Isn't it true that there is a geniuslike cleverness in this plot, a kind of daring trickery, united with *fantasy* and *irony*? In this business Chichikov is a hero among swindlers, a poet of his business: see how he is carried away by his idea when he undertakes his exploit: "And the best thing about it is that the commodity will seem so unusual to everyone, nobody will believe it."[4] He rejoices in his singular contrivance, exults in the future consternation of the world, which was not capable of inventing such a business before him, and he almost ignores the consequences in the ecstasy of his enterprise. The self-sacrifice of the swindler is carried to its ultimate limit in him: he is as

[4] Nikolai Gogol, *Dead Souls*, trans. with an introduction by Helen Michailoff (New York: Washington Square Press, 1964), p. 274. All subsequent citations will be from this edition, with the page number indicated in parentheses within the text.

secure in it as Achilles is in his immortality, and therefore, like him, is fearless and bold.

In order to bring his poetic project to fulfillment, Chichikov had to find the special town of N, and people adapted to it. The hero and his enterprise inevitably brought their fitting environment with them. Some readers blame the author for the persons portrayed by him; it was useless for the author prudently to attempt to forestall a similar reproach when he said, "The readers should not be indignant with the author if the characters who have hitherto appeared are not to their taste; that is Chichikov's fault. Here he is complete master of the situation . . ." (275). Indeed, if he is the hero of the century, if his project is distinguished by a kind of poetry of invention, then of course he could not fulfill it in any other town and with any other people than those depicted with a wonderful, masterly brush by the creator of the poem. Let us attentively go through the gallery of these strange persons who live their own special, full life in that world where Chichikov accomplishes his exploit. We will not violate the order in which they are depicted. Let us begin with Manilov, on the assumption that the author did not begin with him for nothing. Well nigh a thousand persons are collected in this one person. Manilov represents a great number of people who live in Russia, about whom one may say, along with the author, neither fish nor flesh nor good red herring, as the proverb goes. If you want, they are generally good people, but empty; they praise everything and everyone, but there is no meaning in their praise. They live in the country; they do not take care of their estates, but regard everything with a calm and benevolent regard, and smoke their pipes (the pipe is their inevitable adjunct); they fall into idle dreams, like building a stone bridge across a pond and putting little shops on it. The kindness of their souls is reflected in their family affection: they love to kiss, but that is all. The vapidity of their saccharin-sweet and cloyed lives savors of overindulgence as children and a bad education. Their dreamy inactivity is reflected in all their household; look at their estates: they all resemble Manilovka, as his own resembles Manilov. Gray timbered huts; no green any-where; everywhere the same logs; a pond in the middle; two country-women with a fish net, in which two crayfish and a carp are entangled, and a plucked rooster with its head pecked through to the very brain (among such people in the country it is indispensable even for the rooster to be plucked)—these are the sure external signs of their village way of life, which even a light-gray day fits perfectly, because in sunshine the picture would not be so interesting. There is always some defect in their houses: along with furniture upholstered in fancy material, one inevitably finds two armchairs covered in canvas. At every businesslike question they always appeal to their stewards, even if it should be but a matter of selling village products. But propose some more devious deal to them: they will not catch you, as Manilov did not catch Chichikov, because no business thought can be forged in their heads; out of kindness and softness of character, they will quickly agree with you. Visit them in the country—you could not be better received, but look after your servants. The hospitality and softness of the masters are reflected in the lives of their house servants, who will certainly give your coachman more than enough to drink, as happens to Selifan, Chichikov's coachman.

Korobochka is another matter entirely! This is the type of an active proprietress-mistress; she lives entirely for her property; she does not know anything beyond it. From her first appearance, you would call her a penny-wise woman, seeing how she collects pennies and nickels in her various little bags; but if you look at her more closely, you will grant her the justice of her activity and unwillingly say that she is an excellent manager of her affairs. See the tidiness of everything around her! The peasant huts show the prosperity of their inhabitants; the gates do not sag anywhere; everywhere old thin roofing has been replaced by new. Look at her rich hen roost! Her rooster is not like the one in Manilov's village—her rooster is a swell. It is obvious that all the fowl, trained by their solicitous owner, form, as it were, part of her family and come near the window of her house: nowhere but at Korobochka's could the somewhat discourteous encounter between the turkey cock and the visiting Chichikov take place. Her whole household is in complete order: it seems that only Fetinia is in the house, but look at the pastries and at how the huge feather bed took the weary Chichikov to its bosom! And what a wonderful memory Nastasia Petrovna has! How she rehearsed to Chichikov by heart, without any notes, the names of all her perished serfs. You observed that Korobochka's serfs are distinguished from other landowners' serfs by some extraordinary nicknames. Do you know why? Korobochka knows which side her bread is buttered on: what is hers, remains hers; the serfs are branded by special names the way a bird is tagged by an accurate master, so that it may not run away. That is why it was so difficult for Chichikov to settle his business with her: she loves to sell, and will sell every product of her homestead, but she regards dead souls as she regards lard, as she regards hemp, or honey, reckoning that they might come in handy in her household. She tormented Chichikov to the point of making him sweat by her involutions, constantly citing that these goods are new, strange, unprecedented. The only way to handle her is to frighten her by the devil, because a Korobochka has to be superstitious. But it is a misfortune for her to sell any one of her goods too cheaply: it is as though her conscience were disturbed—and therefore it is no wonder that, after having sold her dead souls and thought about them, she would come galloping into town in her watermelon-shaped carriage, on cotton-stuffed cushions, with bread loaves, rolls, doughnuts, pretzels, and other things, come galloping to find out for a certainty what the dead souls are wanted for! and whether she has not missed the mark by perhaps having sold them, God forbid, at one-third the going price.

On the high road, in some dark wooden inn, Chichikov met Nozdrev, with whom he had become acquainted in town: where would one meet such a man if not in such an inn? One meets many Nozdrevs, the author remarks: it is true, you will certainly meet a Nozdrev at the most insignificant Russian fair and of course several Nozdrevs at other more important ones. The author says that this type of person is well known among us in *Rus* under the name of *free-and-easy* fellow: other epithets befitting him are inconsistent, flighty, disordered, a braggart, a squabbler, a quarreler, a liar, a bad lot, an impudent rascal, and so forth. The third time they speak to you they use the familiar second person form; at a fair they buy everything they take a fancy to, as for example, horse collars, pastilles, clothes for the nurse, a stallion, raisins, a silver washstand, Dutch linen, flour, tobacco, pistols, herrings, pictures, a grinding instrument, in short, their buying is as disordered as their brains.

In their village they like to brag and lie without mercy and call everything that does not belong to them theirs. Do not trust what they say, tell them to their faces that they are talking nonsense: they will not take offense. Their great passion is to show everything in their village, even though there is hardly anything to be seen: manifest in this passion is a cordiality (a characteristic of the Russian people) and a vanity (another characteristic native to us). Nozdrevs constantly change their inclinations. Nothing stays with them very long, and everything around them must be in a whirl, as their heads are. Friendly fondness and abuse flow together in their language, mixed in a torrent of indecent words. Lord deliver us from their dinners and from any intimacy with them! When they play they cheat boldly —and are ready to scrap if you remark upon it. They have a special passion for dogs and their kennels are in good order: does this come from a kind of sympathy? For there is something genuinely doggish in the Nozdrevian character. It is totally impossible to settle any business with them: that is why it seems strange at first that Chichikov —an intelligent and businesslike fellow who can immediately size up a man for what he is and how to speak to him—should decide to enter into dealings with Nozdrev. This blunder, which Chichikov later repented, could, however, be explained by two Russian sayings: there is some simplicity in every sage; and the Russian is wise after the event. Chichikov paid for it later: without Nozdrev no one would have given the alarm in town and produced all the confusion at the ball which caused such an important reversal of Chichikov's fortunes.

But Nozdrev must yield his place to the enormous type of Sobakevich. Here we cannot refrain from quoting the author himself, whose words paint this face better than any brush could (if the monstrous, animalistic physiognomy of Sobakevich can be called a face):

> As everyone knows, there are many faces in this world over the finishing of which nature has taken no great pains, using on them no such tools as fine files, fine gimlets and so forth, but has simply rough-hewn them with a full swing of the arm: one stroke of the ax and there is the nose for you; another, the lips; two thrusts with a drill, the eyes; and without any polishing, she thrusts him into the world, saying, "He will do all

right!" Just such a rough-hewn and amazingly solid countenance did Sobakevich have. He held it bent down rather than uplifted, and he never turned his neck; due to this unwieldiness he seldom looked at the person he was talking to, but always either at the corner of the stove or at the door. Chichikov stole another sidelong glance at him as they were passing through the dining room. A bear! A regular bear! And as a strange coincidence would have it, his name was even Mikhail Semenovich.[5] (104–5)

It sometimes happens in nature that a man's exterior is deceptive and you meet a good soul and a gentle heart beneath a strange monstrous form. But in Sobakevich the external completely corresponds to the internal, point by point. His outer mug has left an impression on all his words and actions, and on everything that surrounds him. His house was ponderous: full-weighted and stout beams in the stables, shed, and kitchen; compact peasant huts wonderfully timbered; a well fashioned in firm oak fit for shipbuilding; in the rooms portraits with fat thighs and endless mustachios; the Greek heroine Bobelina with a leg bigger than a torso; a big-bellied walnut bureau on four preposterous legs; a dark-colored thrush; in short, everything around Sobakevich was like him, and, along with the table, armchair, chairs, could sing in chorus, saying, "We are all Sobakevich!" Look at the meal: every dish repeats the same thing to you. The enormous "nurse"[6] made of sheep's stomach, stuffed with buckwheat groats, brains, and trotters; the tarts larger than the plates; the turkey big as a calf, packed with all kinds of things—how like all this fare is to the master! And the radish boiled in honey—we do not know where such a jam exists, but it could be thought up only by a Sobakevich. Listen to his words at dinner: "If we have pork, we have the whole pig served on the table; if it's lamb, the whole of it must be brought in; if it's goose, the whole goose! I'd rather have just two dishes but eat my fill of them, as much as my *soul* craves" (110). Isn't the word soul expressive here? Sobakevich could hardly have any other understanding of the soul. Look at him, how he dumps half the lamb's side onto his plate, devours it, gnaws and sucks at everything

---

[5] *Mikhail* is the name commonly given to bears in Russia.

[6] "Nurse" (*niania*) is the name of a dish something like haggis.

down to the last little bone. Or how after his satisfying meal he emits indistinct grunts, crossing himself and covering his mouth with his hand every minute! Here Sobakevich's bearlike nature becomes swinish: this is a kind of Russian Caliban, stinking like a pig; this is all of gluttonous *Rus* combined in one beast-man. Speak with Sobakevich: all the above-mentioned dishes belch up with each word that comes out of his mouth. All the loathsomeness of his physical and moral nature resounds in each of his phrases. He hacks at everything and everyone, just as pitiless nature has hacked him; to him the whole town consists of fools, cutthroats, swindlers, and even the most respectable people are nothing but pigs in his dictionary. Of course, you have not forgotten Fonvizin's Skotinin[7]: if he is not of the same blood, then he is at least the godfather of Sobakevich; but it is impossible not to add that the godson has surpassed the god-father.

It seemed that Sobakevich's soul "was encased in such a thick shell that whatever stirred in its depths never rippled the surface" (114), says the author. His body had got the better of everything inside him, darkened all the man and had become incapable of expressing spiritual movements.

His gluttonous nature also showed itself in monetary greed. Intelligence operates in him, but only in so far as it is necessary to cheat and make money. Sobakevich is a veritable Caliban, of whose intelligence only an evil slyness remained. But in his resourcefulness he is funnier than Caliban. How masterfully he entered Elizaveta Sparrow on the list of masculine souls! how he ate a whole sturgeon and played the part of a starving innocent! It was difficult to settle any business with Sobakevich, because he was a *kulak;* his stingy nature haggles, but once the business has been settled, it is possible to relax, for Sobakevich is a solid, firm man who will stand behind what he has done.

The gallery of persons with whom Chichikov does business is concluded by the miser Pliushkin. The author remarks that a like phenomenon seldom is come across in *Rus,* where everyone would rather expand than contract.

---

[7] Skotinin is a character in D. I. Fonvizin's *Nedorosl* (1782).

As in the case of the other landowners, Pliushkin's village and his house paint the character and soul of the master in external form. Old, dark beams on the huts; roofs you can look through, like a sieve; paneless windows in the small huts stopped up with rags or peasant coats; a church with yellowish walls, splotched and cracked. The house looks like a decrepit invalid; its windows shuttered or boarded over; on one of them a triangle of dark blue sugar-wrapping paper. Dilapidated buildings all round; a dead indifferent silence; the gate always bolted and a giant padlock on an iron ring—all this prepares us to meet the master himself and serves as a mournful, living symbol of his reclusive soul. You rest from these mournful, heavy impressions in the rich picture of the garden, which, while overgrown and choked with weeds, is still picturesque in its tangles: here the wonderful sympathy of the poet for nature, which comes completely alive under his tender glance, immediately entertains you, but it is as though you catch a glimpse, in the depths of this wild sultry picture, of the story of the life of the master, whose soul is as choked as the nature in the silence of this garden. Go into Pliushkin's house—here everything speaks of him before you have seen him. Piled-up furniture, a broken chair, on the table a clock with a stopped pendulum to which a spider has attached its web; a bureau inlaid with a mother-of-pearl mosaic which had fallen out in places, leaving behind only yellowish grooves filled with glue; on the bureau a pile of papers finely written over, a shrivelled lemon, the broken-off arm of a chair, a wine glass with some kind of liquid and three flies in it, covered by a letter, a bit of sealing wax, a bit of rag picked up somewhere, two ink-stained pens as shrivelled as though in consumption, a completely yellowed tooth-pick with which the master probably picked his teeth even before the invasion of Moscow by the French.... All along the walls pictures blackened by time, a chandelier in a canvas bag, dust making it look like a silk cocoon with the worm still inside, a pile of litter in a corner whence a broken-off piece of wooden shovel and an old boot sole stuck out—and the only sign of a living creature in the whole house was a shabby nightcap lying on the table.... How Pliushkin is seen in every object, and how wonderfully you already know the man from this incoherent pile! But here he is himself, looking from a distance like his old housekeeper, with his unshaved chin which juts out so far forward and resembles a currycomb made of iron wires for cleaning horses in the stable, with grey eyes that dart out like mice from under high bushy eyebrows... We see Pliushkin as vividly as though we had seen him in a picture by Albrecht Dürer in the Doria Gallery... Having depicted him, the poet enters into him, lays bare to us all the dark folds of this hardened soul, relates the psychological metamorphosis of this man: how avarice, having once made its nest in his soul, little by little extended its power over him, having overrun all his feelings, changed the man into an animal which by some instinct drags into its burrow everything that might come across its path—an old sole, a woman's rag, an iron nail, an earthen potsherd, an officer's spur, a pail abandoned by a woman.

All feelings slip across this hard, petrified face almost imperceptibly. Everything dies, putrefies, and crumbles near Pliushkin. It is no wonder that Chichikov could get such a large number of dead and runaway souls from him, all of a sudden significantly increasing his fantastic crowd.

These are the persons with whom Chichikov sets his scheme in motion. They all, apart from special attributes strictly belonging to each, have one feature in common: hospitality, that Russian cordiality toward guests which lives in them and holds on as though by national instinct. It is remarkable that this natural feeling was conserved even in Pliushkin, despite the fact that it is absolutely contrary to his miserliness: he reckoned it necessary to offer Chichikov tea and would have ordered the samovar to be set up, except that, to his joy, his guest comprehended the business and refused the treat.

There are two other persons around Chichikov, two trusty companions: Petrushka, the greasy lackey in the frock coat which he never takes off, and the coachman Selifan. It is striking that the first, who is always near his master and imitates his dress, and even knows how to read, stinks; while Selifan, who is always with the horses and in the stable, preserves his Russian nature fresh and unbroken. In fact, it is always so around Chichikovs: Petrushka the lackey completely takes after the hero; he is his living, walking attribute. The author makes a profound remark about how Petrushka reads everything he comes across, and how the process of reading pleases him most, the perpetual discovery that another word has emerged from the letters. The coachman Selifan is another matter entirely: this is a new, complete, typical creation drawn from simple Russian life. We did not know about him until Manilov's house servants made him drunk and the wine revealed to us all his nice and good nature. He gets drunk mostly in order to speak with a good man. The wine stirred Selifan up: he plunged into conversation with the horses, which in his artless way he thought of almost as his dear friends. His preference for the Bay and the Assessor, and his special hatred for the villain Mottled, whom he pesters his master to sell, is taken from the nature of every coachman who has a special calling to his profession. Our drunken Selifan boasted that he would not turn the carriage over, but when misfortune comes to him, how naïvely he cries: Look, it turned over! With what artlessness and resignation he answered his master's threats: "Why shouldn't I be thrashed if I deserve it, if the master wishes it . . . If one deserves it, thrash him, why not?" (44).

Of all the persons who have thus far appeared in the poem the one who elicits most sympathy is the inestimable coachman Selifan. Indeed, we vividly and profoundly see in all the preceding persons how an empty and idle life can bring human nature down to bestiality. Each of them presents a striking resemblance to some animal. Sobakevich, as we have already said, combined in himself the bear and swine species; Nozdrev is very like a dog which for no reason at one and the same time barks and gnaws and fawns; one might compare Korobochka with a fussy squirrel collecting a store of hazel nuts, all devoted to its own household; Pliushkin, like an ant, driven by the instinct of an insect, drags everything he comes across into his ant hill; Manilov has a resemblance to a stupid hoopoe which sits in the woods, pesters you with its monotonous call, and looks as if it is dreaming about something; Petrushka with his smell is changed into an odorous billy goat; Chichikov by his imposture outdoes all the animals and by that alone upholds the glory of human nature. Of all, only the coachman Selifan, who has lived all his life with horses, has preserved the goodness of human nature.

But there is another person who lives a full integral life in the poem, who is created by the comic fantasy of the poet. This person

is the town of N. In its depiction the poet's creative imagination is at
free play, it is almost divorced from substantial life. You will not
find that the town of N is any specific one of our provincial towns,
but it is a conglomerate of many facts which were observed by the
keen eye of the author in various corners of Russia and, permeated
by his comical humor, were blended into a new, strange whole. Let
us try to depict this town as a single person, combining all its features
which were widely scattered by the author. The official part of the
town of N consists of the Governor, a delicate man who embroiders
tulle; the Public Prosecutor, a serious and silent man; the Postmaster,
a wit and philosopher; the Chairman of Administrative Offices, a
judicious, courteous, and kindly man; the Commissioner of Police, his
people's father and benefactor; and other officials, all of whom are
divided into the fat and the thin. Its unofficial part consists, first, of
educated people who are readers of *The Moscow News*, Karamzin,
and so forth; further, people who never do anything, solitary slug-
gards, and ladies who call their husbands by pet names, such as
Dumpy, Fatso, Belly-boy, Blackie, Kiki, and Zhuzhu. There are two
sorts of these: ladies merely pleasant and ladies pleasant in all
respects. There is a garden in this town where the trees are no higher
than reeds; but on account of an illumination it was nevertheless said
in the newspapers that the garden consisted of shady wide-branched
trees which cool you on a burning hot day... The town drives about
in its own special carriages, among which the loud-rattle and the
squeaky-wheel varieties are the most remarkable. It is of a very kind
disposition, hospitable and artless; conversations in it bear the stamp
of a kind of special intimacy, the inhabitants are all so familial and
informal among themselves. When the town plays cards, it has its
own special saying and expression for every suit and every card.
When the inhabitants talk among themselves, everyone has his own
peculiar name, at which no one takes offense. If you want to have an
understanding of the special language of this town, listen to the
famous tale of the Postmaster, the first orator of the town, about
Captain Kopeikin. All official business is conducted within a family
circle: no one is surprised at bribes, which are a kind of domestic
custom dating from ancient times. Some have accused the author of
a lack of veracity because Korobochka sent the letter of authorization

in connection with the deed in the name of the Father Archpriest;[8] because Pliushkin gave such an authorization from the country in the name of that very Chairman of Administrative Offices who registers the title; because the title deed to all the dead souls was miraculously recorded on the same day. Accusers say this is unnatural because it is contrary to law. We agree completely with the author's accusers that it is contrary to law, but how is it that they do not see that all this is in accord with the mores of that fantastic town created by the author where everything is on a domestic, special footing, and the familial way of life completely overcomes the official way of life? In spite of all that, the town is so alive and natural that we understand that it is only in it and in no other town that Chichikov could bring a part of his extraordinarily daring scheme to fulfillment. This is the material which the poet took from life and brought into his poem! By stating the content, we intentionally laid bare all this life without the charm of the art, in order more easily to bring its meaning to your notice. And now we hear the following questions arising all around us: what is in this life? What is its attraction? What is interesting about it? Why this choice of theme, hero, and persons?

Why this choice of theme, hero, and persons? But don't you know that your censures are unjust, that the poet himself was not free to elect the subject which animated him? How will you explain to me why Raphael perpetually dreamt of the Madonna? Why Teniers readily painted drunkards? Why Paul Potter's brush depicted only beasts and forgot man? How explain why the brain of Homer at various times created Achilles and Thersites, Odysseus and Iris? Or why in Shakespeare's brain there now appeared Romeo, at another time Othello, at a third Caliban or Falstaff? A genuine poet, a poet by vocation, is like history: he has almost no power of choice of heroes and subjects. In resolving the question of choice of subject, it is difficult to separate what is a result of the internal, secret, unfathomable proclivities of the poet himself, as a man, from what the epoch and a look at the life surrounding him has suggested to him.

[8] Shevyrev makes a slight error: the letter was actually sent, not to Father Kiril, but to his son, a clerk at the Revenue Office. Here, and in subsequent citations of objections to the novel, Shevyrev does not seem to be referring to any particular review published in the contemporary press.

Secret proclivity acts more conspicuously in those talents who are limited, whose fantasy is imprisoned in the narrowness of their special characters and personal sympathies; in poets with a genuine vocation, poets of great capacity, secret proclivity coincides with the character of contemporary life. Fortunate is that century in which the poets' vision is pure, ideal, noble, exalted; when Achilles and Odysseus, Orlando and Goffredo appear in their poems, when majestic and beautiful images flit through their artistic imaginations, inspiring young people and prompting wonder in all centuries and peoples! Indeed, genuine poetic creations are achieved like dreams, in which we are powerless. We may continue this comparison. It has been remarked that our dreams depend a great deal on the food we eat and on the impressions of external life; do the visions of the poet then not depend on that spiritual nutriment which contemporary surrounding life offers him? Consider the terrible state of the poet when, instead of ideal visions, horrible nightmares of actual life haunt him constantly; when, instead of Achilleses, Agamemnons, Hamlets, Lears, he dreams of Frogs, Wasps, Harpagons, Don Quixotes, Sancho Panzas, Chichikovs, Sobakeviches, and Nozdrevs. Where can he protect himself from such a race? How can he rid himself of his heroes, whose innocent victim he is? How can his life be reconciled with his art? He will withdraw into the depths of his spirit; from there will he observe the visions pursuing him; he will flash rays of his inexhaustible humor on them; he will insulate himself from them with the aid of his clear, boisterous laughter and secret tears—and he will find rest and quiet either in his soul's solemn lyrical stirrings or in a clairvoyant fantasy which encompasses everything, accepts the whole world into itself and reconstructs it in like proportions. But justify the poet as we may, the same questions still arise around us: what do your poetic nightmares have to do with us? It is enough that Nozdrevs, Chichikovs, and Sobakeviches exist in actuality, why repeat them and through art give them permanent, endless being? Admit that if you knew beforehand that you were bound to meet one of those three persons, then of course you would take a thirty-verst detour, just in order to avoid a Nozdrev or Sobakevich. What reason is there to meet them in your poem? We agree with you in so far as your observation is extremely witty and neat, but excuse us if we do not agree with its substance. It has the same two aspects as the whole problem we are discussing: the aspects of life and of art. Let us take them separately in order to understand the matter better. First, life. You say: it is enough that all this world exists in fact, why transfer it into the world of art as well? But without the poet would you know precisely that it does exist in fact? And if you did know, would you comprehend all its profound meaning, all its secret, invisible, at first glance imperceptible bonds with the world surrounding you? Are you really not curious, is it not even indispensable to you to know that the Sobakeviches, the Nozdrevs, the Chichikovs, the Korobochkas are your compatriots, your countrymen, members of the nation and state to which you belong; that you and they compose one unified, inseparable whole, that they are indispensable active links in the enormous chain of the Russian Empire, that their electric force inescapably acts even on you? What a strange, not only un-Christian, but even un-Russian sentiment has imprisoned you in your quiet and self-satisfied solitude, in the narrowness of your serene and chosen circle which you have formed ideally for yourself according to your own taste!

Oh, no! Come out, quickly come out of your confinement for the welfare of your neighbors, of your compatriots, of your Russia, and thank the poet because with the strength of his powerful imagination he has called forth from a remote corner of our motherland such countrymen, such strange brethren of yours whose existence you may have suspected but have completely forgotten in your magnificent vanities and preoccupations! Moreover, look closely at the poets' visions, listen to their secret, greatly significant prophesies. They have a wonderful, prophetic sympathy with life; they report to you things you could not learn from anybody else. Not for nothing have they always been called teachers of life—they indeed propose such profoundly thoughtful lessons to you as you have heard from no one else. Provided their words be free and open, they pose danger to no one, for they report not out of prejudice, but out of a profound feeling for truth. Yes, there is everywhere a vital bond between art and life, but it is especially vital among us, a practical people incapable of abstraction. A literary work will touch a nerve, will stimulate participation only if its essential foundation is closely bound to the roots of our life, whether on its good or bad side. All genuine poets of our fatherland comprehended this indispensable unity; you will inevitably find it in every living work of Russian poetry—and that is why every educated Russian has the obligation to study a poet's works in relation to life and not to be squeamish about any truth of Russian actuality, if only it is reproduced faithfully, fully, vividly, with the powerful fantasy of a poet. Let us now say in passing (reserving the option to speak about it later) that one of the most important tasks of Russian criticism is precisely that of resolving the question of the relations between literature and life; that literature's indigenous character must be defined from this point of view and must correspond to the purpose of art in our fatherland; that criticism lost in empty abstractions will never say anything sensible and trustworthy about Russian literature; that it is indispensable for it to combine a view of life with a view of art, to reconcile the approach of the French with the approach of the Germans; only then will criticism fully achieve its purpose. But let us halt and not be carried away further by this interesting aside in which our favorite idea was unwillingly expressed. It is clear from what we said earlier that equally wrong are those persons who in their loftiness and pride scorn the content of Gogol's poem, its presentation of actual life, and those who, abstractly enraptured by his art alone, think it unnecessary to turn their attention to the content of his poem. We absolutely do not share these opinions. All this strange world of village and provincial heroes revealed by Gogol's fantasy, a world of which we had a kind of dim understanding, as in a dream, but which is now embodied so clearly and vividly before our waking eyes, according to our way of thinking has an extremely profound and great contemporary significance. Turn your attention to the clear contradiction between this world and the one which so splendidly, so enchantingly surrounds you. The Sobakeviches, the Nozdrevs, the town of N, our countryside, the clear pictures of the ways of life within Russia, clearly presented to you in the very midst of your luxuriant sleep, destroy many serene charms, bring you down from the world of lofty dreams into the world of naked essentiality, and direct your attention to those questions which would otherwise perhaps not enter your mind! Look further. The deal uniting Chichikov with the persons of the poem and making up the main content, the main action which develops in it, is the springboard for many comic scenes. In these the author's inexhaustible talent skillfully presents one and the same motive, providing variations through the characters whom Chichikov encounters. The subject of the deal was very intricately devised by the poet's fantasy; there is nothing in it which would outwardly, at first glance, indispose us—this would be contrary to the very requirements of art. But as you penetrate through the laughter and play of fantasy to the depths of essential life, you become melancholy, your laughter changes to serious musing, and important thoughts about the essential bases of Russian life arise in your mind. Turn your attention to all these villages which are presented to you in turn, with all their landowners: how the character of the master with all his features is mirrored in each of them! And the reflections of Chichikov on the souls bought! How many profound observations on Russian life are in them! And all the empty nonsense in the activities of the town of N! There is a great deal of significant truth in it... Yes, the more deeply you look into this poem, the more important its apparently droll content becomes to you—and you follow the advice the author offers you in one of the last pages of his poem; the laughter wearying your lips will disappear, a profound, internal meditation will close them, and other words the author spoke in another place will prove true in relation to you: "What is amusing can instantly become melancholy in our eyes, and if we were to dwell upon this long enough, God only knows what thoughts might not occur to us" (62).

It is time, it is already time for us to turn from the brilliant external life which captivates us so much to internal being, to the actuality properly Russian, however insignificant and repugnant it might seem to us, captivated as we are by an unworthy pride in foreign enlightenment. Then every significant work of Russian literature which reminds us of the grievous essence of our internal being, which reveals those remote places lying near us which seem to be beyond the mountains only because we do not look at them, every such work which peeps into our life, besides its artistic merit, can in all truth have value and do a noble deed to the benefit of the Fatherland. Russian literature has never avoided this practical purpose but has always called the people to a consciousness of its internal life; and our government (honor and praise to it) has never hidden this consciousness from us, if only it was revealed by genuine talents with a sincere feeling of love for Russia and confidence in its lofty purpose. In the splendid time of Catherine, Fonvizin brought the family of the Prostakovs before us and disclosed one of the deep wounds of the Russia of that time in family life and education. In our time this feat was accomplished by Gogol in *The Inspector General* and is now accomplished again in *Dead Souls*. From Kantemir's time to ours literature has tied its productions to the essence of Russian life—and only the moles of contemporary criticism, who in their blind delirium grasp neither Russia nor its literary development, do not see that profound internal bond between life and literature which we have had from time immemorial. Let us conclude: our Russian life, with its coarse, brutish, material side, is profoundly imbedded in this first part of the poem and gives it an extremely important contemporary, apparently comic but in its depths actually sorrowful significance. The poet promises to offer us another side of our life, to expose the treasures of the Russian soul to us: the end of his poem is full of a noble, lofty presentiment of this other bright half of our existence. We await his future inspirations with impatience: may they come to him quickly, but even now we thank him for the revelation of many internal secrets which lie at the base of Russian life and are accessible only to the clear-sighted gaze of the poet gifted with a powerful clairvoyant view of life.

We agree, our opponents say, that this rough life, like anything else in the world, may be the object of the observations of a practical philosopher and of a statesman who studies it as a naturalist studies a reptile or any other lowly creature in nature.

But of what possible interest can it be to the poet? What connection is there between such life and art?

In just one moment we will answer your question, which is the next topic of our deliberations. But let us at first recall one of the remarks on the novel whose witty formulation stuck in our mind—the right time to respond to it is now, when we are turning from questions of life to questions of art and the artist. You asked us: "Is it not true that when you travel around Russia you would rather make a detour of thirty versts than meet a Sobakevich or Nozdrev? Why should one wish to meet them in a poem, when they are such a horrible nightmare even in waking hours? Could you let any one of the poem's characters come any further into your house than the anteroom?" Let us, in our turn, pose some questions. Take a look at the street: a drunkard is staggering on the sidewalk, a coachman races by in his reckless troika. You will, of course, give the drunkard a berth of several feet and will not invite the coachman, especially with his troika, into your drawing room. But if Teniers paints the drunkard with his gay brush and Orlovsky draws the daredevil coachman on a reckless troika with his immortal pencil, then Teniers's drunkard and Orlovsky's troika will both be given prominent, respectable places on the wall of your drawing room—indeed, more prominent places than those for pictures weightier in subject matter but less skillfully executed. Such is the privilege of art.

God's world is great, wide, and wonderfully diversified: there is a place in it for everything. Sobakeviches and Nozdrevs also live in it. The world the artist creates is like God's world: in it, too, there must be a place for everything. The poet's all-embracing fantasy scorns nothing; the whole world from the stars to the infernal regions is within its realm; it apprehends everything freely and re-creates it with its wondrous power. Art's specific concern is not *what* the artist chose, but *how* he re-created it, how he joined the real world with the world of the beautiful.

The first question, that of *what* the artist represented—a question demanding a definition of the link between his work and life at large —has already been decided by us. Let us now turn to the second question: *how* did the artist represent the life selected by him? One of the primary requirements of any work of art is that it should invest our inner being with a full and blissful harmony not common to everyday life. But a representation of objects taken from rough, base, animalistic human nature would produce a directly contrary reaction and would fail to meet the primary requirement of artistic impression —the creation of harmony in our soul—if it were not aided by an intensification of something else, that is, by an elevation of the subjective spirit of the poet who re-created this world. The baser, rougher, more materialistic, more animalistic the objective world depicted by the poet, the loftier, freer, fuller, and more concentrated must be his creative spirit. In other words, the baser the depicted object, the loftier must be the poet's subjective personality, the more it must renounce the object and free itself from it.

The poet's subjective personality is manifest in his humor, a wonderful mixture of laughter and tears, by means of which the poet unites all the visions of his fantasy with his own human essence. Gogol's comical humor is inexhaustible; by his deliberate will all objects arise before him showing their ridiculous sides; even the names, words, and comparisons that come to his mind evoke laughter. As might be expected, *Dead Souls* brought contagious laughter to all parts of Russia, wherever it was read. But he who does not notice a profound, secret sadness in Gogol's lively laughter neither hears nor sees very far. Gaiety turns into pensiveness and sorrow especially frequently in *Dead Souls*. For Gogol laughter is the attribute of the artist, the only medium through which he can absorb the whole crude bag and baggage of the lowly nature of mortals. Sorrow, on the other hand, is the attribute of the man in him. It is as though two beings peered at us from his novel: the poet who carried us away by his clairvoyant and whimsical fantasy, amusing us with his tireless game of laughter through which he saw everything base in the world; and the man who wept profoundly, experiencing feelings of quite a different order at the same time as the artist laughed. We see a dual or split personality in Gogol; his poetry is not whole, not integrated, but dual, broken asunder. We will see below how this dichotomy is reconciled and reaches full harmony in him.

The poet's clear laughter, passing through profound reflection and sorrow, often turns into lofty lyrical flights. The same man who laughed so lightheartedly before you and made you laugh just a minute ago, changes into an inspired oracle with solemn thought on his grave brow. This ability to pass so easily from laughter to all the nuances of sentiment, to the loftiest lyrical transports, shows that the poet's laughter originates not in a cold intellect which negates and therefore ridicules everything, but in a depth of feeling which splits into gaiety and sadness by the very nature of man. This is what distinguishes Gogol's comical humor from that empty banter (*persi-*

flage) which we often see in French literature and which derives from Voltaire. The banterer ridicules intellectually, but does not laugh with feeling; his empty laughter eventually becomes tiresome, while laughter with feeling often makes us reflect.

Let us corroborate our opinion of the character of Gogolian laughter by his own words, in which he so precisely and forcefully expresses himself and reveals the secrets of his soul. One rarely meets a poet conscious of his own character and art: Gogol is one of these rare exceptions. By his analysis of Khlestakov's character (*The Inspector General*) he has proved how clearly he understands his own creations.[9] *Dead Souls* is also full of profound remarks about the poet's state of soul and about how he regards his works. We have already cited one such passage in the first half of this review: we will repeat it now at greater length, since it is to the point.

"What is amusing can instantly become melancholy in our eyes, and if we were to dwell upon this long enough, God only knows what thought might not occur to us." And further: "Why . . . during unthinking, gay, carefree moments is another, wondrous strain suddenly felt: laughter has not yet died on the lips but it has already changed and in the faces of the very same people there shines a different light" (62). Is there not the same thing in these words as what we said above?

Here is another passage in which the same thought in relation to the poet is expressed much more clearly: "And for a long time yet I am destined by some wondrous power to go hand in hand with my strange heroes, to observe life in its entirety and immensity rushing by, to contemplate it *with laughter apparent to the world and through tears unseen and unsuspected by it*" (150). These words are precious, profound, brought up from the deepest recess of the soul and uttered at one of those rare bright moments when the poet and the man clearly understood himself!

These tears, unseen and unsuspected by the world, do in fact very often appear in Gogol's poem. One who wishes to look more deeply will notice them through the playful ring of comic laughter; we have

[9] A reference to "Otryvok iz pisma, pisannogo avtorom vskore posle pervogo predstavleniia *Revizora* k odnomu literatoru" which was published as a preface to the second edition of *Revizor* (1841).

several times experienced the transition from boisterous gaiety to sad thoughtfulness in ourselves. Let us support this with the evidence of the work itself. The central motive on which the whole comic action of the poem turns, the selling of dead souls, at first seems merely amusing, a clever invention of the artist's comic fantasy: there is nothing offensive, nothing harmful to anyone in it. What are dead souls? They are nothing, they do not exist, yet such a fuss is made because of them. Here is the source of all the comic scenes between Chichikov and the landowners, of all the commotion in the town. The motive is apparently only amusing; it is a veritable gold mine for the comic author; but when you pay more attention to Chichikov's dealings with the landowners, when you start thinking with him—or rather with the author who here made a mistake in yielding place to his hero—about the fate of all these obscure beings who suddenly come alive in front of you as divers types of the Russian peasant (in chapter seven of the poem), then a profound irony in the central motive emerges, and an involuntary thought casts a shadow on your cheerful expression.

Look at the arrangement of the characters: are they introduced in this sequence for no reason? In the beginning you laugh at Manilov, you laugh at Korobochka; you look at Nozdrev and Sobakevich somewhat more seriously; but when you see Pliushkin you will become entirely thoughtful: you will be sad at the sight of this ruined man.

And the hero of the poem? He will make you laugh many a time as he boldly sets his strange scheme in motion and raises all this commotion among the landowners and in the town; but when you have read the whole story of his life and education, when the poet has revealed to you the whole inner essence of the man—will you then not become profoundly thoughtful?

Finally, let us consider the whole town of N. Here it seems that Gogol's comical humor was given entirely free play, as though it was concentrating its powers before the end of the volume. The townsmen's talk about Chichikov's souls and about their behavior, the Governor's ball, Nozdrev's appearance, Korobochka's arrival, the scene of the two ladies, the town rumors about the dead souls and about the abduction of the Governor's daughter; all the nonsense, alarm, commotion, confusion; the news about a new governor general; and the gathering at the Police Commissioner's where the tale about Captain Kopeikin is told!... One is amazed at how the comic action grows by degrees and how new waves of the author's satire, which is here given full freedom, keep rolling in. It is as though the very demon of confusion and stupidity were flying over the town blending all the citizens into one; here, in Jean-Paul's words, there is not just one fool and not just one individual stupidity, but a whole world of nonsense incarnated in the entire town population. This is the second time Gogol has shown us such a fantastic Russian town: he did it first in *The Inspector General*. There too, we could hardly distinguish among the Mayor, the Postmaster, the Director of Charities, Bobchinsky and Dobchinsky; there too the whole town was blended into one person, of which all those gentlemen were merely parts; the same provincial folly, called forth by a comic fantasy, inspired them all, hovered over them all, and goaded them into actions and utterances each more ridiculous than the other. This same folly, only elevated to the level of a provincial capital, is embodied and is at work in the town of N. One cannot help but wonder at the resourcefulness of Gogol's talent, which has presented the same idea a second time, but has not repeated the forms or recalled one feature of the town of *The Inspector General*. This technique of comically portraying official life inside Russia calls attention to the poet's artistic instinct: he catches all the malpractices, all the strange customs, all the prejudices in the same net of light mocking irony. This is as it should be: poetry is not a denunciation, not a wrathful indictment. The only colors it can use are the colors of the laughable.

But even here, where laughter has reached its furthest limits, where the author, carried away by his humor, took his fantasy at times beyond the realm of real life and thereby violated, as we shall point out, real life's character—even here laughter turns into pensiveness at the end, when, in the midst of all this pointless bustle, the Prosecutor suddenly dies and all the turmoil terminates in a funeral. One cannot help but recall the author's words: what is amusing can instantly turn into melancholy.

The whole poem is studded with a large number of brief episodes, brilliant remarks, and profound insights into the essential side of life, all of which betray an inner propensity for a warmhearted thoughtfulness, for a serious contemplation of human life in general and Russian life in particular.

In order to complete this series of forceful examples supporting our view of Gogol's humor, we shall quote a passage from his poem which reveals the dynamics of the poet's feelings with amazing completeness and reflects, as though in a miniature, the character of his whole poem, not only of the first half which we are now reading, but also of that future second half which the author promises us. It is a description of the Russian highway:

> Again milestones began flashing by on each side, again the familiar sights: stationmasters; wells; strings of peasants' carts; gray villages with samovars; country wives; a brisk, bearded innkeeper coming hastily out of his inn yard with a bag of oats for horses in his hands; a wayfarer who has covered some eight hundred versts, plodding along in his worn-out bast shoes; little towns put up in a hurry, with their miserable small shops displaying barrels of flour, bast shoes, loaves of white bread and other sundries; striped outpost barriers; bridges under repair; then on both sides of the road, boundless fields as far as the eye can see; landowners' unwieldy carriages; a soldier on horseback carrying a green box with grapeshot in it and an inscription on the outside: such and such artillery battery; the steppe streaked with green, yellow or, where the land has just been upturned, black stripes; a song in the distance; the tops of pine trees crowned with mist; the tolling of church bells resounding and dying far away; rooks thick as flies; and the horizon without limit, without end... Oh, Russia, Russia! I envisage thee from my fair distant retreat; I behold thee: everything in thee is poor, scattered about and comfortless; thou hast no audacious marvels of nature crowned by daring marvels of art, no cities with many-windowed lofty palaces rooted in rocks, no picturesque trees, nor ivy sprouting right out of the walls of dwellings while waterfalls murmur ceaselessly and bedew them with white spray; thou hast nothing to gladden the eye or inspire the heart with awe. No one will throw back his head for a look at the tall rocks piled up high above; no eternal outlines of glittering mountains that soar into a clear silvery sky gleam through endless rows of dark arches entwined with vines, ivy and innumerable wild roses. No, thou art open, desolate, flat; like dots, like punctuation marks, lie thy lowly towns, hardly perceptible amidst the plains; there is nothing about thee to allure and charm the eye. But what

is that inexplicable force that draws me to thee? Why does thy plaintive
song, which rises all over the length and breadth of thee from sea to sea,
constantly resound in my ear? What is there in it, in that song? What is
there in it that calls, and sobs, and grips my heart? What are those
strains that poignantly caress and torment me, that stream straight into
my soul, that entwine themselves around my heart? Russia! What dost
thou want of me? What is the incomprehensible bond that mysteriously
ties us together? Why dost thou gaze at me thus, and wherefore hast
everything within thee turned upon me eyes full of expectancy? And
while I am still standing motionless in deep bewilderment, a thunder-
cloud heavy with coming rain has gathered over my head and my
thought is numb before thy vast expanse. What does this infinite expanse
foretell? Is it not here, in thee, that a boundless idea will be born, for
thou, too, are without bounds? Where else, if not here, will a titan be
brought forth into the world, since here he has enough room to stretch
his limbs, to move about freely? And thy overpowering expanse encompasses me menacingly and is reflected in the very depth of my being;
some supernatural power has lent light to my eyes: oh, what a dazzling,
wondrous horizon unfamiliar on this earth! Russia! (250–51)

Give careful consideration to these two pages in which the author's
feelings are poured forth so completely: you will notice that at the
beginning his comical humor brought to his attention only base
objects of the Russian highway, the milestones, the carts, the gray
villages with samovars, the country wives, the bearded men, the little
towns with their small shops, bast shoes and loaves of white bread...
His fantasy, drawn to one side, did not notice the expanse of our
fields which bear rolling waves of a limitless and varied harvest; the
fallow fields left by the plowman because of an overabundance of
land; the special features of our nature: the rich soil that keeps the
meadows green all summer long; the marshlands and the glades
luxuriantly colored now with lilac, now with blue, now with yellow
flowers; the thick-leaved oak; the rowan tree adorned with coralline
curls; our rivers which unexpectedly obstruct the highway in front
of the horseman; the physiognomy of the Russian peasant and his
bright red shirt; the fair-haired little boys hopping along the streets;
the ancient cities rising high above the steep banks of deep rivers; the
file of icon painters who plod their way, Heaven only knows from
what regions, for many thousands of versts across boundless Russia

subsisting on prayer and alms; the temples of God surrounding you, as though in prayerful chorus, all round the horizon, rising to the heavens and standing, brightly painted and crowned with golden crosses, in lonely majestic splendor over the humble dwellings where the Russian peasant drags out his obscure existence, earning his bread by the sweat of his brow and feeding the whole of Russia... Comical humor could not notice all this. Also, luxurious Italy, with the wonders of her art and nature, overshadowed everything that might have spoken to the poet's heart on the monotonous Russian highway... But at the mention of the name *Rus* a distant native song resounded in him with elementary force. His heart began to throb, the smile instantly vanished from his face, tears started from his eyes, an inexplicable desire drew his soul to the distant native land, lofty lyrical stirrings filled his breast and issued forth in sonorous, exalted, prophetic words!

The same quality we see in this passage was noted by us earlier in the central motive of the poem, in the arrangement of the characters, in the hero, and in the depiction of the town. Will it not be seen in the work as a whole? Yes, it will be, it must be, judging by the spirit of the poet himself so brilliantly incarnated in his creation. So he himself predicts at various points in the poem, especially in its conclusion:

> ... Possibly in this very same novel some different, hitherto untouched chords will be struck; perhaps through these pages will pass a man endowed with divine valor and virtue or a wonderful Russian maiden such as cannot be found anywhere else, possessed of all the miraculous beauty of a woman's soul, who is all generosity, disinterestedness and self-denial. And beside them the virtuous people of other nations will look lifeless, as lifeless as a book is beside the living word. Russian passions will be stirred up, and the whole world will see how deeply the Slavic nature has been filled with that which only glides superficially over the nature of other peoples .... (253–54)

And further:

> The entrance to any city, even to a capital, is always somehow unimpressive: at first everything is bleak and monotonous; smoke-begrimed

factories and plants stretch endlessly on and on; and only after some time, corners of six-story houses will come into view together with stores, signboards, vast perspectives of streets lined with belfries, colonnades, statues and towers, with the city glitter, noise and rumbling, and everything the hand and mind of man has so miraculously produced.

How the first purchases were accomplished the reader has already seen; how things will develop further, what success and failures will fall to our hero's lot, how he will deal with and overcome difficult obstacles, how colossal images will appear, how the hidden springs of our novel will come into motion, how its horizon will expand, and how *it will take its majestic, lyrical course*—all this the reader will see later. (275)

Even if the author had not opened doors into the future of his narrative by these clear words, we could still have guessed his further intentions by the demands of the beautiful, by the power and plenitude of his gift, and by the character of his humor. We have laughed much, very much over the first volume: it is hard to make a guess in such an affair, but it seems inescapable that *what is amusing will become melancholy* and that we will weep over the subsequent volumes. Our feelings will be split into two halves which will complement each other and will perhaps become reconciled at the end in the poet's radiant, reassuring, lofty, and all-embracing fantasy.

When you speak of Gogol and come under the continuous influence of his work, poetic images will enter your mind spontaneously, and the critic's cold language will turn into the language of a poet. We therefore hope it will not seem strange to the reader if we use a comparison in order to elucidate the development of inner feeling and fantasy in the whole of the poem. Look at the wind before a storm: at first it rushes by lightly, close to the ground; it stirs up the dust and all sorts of litter; feathers, leaves, scraps fly upwards and spin; and soon the air is all caught up in this capricious whirligig. It seems to be light and insignificant at first, but nature's tears and a frightening storm are hidden in this wind. Gogol's comical humor is exactly like this... But watch, the clouds have hung low. Lightning has flashed. Thunder has rolled across the sky. Rain is falling in torrents. Earth and sky are jumbled together... Isn't this just what the second part of Gogol's poem will be like, the part in which he promises us a *lyrical course, expanding* horizons, and the *majestic thunder of different words?*

But we know that above the wind, above the lightning, thunder, and clouds with which heaven battles earth and cleanses it—high above them all a clear, imperturbable, azure sky with its constant sun stretches away. Is it not likely that above the poet's humor, in which his free spirit is separated from the essence of real life, there lies the world of his radiant fantasy where his feelings, torn in two opposing directions by life, are reconciled, where the man with his laughter and tears grows calm and is converted into an artist, single and whole?

Having explained the significance of real life in the first part of Gogol's poem and having shown how this real life is joined to the world of art, we will now turn to the purely artistic element, to the realm of his fantasy, and will offer a characterization of it. Gogol's talent would be entirely one-sided if it were bounded by comical humor alone, if it embraced only one inferior sphere of real life, if his personal (subjective) feeling did not shift from lively laughter to a lofty storm of exalted passion, and if the two opposing poles of his feeling were not eventually reconciled in his radiant, creative, all-comprehending fantasy. Let us remember that one and the same pen depicted the quarrel of Ivan Ivanovich with Ivan Nikiforovich, the old-world landowners, and Taras Bulba. Gogol's artistic talent accomplished such remarkable transitions when he lived and worked in the sphere of his native Little Russia. According to all the facts and in all probability, one must suppose that he will accomplish the same transitions in the new, enormous sphere of his activity—in Russian life, which has evidently become the dwelling place of his fantasy. If *The Inspector General* and the first part of *Dead Souls* correspond to "Shponka" and to the notorious quarrel of the two Little Russians, then we have a right to expect new lofty creations, of the same kind as *Taras Bulba*, but taken this time from the Russian world.

But even now, when everything of this world re-created by Gogol bears the distinct stamp of his comical humor, even now we notice in him the presence of a radiant creative fantasy which conducts his abilities like concordant voices in a chorus, rises above all the subjective sentiments, and would be ready to pass over entirely into the pure, ideal world of art if the all too lowly objects of earthly life did not tie down its powerful wings, and if the comical humor did not hinder its free, full, and calm contemplation of life. Let us now attempt to outline its features and to make closer acquaintance with the personality of the poet which is clearly reflected in his new work.

The first feature of Gogol's fantasy is a live, *clairvoyant* insight into the world which he transfers from real existence to the ideal existence of art. We have every right to call Gogol's fantasy clairvoyant in the highest sense, because it clearly sees in every depicted object both the internal and the external sides and their mutual relationship. Without a special calling, without the gift of God, Gogol could not have developed this ability in himself; it cannot be acquired by mechanical learning. We must observe, however, that he has had excellent teachers: Italy, with her poetry, painting, and nature gave scope to the external side of his fantasy; Shakespeare and Walter Scott gave scope to its internal side and accomplished its development.

Any reader will notice the rich painting of the external world in *Dead Souls:* the warm pictures of Russian nature; the representations of all the minute details of urban and country life; the external physiognomy of all the characters who literally move before your eyes; and finally the bright plastic comparisons which are always rounded off and carried to their conclusions with painstaking art. We would have to cite a great deal from the poem if we were to demonstrate this aspect of it to the readers, but we assume that many of them know it already almost by heart and that the pictures painted by Gogol's brush have left a lively impression on their imaginations. Everything his magic fantasy touches in the external world becomes enchanting, its colors glitter, and it shines through his bright, precise, copious, and expansive language.

We have already seen this aspect of Gogol's fantasy in *Evenings on a Farm near Dikanka,* in "Old-World Landowners," and in *Taras Bulba.* Who does not remember the Little Russian steppe and fertile garden? It must be said that this aspect is even more striking in *Dead Souls.* Only the blind do not notice that here the sky of Italy, her transparent air, the clear outlines of her objects, her picture galleries and artists' studios, which Gogol frequented, and finally her poetry fostered that side of Gogol's fantasy which turned toward the external world and gave it such a pictorial direction, such fullness and completeness.

When speaking about this it is impossible not to pay attention to Gogol's sympathetic feeling for Italy, his spiritual fascination with the land of the beautiful. How can one explain this? Simply by the fact that he is a genuine artist, and that art is his vocation. Indeed, Gogol is the only one of our writers who remains faithful to his calling, who is not carried away by anything alien to it, who serves art firmly and constantly, and lives for it alone. A noble, beautiful, worthy service! Praise to him for not having exchanged it for anything else! And if this is so, what land could have satisfied him besides Italy, where everything breathes a world close to his soul? And in Italy itself, what city could he have chosen other than Rome, where the grandeur of the past, nature and art have combined to offer the contemporary artist a wonderful shelter and enchanting surroundings? From here, from his *fair distant retreat*, thanks to the transparent southern sky, he can contemplate Russia more clearly and fully. Nightmares, with the figures of Sobakeviches and Nozdrevs, visit the dreams of his fantasy, while he may rest his eyes on the well-proportioned outlines of the Colosseum and of St. Peter's Basilica, on the pictures of Perugino and Raphael, on the delicate silhouettes of hills, and on the wonderful azure of the Italian sky! This is what a genuine artist demands. May he have a blissful sojourn there, may the moments of inspiration come to him as often as possible!

The bright stamp of the nature, painting, and poetry of the aesthetic European South overlays the colors of *Dead Souls* and everything comprising the external side of the world depicted in them. In connection with this remark, I must beg the reader not to confuse the content and the art: the content, naturally, was given by Russia and the poet remained always faithful to it; but the clairvoyance and the power of fantasy with which he re-creates the distant world of his fatherland were developed in Gogol by the Italian environment. In one passage it is evident that Italy involuntarily lent some of her burning colors even to the content of the picture: this passage is the description of Pliushkin's garden in which the green clouds and trembling cupolas of foliage, set against celestial horizons, remind one of southern landscapes.

When speaking of this Southern element in Gogol's poem one cannot forget the wonderful similes which turn up quite frequently in *Dead Souls!* Their full artistic beauty can be appreciated only by those who have studied the similes of Homer, of the Italian epic poets, of Ariosto and particularly of Dante, the only poet of the Christian age who has achieved the simplicity of the Homeric simile and reinstated that well-rounded fullness and completeness with which it appeared in the Homeric epic. Gogol has followed in the footsteps of his great teachers in this respect. In his hands similes assume the shape of a separate, complete little picture, in which he is as absorbed as an epic poet, and which he skillfully inserts into the body of the narrative poem without disturbing its unity or interrupting the development of its plot. There are many such similes in Gogol, but we shall single out one where completeness and simplicity of image recall Homeric similes:

Black evening coats flitted about, singly and in clusters, like flies moving over a gleaming white sugar loaf on a hot July day when an aged house-keeper breaks and splits it into glittering lumps before an open window; children gather around to watch with curiosity the movements of her roughened[10] hands lifting the mallet, while the light squadrons of flies riding on the air stream fly in boldly as if they owned the place, and taking advantage of the old woman's failing eyesight and the sunshine that dazzles her, scatter over the sweets, here singly, there in thick clusters. Sated with the riches of summer, which spreads delectable repasts for them at every step, they come in not to eat but to show off, to swagger up and down the sugar heap, to rub their hind- and forelegs

[10] When reading this word one cannot help but recall with indignation the *dirty tricks* of a Petersburg journal which distorts the text of Gogol's poem and then throws abuse on its very own distortions. Read page 29 of the "Literary Chronicle" section in *Library for Reading*. The editor prints "the movements of her woman's (*zhenskikh*) hands" instead of "the movements of her roughened (*zhestkikh*) hands," and then adds in parentheses: "that is, the hands of the aged woman housekeeper who could not have had any other hands but those of a woman." Really, you cannot believe your own eyes when you see to what extremes the unfairness of a critic, blinded by a strange hatred for a talent, can go. It is a long time since any article has evoked such grievous revulsion in us as this review of *Dead Souls* in which both the text and the content of Gogol's work are deliberately distorted. We are ready to prove our statement and regard it our duty to reveal the indecency of such an act before the eyes of the public. (Author's note.)

against each other, to scratch themselves under the wings, or, stretching up their forelegs, to rub them over their heads; then they turn around and fly away, only to be replaced by new harassing squadrons. (12–13)

Take a close look at these flies: how graceful they are, and how subtly the poet has caught all their minute movements! Let us quote a few like similes from Homer:

Even as when the tribes of thronging bees issue from some hollow rock, ever in fresh procession, and fly clustering among the flowers of spring, and some on this hand and some on that fly thick; even so from ships and huts before the low beach marched forth their many tribes by companies to the place of assembly.[11]

And as when a lazy ass going past a field hath the better of the boys with him, an ass that hath had many a cudgel broken about his sides, and fareth into the deep crop, and wasteth it, while the boys smite him with cudgels, and feeble is the force of them, but yet with might and main they drive him forth, when he hath had his fill of fodder, even so did the highhearted Trojans and allies, called from many lands, smite great Aias, son of Telamon, with darts on the centre of his shield, and ever followed after him.

(11.201)

And ever men thronged about the dead, as in a steading flies buzz around the full milkpails, in the season of spring, when the milk drenches the bowls, even so thronged they about the dead.

(16.307–8)

Here are some similes from Dante:

As sheep come forth from the pen, in ones, in twos, in threes, and the others stand all timid, casting eye and nose to earth,
     and what the first one doeth, the others do also, huddling up to her if she stand still, silly and quiet, and know not why,

---

[11] *The Iliad* done into English prose by Andrew Lang, Walter Leaf, and Ernest Myers, *The Complete Works of Homer* (New York: The Modern Library, 1950), bk. 2, p. 21. The subsequent two quotations are also from *The Iliad;* the book and page numbers will be given in parentheses within the text.

so saw I then the head of that happy flock move to come on, modest in countenance, in movement dignified.[12]

As doves when gathering wheat or tares, all assembled at their repast, quiet and showing not their wonted pride,

if aught be seen whereof they have fear, straightway let stay their food, because they are assailed by greater care;

so saw I that new company leave the singing, and go towards the hillside . . . .

(2.204)

The technique of his famous teachers is very evident in Gogol's similes. Let us recollect the best ones: the simile of Manilov and a cat tickled behind its ear; of an oval face and a transparent egg; of a joyous feeling in the midst of sorrow and a glittering carriage dashing through a poor village; of Pliushkin's eyes and mice; of the nervous attention of an impatient lady and a Russian gentleman hunter waiting for a hare; of town ladies and a scholar expounding a bold hypothesis; and of the town's citizens and a schoolboy into whose nose his roommates thrust a "hussar." We cannot, however, resist quoting in full the wonderful picture of barking dogs and their comparison with a choir:

Meanwhile the dogs were barking furiously in all sorts of voices: one, throwing up his head, drawled out his notes with as much zeal as if he were paid God-knows-what high salary for it; another chopped off his barks hastily like a sacristan; between them the indefatigable treble of an apparently young puppy rang like the bell of a mail coach; and finally all that was topped by a bass, possibly an old fellow, endowed by a sturdy canine nature, because he was as hoarse as a contrabass in a choir when the concert is in full swing: when tenors rise on tiptoes in their intense desire to hit a high note and all strive upward, their heads thrown back while he alone, with his unshaven chin thrust into his cravat, squatting and almost sinking to the ground, lets out a note that sets the windowpanes to shaking and tinkling. (45–46)

[12] Dante Alighieri, *Purgatorio, The Divine Comedy*, trans., John A. Carlyle, Thomas Okey, and Philip H. Wicksteed (New York: The Modern Library, 1932), canto 3, p. 208. The second quotation is also from *Purgatorio;* the canto and page number will be given in parentheses within the text.

We shall not cite a whole host of other, briefer similes which are scattered through the work: let us just recall the roads that crawl in all directions like crabs thrown out of a bag, or the covered chandelier in Pliushkin's house which looks like a silk cocoon with the silkworm inside. Whatever Gogol's magic art touches lives in his bright words; every object shines through them and emerges with its shape and color. The Russian poet could raise this quality of his fantasy to such a degree of art only in that country where Dante had worked and where Ariosto, as a friend of Raphael's, had watched his immortal brush in his studio, and transformed its vivid colors into flaming Italian words. Only those who comprehend Gogol's feeling for Italy can fully appreciate the beauty in the plastic, external element of his fantasy.

But the objects of external nature receive another, special life in Gogol, because they are tightly bound to man. They are there, not for their own sakes, not for the sake of epic description, but most often in order to expose us to ourselves, to serve as symbols of individual characters or of the whole nation, to express the inner life and actions of man. Remember the landowners' villages, Korobochka's hen roost, Sobakevich's furniture and dinner, Pliushkin's house or rather storeroom, Nozdrev's kennels, Selifan's horses... The man himself lives in every dead, soulless object; his personal qualities and character are reflected in it. The poet tells us how this humble observation of objects developed in him from childhood: how in town or village *nothing eluded* his *fresh, keen attention;* how he followed the movements and examined the clothes and exterior of people who passed by him and *in his thoughts* was *carried after them into their meager lives;* how he tried to guess what landowners were like by looking at their houses and gardens. This stock of impressions of a distant childhood evidently became useful and served as raw material for his poetry.

We have explained the external side of the poet's clairvoyant fantasy, have shown its development and its relation to the internal side: let us now turn to the latter. By the internal side we mean a perceptive contemplation of the inner man in its various manifestations. In this respect Gogol is a worthy pupil of northern poetry, particularly of Shakespeare and Walter Scott. Here the creation of integrated characters comes first. Gogol is able clearly to see every person he creates and to trace him through every possible situation in life, through all windings and movements of body and soul. It is here that a poet's creative power particularly appears.

The characters created by Gogol are not individual cases, not isolated phenomena recorded by an observant mind. No, the artist elevates each of them to the level of a general type and even hints at this intention. We remember what he says about Nozdrev and Sobakevich. Indeed, you will find parts of Sobakevich, this clenched fist of a man with a sturdy nature all compressed within itself, in many people in different layers of society, up to the highest. Some have scorned this man, especially when they saw him over his "nurse" and after dinner. A strange thing! They are squeamish about him in the poem, as though they did not often see him around themselves, as though they did not often dine with the likes of Sobakevich, who stuff themselves, if not with "nurse," turkey, and tarts, then with enormous truffled cutlets, who boast of education because they speak French, and who are morally even more odious than Sobakevich himself. Do you know that there are Sobakeviches even in literature? Take for instance all those writers who regard literature as the easiest way to make money; all those literary *kulaks* who talk about a writer's talent in exactly the same terms as Sobakevich talks about the Governor and other officials, and who constantly enact Krylov's famous fable in their critical reviews.[13] Are all these fine fellows really not Sobakeviches, even though they may seem to stand a little higher in rank? Just take the trouble to collate with the original what they innocently quote from a book supplying parenthesized remarks[14]— and you will come across more than one Elizaveta Sparrow, whom they can cleverly slip in for their own clandestine purposes! And Manilov? Oh, there are many Manilovs in the capitals: unfortunately, you cannot escape this breed of idle dreamers in our Russia. They seem to be insignificant people, but if you look more closely, they really are very harmful in their indolence. And Korobochka? There are Korobochkas all over Moscow, in all the back streets of our vast capital; they gather at the market places in throngs, only they buy

[13] A reference to the fable "Osel i solovei."
[14] See above, p. 49, n. 10.

more than they sell. And Nozdrev? We are overcrowded with crotchety Nozdrevs. They have insinuated themselves into literature together with the Sobakeviches. The quill driver who yesterday sent you polite, deferential letters and praised you in print yet turns on you with abuse today, also in print, without any reason; who springs out from behind the gate and barks incessantly at all the passers-by as if he were paid God knows what for it; who reviles all the possible glories of the world, the glories of Italy, France, and Russia, and starts worshipping someone who has not asked for his praise, shouting to him at the top of his voice: "You are greater than Shakespeare!"—just as Nozdrev assured Chichikov that he was dearer to him than his own father; and who, finally, develops his impertinent bragging and self-praise to the level of an accomplished craft; tell me, isn't such a blackguard of a quill driver also a Nozdrev —a Nozdrev who has, Heaven only knows by what accident, put his hand to pen and literature? He is probably worse than Nozdrev, because Nozdrev abuses and praises, barks and licks boots, lies and brags entirely instinctively, while the blackguardly quill driver does the same in the full consciousness of his actions. And can you deny that there are also Chichikovian deeds in our literature? For instance, somebody collects subscriptions for a book which exists—like the dead souls bought by Chichikov—only in his imagination: is that not a Chichikovian act? But enough of this.

Gogol has a great talent for creating characters, but we must also frankly state that we notice he has a shortcoming with regard to his completeness in portraying characters and setting them in motion. The comical humor which conditions the poet's view of all these people and the comicality of the events in which they are entangled are both obstacles to presenting them with all their sides and to revealing their full lives through their actions. We surmise that in addition to the characteristics now visible there must be other, good traits in them which would be revealed in different circumstances. Manilov, for example, for all his idle dreamfulness, must be quite a well-meaning man, a kind and undemanding master to his servants, and honest in everyday affairs. At first sight Korobochka is only a thrifty woman, engrossed in the material interests of her estate, but she must also fear God and give alms. It is more difficult to unearth something good in Nozdrev and Sobakevich, but even in them there must be some more human inclinations. This general human side is revealed more deeply and fully in Pliushkin, especially in the former Pliushkin, because the poet looks at his character much more seriously and sternly. It seems as though his comic and ironic demon left the author alone this time and his fantasy had greater scope and freedom, so that he might examine the person from all sides. He acted the same way with Chichikov when he revealed his education and whole biography.

The demon of comedy sometimes carries away the poet's fantasy, so that the characters go beyond the limits of verisimilitude, although this happens very rarely. It seems unnatural to us, for example, that Sobakevich, a practical and solid man, should start praising his dead souls and let himself be carried away by such fantasy. Nozdrev would have been more capable of such transports if the deal had been arranged with him. The scene, if you please, is very funny: we roared with laughter at the oratorical pathos of Sobakevich; yet as far as the verisimilitude of the fantasy is concerned, it does not ring true to us. Even his eloquence, the gift of words he suddenly displays by some special inspiration in his panegyrics to Mikhei the coachman, Probka the carpenter, and other dead souls, seems to contradict his ordinary style, which is terse and roughhewn, just as nature roughhewed him. The transgression against one truth has brought with it a transgression against another. The author felt this himself, and his tongue slipped when he remarked of Sobakevich: "His pace and power of expression were truly surprising" (116). The same can be observed about Chichikov: his reveries in chapter seven about the dead souls he had bought are beautiful, but they are mistakenly attributed to Chichikov himself who, as a solid man, could hardly have thought up such wonderful, poetic legends about Stepan Probka and the bootmaker Maksim Teliatnikov, and especially about the literate Popov who traveled without a passport, and Fyrov Abakum who roamed about with the barge haulers. We do not understand why the poet did not express these reflections in his own person. It also seemed unnatural to us that Chichikov should have got so drunk as to order Selifan to make a roll call of all the dead souls. Chichikov is a solid man, and he will hardly drink enough to fall into such dreaminess.

What we have said about the characters must be repeated about the reproduction of Russian life at large in Gogol's poem. Gogol's fantasy reveals life's texture, which is invisible to the naked eye because of all its threads and knots, with wonderful clarity. The more we look at the invented details, the more amazed we are at how masterfully they are fitted to the whole and to each other. We become convinced that this can be achieved only by an integrated, creative, clairvoyant insight into life, and not by an artificial, mechanical process which, try as it might, will never fit the pattern of life, will never be able to imitate life. This can be achieved only by a fantasy imperiously in control of all the poet's abilities while they, in their turn, are ready to serve it with their gifts, with the fruits of their experiences and observations, and with all other means. We have already hinted at this in our account of the contents; now we shall refer to a few minor details which, minor as they are, still constitute hidden threads in the texture of the whole narrative.

How lifelike it is that the coachman Selifan gets drunk visiting Manilov's household servants! When he drives away from Koro- bochka's house he is an entirely different coachman: he is orderly and diligent. From Nozdrev's he drives off in a foul mood and in the same disturbed state of mind as that of the man he and his master have just visited. No wonder that on the first occasion he lost his way and over- turned the carriage in his drunkenness; on the second, he drove very respectably; and on the third, he senselessly ran into another carriage, entirely in Nozdrev's manner. These details may appear as minutiae at first sight, but they are very important in the general texture of events which make up the action of the plot. Observe Nozdrev's escapades: they arise from his character. It is totally impossible to make a deal with him; he alone is capable of setting the town aflutter during the Governor's ball and of ruining Chichikov's whole enter- prise; he is the one whose visit and frankness make Chichikov realize that it is time to leave fast. Is Korobochka not faithful to herself all through? Who else could have driven to town in such a hurry and raised such an alarm? The lightning comes out of the blue; this is a common rule of the world. The Korobochkas are very important and significant in such enterprises.

But here, too, we have the same reservation: the author's comical humor sometimes hinders him in embracing life in its fullness and broad extent. This is especially clear in those brilliant remarks about Russians which are scattered all through the poem. In most of them we see only a negative, laughable side, a grasping of only one half, not the whole, of Russian life. Any nonsense and stupidity yields itself readily to the comic poet's keen brush. The coachman Selifan boasted that he would not overturn the carriage, yet he overturned it immediately. The little girl knows how to show the way, but she cannot tell left from right. Uncle Miniai and Uncle Mitiai fuss and fuss about the *brichka* and the carriage but, muddleheaded as they are, do nothing but exhaust the horses. From one point of view, we see here a good trait of the Russian people: its cordiality and selfless readiness to help a neighbor in need which you will seldom find in the civilized West; but from another point of view it is a pity that all this cordiality is combined with muddleheadedness, which is very funny but does not provide a complete picture. For, in general, the Russian peasant is far from muddleheaded: in a matter demanding common sense he will do better than any learned foreigner. It is true that misfortune will sometimes overtake him as it overtakes Selifan; he will sometimes boast and topple a carriage in a drunken state; but it also happens frequently that he gallops through the devil knows where, happy-go-luckily drives across a straw bridge, and, unlike some Germans, never forgets that he is driving horses while the reins are in his hands, nor lets his master fall out of the carriage. Show us such coachmen, too. The misfortune that he works and works, yet finds himself sent away without a kind word, can also befall the Russian peasant, as it befell Uncle Mitiai and Uncle Miniai; but as a general rule, if a mishap occurs on the highway, who helps better than our peasant, who is more sensible and efficient than he? How could he be otherwise when, in addition to his natural endowment of common sense, the highway itself has helped him with its bitter lessons, with its pits and bumps and ruts, with its mud up to the horses' belly, with its melodramatic bridges, and with all those discomforts which cause so much bitterness to the educated traveler inside Russia and which would cause even more bitterness were it not for the Russian peasant, with his patience, his selfless cordiality, and cleverness!

Let readers not think that we are accusing Gogol of anything. God

spare us any such thought, or rather, any such feeling! Gogol loves
Rus, knows her and divines her with his creative sensibility better
than many: we see this at every step. His depiction of the very shortcomings of the nation, if such description is taken in a moral and
practical sense, leads him to profound meditations on the Russian,
his abilities, and particularly his education, on which his happiness
and strength depend. Read Chichikov's reflections about the runaway
souls (151–56): after your laughter you start thinking deeply about
how the Russian of the lowest social status grows up, develops, is
educated, and lives in this wide world.

Let readers not think either that we regard Gogol's talent as one-
sided, capable of contemplating only the negative half of human and
Russian life. Of course we do not think so, and everything we have
said above would contradict such an assertion. If comical humor
predominates in the first volume of his poem and if we see *mostly* the
negative side of Russian life and the Russian in it, it does not follow
that Gogol's fantasy could not rise to a full comprehension of all of
Russian life. He himself promises that he will present us with the
whole *incalculable wealth of the Russian spirit*, and we are convinced
that he will gloriously make his word good. Even in this first part, in
which the content, the characters, and the theme absorbed him in
laughter and irony, he felt a necessity to make up for the deficiency of
the other side of life. This is why he introduces frequent digressions
and scatters about brilliant observations, giving us a presentiment of
this other side of Russian life, which he will reveal in its entirety
when the time comes. Who does not remember the digressions about
the apt words and nicknames the Russian gives, about the boundless
Russian song carried over the vast expanse of our land from sea to
sea, and finally about the dashing troika, this troika-bird, which only
a Russian could have invented and which suggested to Gogol an
inspired page, a wonderful image for the rapid flight of our glorious
Rus? All these lyrical digressions, especially the last one, seem to give
us a glance into what lies ahead, a presentiment of the future—a future
that must vastly unfold in the work and show us all the fullness of our
spirit and life.

We cannot resist quoting the wonderful digression about the Russian nickname and the Russian word:

The Russian people are good at using strong language. And if they bestow a nickname on anyone, it will stick to his lineage and posterity, he will take it with him to the place of his work, into his retirement, to Petersburg, to the end of the world. And no matter how cunningly he may try to ennoble it, how many scribblers he may hire to trace his name from an ancient princely line, it's of no avail: the nickname will burst out crowing with all its crow's might, and will proclaim to all from what nest the bird has flown. An aptly spoken word is like a written word: it cannot be hewn out, not even with an ax. And how apt are some of those phrases that have sprung out of the very heart of Russia, in places where there are no Germans, no Finns, no other foreign tribes, but only the native Russian wit, lively and quick, which is never at a loss for a rejoinder, which loses no time in hatching it, like a hen sitting on eggs, but stamps a man with it then and there, as if issuing him a passport he is to carry with him as long as he lives; and there is no need to add what nose or lips he has—all his characteristics are in that one word.

Just as there is a multitude of churches and monasteries, with their domes, spires and crosses scattered all over our holy and pious Russia, so does a multitude of various tribes, generations and peoples swarm, color and agitate the face of the earth. And each people, bearing within it the seed of strength, endowed with creative spiritual faculties, with vivid individuality and other gifts of God, is distinguished from the others by its own word, which, at the same time it expresses an idea, reflects part of the people's character. A profound knowledge of the heart and a wise understanding of life resound in the word of the Briton; like an airy dandy, the short-lived word of the Frenchman dazzles and soon fades away; artfully will the German concoct his word, intellectual but dry, and not within everybody's grasp. But there is no other word that can be so wide in its sweep, so quick to hit its aim—no other word that, bursting out from the very heart, can bubble and vibrate with life so buoyantly as an aptly spoken Russian word. (122–23)

It is noteworthy that the poet's sharp pencil does not tick off Italian in this enumeration of languages, although he of course had all the data before him to be able to judge it. Is this perhaps because the Russian people has an affinity to the Italian artist in the aptness and liveliness of its word as well as in much else, despite the fact that heat and frost have separated the two peoples?

Let us conclude: the teachers of the South and the North, Italy and Shakespeare, have put their stamp on both the external and internal sides of Gogol's fantasy with regard to a clairvoyant insight into life. Such a combination of two elements, evident in our other poets as well, particularly in Pushkin, promises a many-sided and complete future development for Russian fantasy and for Russian art. Oh, if we could unite in ourselves the external quality of the South and the internal quality of the North, the graceful plasticity and form of the first and the profound idea of the second—we would achieve the ideal in art! It is pleasant to dream of this, and even more pleasant to see that our dream has begun to be realized in certain representatives of Russian art. What we now see augurs well for the future, especially if we refuse to be limited by any one-sided trend and do not pervert the bountiful Russian gift by an exclusive alien influence—be it French as formerly, or German as sometimes happens now. Comical humor, capturing the poet's fantasy and presenting to it only one half of life, keeps the internal and external clairvoyance from completeness. We are not saying that this is a shortcoming of Gogol's fantasy: it is one of its qualities; but we also think that the poet is capable of allowing his fantasy the freest and most extensive flight which would embrace the whole of life; and we suppose that his fantasy, developing further and further, will grow even richer in its fullness and will encompass the life not only of *Rus*, but also of other nations, a possibility we have already clearly seen in his *Rome*.

The relationship between humor and fantasy is a matter of primary importance for Gogol's poetic talent. They are both God's gifts, and necessary gifts: to strike the appropriate balance between them is the greatest task for the poet's development!

This relationship between the two is excellently defined by the second feature of Gogol's fantasy, which is its close correspondence with the essential reality of the life portrayed. Neither in this work, nor in the best of his previous creations does his fantasy disappear into a whimsical dreamworld: rather, its whole poetic content rests on the deep foundations of human life and of nature, into which it breathes life. His poetry is not like clouds, shapelessly and meaninglessly floating above the earth, but like the Fata Morgana, an ideal reflection in the sky of everything that really happens on earth. Like his fantasy, Gogol's humor is tightly bound to the roots of life itself.

This feature of Gogol's fantasy and humor is an especially Russian characteristic. Our poetry, like our philosophy, is unable to renounce life and pass into an abstract, whimsical existence, devoid of meaning. A Hoffmann is impossible among us. The whole abstract side of Goethe's poetry, all its indefiniteness, is also alien to our character and could not be grafted into it. Jean-Paul's humor is magnificent, but it differs from the Gogolian in that it is too trivial and divorced from what is essential in life.

Gogol felt this himself in his new work, and on its last pages (276–77) has pointed out the profound connection between his poem and life.

The least successful of Gogol's earlier works were "Viy" and those stories in the volume *Arabesques* in which he submitted to a German influence. We also count among these "The Nose," published in *The Contemporary*.[15]

The deeper Gogol's fantasy and humor penetrate into the essence of life, the mightier they are, the higher they rise, enriching with content the poetry they create. Every poet, like the Titan Antaeus, must touch the earth: the closer his contact with it, the greater his strength becomes and the freer he flies to the heavens; but if he is entirely torn away from the earth, he loses his strength. This is true of the poet in general; it must be even more so of the Russian poet, judging by the character of his nation; it is certainly true of our Gogol.

Let us repeat: those who pay no attention to the content of Gogol's poetry and see only an abstract artistic side to it, are wrong. Their attitude is no compliment to him, and it also reveals an ignorance of the character of Russian poetry.

For this reason we will tell the poet sincerely: his fantasy and humor must always, unfailingly touch real life, even if they do not live in it entirely, since art is free; but the more deeply they penetrate reality, the greater will be their effect and the more correctly will they

---

[15] In 1835 Gogol submitted the original version of this story for publication to *Moskovsky nabliudatel*, one of the editors of which was Shevyrev. The editors found the story "trivial" and "dirty," and refused to publish it. Gogol revised the story and eventually published it in *Sovremennik* 3 (1836).

establish a mutual relationship, on which the future development of our poet largely depends. All the power and all the beauty of his work have this source, just as all its flaws, all its weak sides are caused by the opposite—they appear wherever the poet has betrayed his basic nature. Whenever he leaves the reality of life too far behind, his humor, deprived of content, becomes trivial, blowing, as it were, soap bubbles; and the laughter, without its profound meaning, is wasted like idle chatter. This happens rarely, but it does happen every time the poet is carried away by his comic demon, gets *muddled up*, and leaves the reality of life too far behind. It occurs most frequently in the description of the town, especially in the description of the Governor's ball and the ladies' society, when Gogol positively rants and raves around Chichikov. It seems to us that in this case his material has failed the poet, he has unwittingly turned away from life and given himself over to the whims of his comical humor, which in its turn carried him away and transgressed against the character of his true-to-life fantasy.

We have called Gogol's fantasy *clairvoyant* and *true-to-life*, but there is a third feature of its artistic character, a feature which is just as Russian as the second: we could call it a *hospitable* quality. Yes, there is a generosity and largess verging on extravagance in the fantasy of our poet, a quality expressed by the old saying: whatever is on the stove is meant for the table. Let us explain. Reading *Dead Souls* you may have noted how many wonderfully complete pictures, brilliant similes, observations, episodes, and sometimes even lightly but convincingly outlined characters Gogol throws in just like that, simply as gifts, as an addition to the poem, over and above what necessarily pertains to its content. Remember the companion at Sobakevich's table, or Nozdrev's fair-haired brother-in-law who looks resilient on the outside but is soft inside: Gogol has thrown them in free, even without names, as additions to the characters. The poet happens to mention Moldavian pumpkins: they remind him of balalaikas and of a village swain, an ogler and dandy of twenty, who whistles at snowy-breasted maidens (104). His imagination strays into Pliushkin's workyard, and the clear picture of a Moscow timber market presents itself to him (131). Pliushkin, by contrast, reminds him of a spendthrift landowner who squanders his wealth with all the expansiveness of Russian recklessness and lordly unconcern; and there appears in the same context the illumination of the garden, the branches wonderfully lit from below, the dark, threatening sky above, and the somber treetops. Everyone has fallen asleep in the tavern where Chichikov is staying, only in one window may a light be seen: and here is something else for you thrown into the bargain—a joke about a lieutenant come from Riazan, a great devotee of boots, who is trying on his fifth pair and cannot look at it enough. One could compare Gogol to a wealthy Russian host who not only lays his abundant table with a two-arshin sterlet, Arkhangelsk veal, and other solid dishes, but also offers you a great variety of hors d'oeuvres, niblets, dips, and expensive sauces, which are all additions to the immense feast and are all invariably eaten up, even though they may be overshadowed by the main attractions of generous Russian hospitality. These additions of Gogol's fantasy sometimes have a lofty character, sometimes turn into a joke, after the manner of Russian songs and folk tales which sometimes offer you lofty sayings of the following kind:

> High is the height of the sky,
> Deep is the depth of the sea,
> Wide are the plains of the earth,
> Deep are the whirlpools of the Dnepr,[16]

and sometimes playful ones, like the famous facetious sayings in our popular stories.

The main qualities of Gogol's fantasy are reflected in his language. We intend to devote a special article to the language and style of *Dead Souls;*[17] right now we shall point out only a few features which are relevant to what we have been saying. The clairvoyance of his fantasy is reflected in his style with singular clarity. Its external side makes it a painting: Gogol's style is a brilliant brush applying all shades of color. We have already had occasion to speak about this. The internal side is manifest in the wonderful variety of the dialogue of

[16] The verse cited is one of the so-called *bylinnye zachiny;* see *The Oxford Book of Russian Verse* (Oxford: Oxford University Press, 1924), p. 1.

[17] This apparently remained only an intention.

the persons portrayed, which always vividly expresses the particular character of each. The correspondence between the fantasy and real life is reflected in the style in that it is *ingenuous*, artless: we notice only the exceptions, when the poet betrays the basic character of his fantasy. Finally, the third characteristic of this last, Russian hospitality, stamps his style: Gogol's language is broad, full, expansive, and prolific. His speech is crisp, like well-cooked dough; it overflows like a glass filled by the hand of a generous host who does not worry about the wine and the tablecloth; and his periods are sometimes overloaded, like the meat pies of an ingenious gastronome who has bought countless supplies and spares nothing for the stuffing. In short, the full hand of an extravagant rich man is seen everywhere; there is enough of everything; it often occurs to one that a little moderation and discrimination might be appropriate, but one is afraid of offending the host's noble generosity and of depriving oneself of the many wonderful delicacies which he liberally spreads on his table.

At the conclusion of this aesthetic analysis of *Dead Souls* a clarification of the term *narrative poem* may be expected of us. A complete response to this question will be possible only when the whole work is finished. Now the term *narrative poem* seems to us to have a double meaning: if we look at the work from the point of view of the fantasy which is in it, we can take the term in its normal, poetic, even elevated sense; but if we look at the comic humor which dominates the content of the first half, then the term tells us that a profound, significant irony informs the poem and we say to ourselves: "should there not be added to the subtitle: A Poem of Our Time?"

Apollon Grigorev

A NEST OF THE GENTRY
BY IVAN TURGENEV

Originally published in the journal Russkoe slovo, *nos. 4, 5, 6, and 8 (1859), under the title "I. S. Turgenev i ego deiatelnost; po povodu romana* Dvorianskoe gnezdo. Pisma k G. G. A. K. B." *The addressee of the letters was Count G. A. Kushelev-Bezborodko, publisher of the journal. The present selection comprises passages from chapters 2, 4, 5, 7–9, 12, 15–19, 22, and 23 of the essay. It was characteristic of Grigorev to digress at length about contemporary literary criticism and aesthetic theory in its social setting; these digressions have been omitted as unnecessary to the main drift of Grigorev's argument. This particular essay, out of Grigorev's large literary output, has been chosen because it contains most of Grigorev's cherished ideas, including his views on Lermontov and Gogol, his interpretation of Goncharov's* Oblomov, *and his general appraisal of Turgenev's literary work up to 1859.*

In his brilliant article on Turgenev's work, A. V. Druzhinin called the distinctive feature of his talent *poetry.* The word chosen by him will be absolutely right for a contrast of Turgenev's work with that *pure* naturalism which prevails, or at least has prevailed all this time in our literature; and although the word *poetry* is one of the vaguest, still everyone understood just *what* the respected editor of *Library for Reading* wanted to say.[1] In this respect Turgenev really does show some resemblance to Sand, the sole poet-idealist of our age, although he lacks the mighty, enchanting powers of Sand. Like Sand, and like Sand alone, he loves to create a rather fantastic world, to devise for

[1] See A. V. Druzhinin, "*Povesti i rasskazy* I. S. Turgeneva, SPB, 1856," *Biblioteka dlia chteniia* 2–3 (1857).

this world a wholly individual setting, to affect the finest strings in the soul—and you trust him implicitly, although not so completely as you trust Sand. You believe in this fantastic world because of the correctness of the psychological analysis; you do not call the individual setting aberrant, for you palpably see its *poetic* truth, its ideal *possibility* of being; you will enter a world of the finest sensations, lured by their detailed and artistically scrupulous analysis. But Turgenev does not have that ideal power which compels everyone to put aside his doubts and believe in the twilight world of *Le Piccinino*, in the exceptional circumstances and types in *Teverino*, and so forth. There is a kind of incompleteness to his work, and therefore some of his tales leave you with a kind of moral irritation rather than belief and satisfaction. "Three Meetings," for example, is so poetically conceived, so luxuriant, so sweetly furnished with details, yet offers so little gratification for the thirst it has aroused. This happens with other passages in his tales, even though they are *poetic*, as, for example, the scene of the morning meeting in the woods between Veretev and the heroine of the tale "The Calm." We always feel something queer in these poetic tendencies of Turgenev: we feel that his nature thirsts to express these tendencies while he is apathetic to all others; yet at the same time we feel that his personal experience and the trends of public life have smashed all his belief in these tendencies. Sand, on the other hand, believes in poetic tendencies firmly and steadfastly, and at times the faith of her great talent works genuine miracles even in her most eccentric creations.

Therefore, the word *poetry*, applied to Turgenev's work, takes on meaning in contrast with pure naturalism.

I must point out to you that by pure naturalism I do not mean Gogol's work, nor what has long been called "the natural school." I mean rather the simple depiction of actuality without an ideal, without rising above it. This is partially manifested in the details of Goncharov's *A Common Story*, fully and clearly in the solid genius of Pisemsky, brusquely and roughly in the works of Potekhin.[2] Gogol's work is imbued with the consciousness of an ideal, the so-called

[2] A. A. Potekhin wrote novels, short stories, and plays on peasant life, on petty officialdom, on businessmen. Grigorev probably has in mind, above all, his comedy *Mishura* (1858).

natural school with the morbid humor of protest. It is quite understandable that the talent of Turgenev—which is impressionable and sensitive to everything, which responded to the natural school with the remarkable story "Petushkov" and with the bad drama *The Bachelor*, which even echoed dramatic proverbs and platitudes from the life of "high society," and was somehow effeminately subordinated to every trend—this talent did not respond only to contemporary *pure* naturalism. This was outside his sphere, outside (but no higher than) his talent.

In this sense, A. V. Druzhinin is absolutely right when he calls poetry the distinct property of Turgenev's talent. In any other connection the word *poetry* expresses nothing. Why, in other senses, is poetry reserved to Turgenev? Is there really no poetry in Ostrovsky, who was able to endow the well-known scene in *A Protégée of the Mistress* with such warm colors, the scene in the garden which in anyone else's hands would have descended to triviality and even below triviality? Is Tolstoy really not a poet in passages of *Childhood, Boyhood, and Youth:* in the chapter "Holy Idiot," in the charming episode of love for Sonechka, in the depiction of the night in the garden (*Youth*)? Finally, did not even the pure naturalism in Goncharov and Pisemsky (remember the provincial town, the monastery in *One Thousand Souls*) rise at times to poetry?

It is clear that A. V. Druzhinin meant the word *poetry* only in connection with the general artistic aspirations of Turgenev, in contrast with the aspirations of our time for a most actual, a most graphic presentation of the simplest, most everyday actuality from a point of view borrowed from actuality itself.

But this is only a coloring, a tone. The reason that this side of Turgenev's gift is more prominent than the others is explained by his spiritual development.

With his nature for the most part impressionable, effeminately submissive to every trend of our age, Turgenev, as I have said, was responsive to everything except pure naturalism.

He began directly with the most extreme tendency left us as our heritage after the decease of Lermontov. In his *Parasha*—in which only Belinsky's perceptive genius divined a deposit of extraordinary, though as yet misdirected, gifts—he powerfully preached that "pride is a virtue, gentlemen!"[3]

In his *The Landowner* he hotheadedly and impressionably made obeisance to the bitterly satiric tendency. He was *tormented* by the odiousness of the *goatish* (rather than goatskin) shoes worn by provincial misses, and, under the influence of Lermontov, consigned them to suffering with his blessing—although the stanza about this was not altogether devoid of charm and feeling. In his "Three Portraits" he went so far as to create an original, purely Russian but cold and gloomy type; but then a revulsion occurred in him. The nature of his hero, Vasily Luchinov—cold to the point of reflection and passionate to the point of licentiousness—terrified him. While some sympathized with his hero, others pointed at everything unethical and actually corrupt in the Lermontovian type, a type Turgenev had depicted so much in his own way, so originally. At last Turgenev stopped before the type in perplexity and hesitation. He had no gloomy and evil belief in this type of Lermontov's. The hesitation led to a moral disease; it was expressed by the convulsive self-derision of his "Prince Hamlet of Shchigrovo" and by the plaintive, sincere wails of "the superfluous man."

"Prince Hamlet of Shchigrovo" revealed this sick, transitory phase in his thinking and in his internal development especially clearly. The hero of the story is not at all a parody of Hamlet, as it has seemed to some. The natures both were given might actually be identical; they both were equally entangled, almost to self-destruction, in the circumstances surrounding them; but Shakespeare's Hamlet was called to a tragic fate by "a most unusual event" beyond his powers, while the Hamlet of Shchigrovo, to whom only the most normal of normal things happened, remained "a young man of twenty years, near-sighted and fair, dressed from head to foot in black clothes, but caustically smiling." The claims of the Hamlet of Shchigrovo are not in accord with his own power: his brain is accustomed to follow through the relentless sequence of every thought, while his action, which generally demands the exercise of the will, is completely separated from his thought. The craving for logical consistency is

<hr>

[3] Belinsky's praising review of Turgenev's narrative poem was published in *Otechestvennye zapiski* 5 (1843). See V. G. Belinsky, *Polnoe sobranie sochineniy*, USSR Academy of Sciences, vols. 1–13 (Moscow: 1953–55), 7: 65–80.

finally expressed in him only by regret that "there are no fleas where they ought to be"; the absence of will bred in him a shyness before everything, before all and each. He is right to complain that he has no originality, that is, a cognizable, definite character. By nature he is intelligent, only with an absolutely fruitless, diffuse mind; he understands much profoundly, but sees only what *has been accomplished*, with no sense of what is *being accomplished*. It goes without saying, the raw material for the constitution of such a character already lay in the very nature of the Turgenevan hero, although it was for the most part developed under the influence of divers trends, trends which make perfectly understandable the vexation of the poor Hamlet over the student circles. In only one thing does the poor Hamlet make a mistake. The cause of his sickness does not lie in the study of the German philosophers and Goethe. Let him say, "I studied Hegel, my dear sir. I know Goethe by heart," and raise himself a little from behind the corner, like a spectre in his nightcap. Neither Goethe nor Hegel is to blame for his having thought it his duty to "read German books in the land of their birth" and to fall in love with a professor's daughter; nor was philosophy to blame if his *circle* talked of nothing but "the eternal sun of the spirit and other abstruse subjects." The poor Hamlet of Shchigrovo, *first*, always was a great dreamer; and *second*, he was an encyclopedist, not a specialist, a man not attached to any serious labor, not a serious lover of any definite business: he was ruined by superficial encyclopedism, or, to put it better, by scrappy knowledge. He was conscientious enough not to be able to "babble, babble, babble without stopping, yesterday in Arbat, today in Truba, tomorrow in Sivtsev Vrazhok, always about the same thing."[4] But on the other hand, he was not sufficiently firm for isolated, original, and recondite thought which, sooner or later, would have led him to an empathy with reality and, consequently, to an understanding of reality, at least in a certain degree. In love, he loved not the object of his passion, but only the process of love, *he loved to love*, like Sterne's Yorick, and like Shakespeare's Hamlet himself.

What was expressed in "Prince Hamlet of Shchigrovo" with convulsive laughter also came forth with painful, plaintive wails in *The*

---

[4] The references are to squares and streets in Moscow.

Diary of a Superfluous Man. Both works are bitter admissions of moral weakness, of spiritual incompetence. Those tendencies which ruined the impressionable and feeble nature of the Hamlet of Shchigrovo are not laughable in themselves; Turgenev himself poeticized them later, that is, he presented them in their true shape in his account of Rudin's university years. His Hamlet laughs not at them but at their absurd application, laughs at himself, who has sincerely and quixotically taken up the burden without the strength for it, at the dichotomy between thought and life which has been effected in him and in many others.

The moral process laid bare in "Prince Hamlet of Shchigrovo" and in *The Diary of a Superfluous Man* is strikingly similar to that process which gave birth to Pushkin's Ivan Petrovich Belkin,[5] both in its commencement and in its result. The way out of the painful, dichotomous situation—both for Ivan Petrovich Belkin, who was intimidated by the gloomy determination of Silvio and Hermann,[6] and for the Hamlet of Shchigrovo, who was frightened by the figure of Vasily Luchinov as well as shattered by philosophical analysis—could be only simple actuality. And this is where Turgenev begins the whole series of *A Huntsman's Sketches*, on the one hand, and the series of experiments in sentimental naturalism, on the other, of which the most felicitous is "Petushkov," the most infelicitous the dramas *The Bachelor* and *The Family Charge*. But his attitude to actuality is not at all so direct and simple as the attitude of Ivan Petrovich Belkin; everywhere in actuality he sees only himself, his morbid temper, and either the tonality of this temper is transferred to everything he touches, or he idealizes simple actuality. His first experiment in this kind of idealizing is "Khor and Kalinich," which was rapturously endorsed by the so-called Slavophiles, as they even more rapturously endorsed one of his last works, "Mumu." But Turgenev is too much a poet to write in accord with a set theme, and his talent is too lofty to submit to a theory. He remained true to himself, to his own inner

[5] The Belkin of whom Grigorev is speaking is both the central character of Pushkin's posthumously published *Istoriia sela Goriukhina* and the narrator of *Povesti Belkina* (1831).

[6] Silvio is the central character of "Vystrel," the first of the *Povesti Belkina*, and Hermann is the hero of Pushkin's later story "Pikovaia dama" (1833).

process, and it is this sincerity that lends unfading charm to *A Hunts-man's Sketches*, as it has long done to Yorick's "sentimental journey." There is neither need nor reason to try to explain this by anything other than Turgenev's poetic personality. This poetic personality is dear to us both in "The Singers" in whose performance the poet senses only *his own* tone, and in "Bezhin Meadow" in the counte-nance of the *Byronic* boy and in the house serf Ophelia—in everything and everywhere. To nature alone does he relate directly; it is not in the tone, of course (I have already spoken about that), but in signi-ficance of the moral process that his relations to nature may be equated with those of Rousseau and of Sénancour's *Obermann*—but, I repeat, not in tone, for in his tone Turgenev remains uncommonly original.

There is a passage in *The Diary of a Superfluous Man* which—especially if you come to it through a reading of everything that preceded it—you cannot read without a profound nervous shock, if not without tears—a passage which always has the same effect, giving us the key to a comprehension of Turgenev's relations with nature. This passage is the end of the diary.

It is remarkable in two respects. First, the dominant feature of Turgenev's talent here appears especially clearly: a profound feeling for nature, a feeling almost of a kind of merging with it. Here spring softly fans the reader, here he savors the odor of newly turned earth. Really only that chapter of Tolstoy's *Youth* where the window frame is removed and the reader is suddenly fanned by a tart, fresh spring breeze can be compared with this passage. But there will be more to say about the special tone of Turgenev's relations with nature when the long-awaited second edition of *A Huntsman's Sketches* is pub-lished. In the present essay I opted for the purely psychological problem, and it is in this respect that the passage takes on a twofold value. Here we perceive the bitterest disbelief of a person in his personality, a disbelief which obviously arose as a result of a lost battle. With this disbelief of a person in himself, in the significance of his own being, was united a bitter feeling of doubt in, if not complete negation of, the sympathy of others. Hence the convulsive laugh of Prince Hamlet of Shchigrovo at a tragic moment, and the total abolition of himself in the face of the eternity of the enormous external world. This is obviously a pantheistic notion, but the pantheistic here is morbid, as it is in the diary of Obermann.

I must remark that a notion like this is not accidental, that it is a result as much of a moral process as, perhaps, of the purely physical conditions of that region, of that soil of the great Russian part of the Ukraine which is poetically reflected in the lofty talent of the author of *A Huntsman's Sketches*.

You will recall with what a cynically bitter abuse of personality *The Diary of a Superfluous Man* ends. The following affront could not have sprung from anything but an extreme, a tense, a morbid state of soul:

> *Publisher's Note:* Under these last lines is found the profile of a head with a large forelock and moustaches, with eyes *en face* and effulgent eyelashes, and under the head someone has written the following words:

> This Manuscript Was Read
> And Its Contents Not Approved
> By Petr Zudoteshin
> MMMM
> Dear Sir
> Petr Zudoteshin
> my Dear Sir

> But since the handwriting of these lines does not in the least resemble the handwriting in which the preceding part of the notebook is written, the publisher considers himself correct to conclude that the above-mentioned lines were added later, by someone else, the more so since it has come to his (the publisher's) knowledge that Mr. Chulkaturin died during the night of April 1–2, 18——, on his ancestral estate, Lambs-water.

Everything is priceless here—the Belkin tone of *the publisher*, the obvious analogy between the idea of this passage and the idea of Hamlet's thoughts on the skulls, and, finally, that Chulkaturin really did die on the first of April, because "it fits him!" All this is priceless as a profound, sincere confession of a morbid spiritual state, experienced by many, perhaps by an entire generation.

When, wearied by this bitter and cheerless exposure of personality,

Turgenev, following contemporary trends, plunged into a search for tranquillity in simple, typical, and unartificial actuality, he amazed everyone by the portrait of "Khor and Kalinich"; but the idealists of Russian life rejoiced too naïvely over this portrait. Along with the idyllically sympathetic portrayal of "Khor and Kalinich," the old type whose alarming aspects are so fascinating emerged once more with the brilliant sketch of Vasily Luchinov in the tale "Three Portraits."

Whatever you say about the immorality of Vasily Luchinov, there is, without any doubt, poetry in this figure, there is fascination. This poetry, this fascination (for which neither Turgenev nor we who sympathize with his character are to blame) is in a sense stronger and more meaningful than the fascination of Lermontov's Pechorin, just as the unfinished but eternally tormenting Arbenin or Arbenev was more poetic and more fascinating for Lermontov himself than the cold and often petty Pechorin.[7] Turgenev several times attempted to repudiate the fascinating aspects of this type, which had tormented Lermontov and all our generation so long—but, although craving a logical train of thought, he always betrayed it in the character created. He wanted to repudiate in this type the aspect of mad passion or flaming and limitless love for life united with a kind of daring carelessness and trust in the moment—and he created Veretev in "The Calm," *inventing* and *contriving* a fitting punishment for his futile existence. And what of it? The futile existence was indeed shown to be futile. But the person created by the poet was still captivating in his passionately enthusiastic moments, remained fascinating, did not lose his poetic tonality. It goes without saying that you censured the wickedness of Vasily Luchinov by a moral judgment, but that threatening and ominous element in him, which was passionate to the point of madness, yet self-aware to the point of reflection, was not repudiated by the artist, nor could you repudiate it —and your inward soul could in no way agree with the critic who called Vasily Luchinov a *corrupt* man.[8] Vasily Luchinov, if you please,

[7] Pechorin and Arbenin (Arbenev in some variants) are the central characters of *Geroi nashego vremeni* (1840) and *Maskarad* (1835), respectively.

[8] See Shevyrev's review of *Peterburgsky sbornik*, in which "Tri portreta" first appeared, *Moskvitianin* 2–3 (1846).

is not merely corrupt, he is infamous; but his strength, this almost southern passion united with a northern self-possession, this ardent reflection or reflexive ardency, is a *typical* feature. You cannot dislodge a typical feature from a place in your mind—if it occupies a place in it—by a *logical judgment* alone. In order to destroy it you must prove that it is not a typical feature, or, to put it better, you must *give visible evidence* that it is not typical in the particular form it has assumed. Until you are able to do this, you will struggle in vain with its fascinating, and therefore viable, aspects. The Pechorin type, for example, is not destroyed by making him shallow and turning him into a Tamarin;[9] he alters only his form, and appears again in a new one. Such is the law of the eternal existence of types—and especially of this type. I assign special importance to Turgenev's Vasily Luchinov because the old type of Don Juan, Lovelace, and so forth, first took our Russian, original form in this person.

But the Don Juanesque or Lovelaceian principle does not exhaust all the content of the type with which Turgenev entered into open, conscientious but naïvely weak battle.

Turgenev took it into his head to measure his strength, before his readers, with a reflection of this type in the form of Rudin. If there are aspects of irresistible allure, of fascination, in the reckless, spendthrift Veretev, or in the depraved and cold Vasily Luchinov, then there should be all the more in Rudin, a man full of all the propensities to conviction, if not of conviction itself, a man whose natural gifts allow us to conclude that his life ought by no means to be ended as it is ended in the epilogue of the tale—even though the epilogue concludes with the glorification of Rudin. As you know, I have a special weakness for the tale of *Rudin*—for the following reason. Something peculiar happens in this tale before the eyes of the reader. The artist, having begun with a critical attitude to the figure he was creating, apparently gets entangled in this critical attitude and does not know what to do with his anatomical knife. Finally, enthused by a transport of the sincere old emotion, in the epilogue he glorifies what he had attempted to treat critically in the story. It is impossible even to think that the criticism was a clever approach to the glorification—so

[9] The hero of the novel *Tamarin* (1852) by M. V. Avdeev, an imitator of Lermontov.

quickly and abruptly is the change accomplished before the eyes of the reader. It becomes clear after a reading of the epilogue that everything—aside from the epilogue itself, and aside from one moment when Rudin, standing at the window at nightfall and concluding his colloquy, his preaching by the legend of the Scandinavian king, reminds one of the style, the method, and the entire image of one of the most beloved people of our generation [10]—aside from the epilogue, I say, everything else was made, not born, made artificially, although by no means dexterously, by a violently tormented soul. In short, a remarkable confusion is here laid bare, both for the artist with his attitudes to the type he had created and for those of us who are conscientious. What is Rudin in the tale? A phrasemonger? But whence the phrasemonger's strength, which operates both on the profound nature of Natalia and on the pure, youthful, generous nature of Basistov? A weak and characterless man, a "scanty" figure, to use Pigasov's expression? But why was Pigasov so glad once he had observed he was *scanty*, and why does Lezhnev, who knows him inside out, *fear* his influence on others? Why was the *generous* fellow Volynsky so *afflicted* by his own generosity, and why was it his fate, according to the matter-of-fact Lezhnev's prediction, to be under Natalia's foot? How terrible it is to be good and generous fellows in our literature! Either they are phantoms or they are beaten. Indeed so.

The most important point is that so long as certain aspects of some type have not passed into the domain of the comic, your soul will struggle in vain with a certain kind of sympathy for them. Humor is the sole death for a type, or, to put it better, for certain of its aspects; but the humor must not be at all strained, for if it is even slightly strained it will not achieve its goal. Tamarin, for example, crushed the *external* aspects of Pechorin, but that made his internal ones stand out in relief. The goals neither of Pisemsky's Batmanov, that figure coarsely daubed-on yet in living colors, nor of his more felicitous image of Bakhtiarov in "The Simpleton" were achieved, perhaps precisely because the artist, now daubing, now charcoaling them, having proposed a certain goal to himself, entered into battle with them from the start. Ostrovsky's Merich, that dandy from Zamoskvoreche

[10] The author has T. N. Granovsky in mind.

with pretensions to Childe Harold, a pallid person but fully outlined, obliterates only the pettiest aspects of Pechorin.[11] Finally,
the persons with whom Turgenev conducts his most naïve battles
either miss the target, like "The Bully," or tease us with the fascinating aspects of the type, like Veretev, or else raise the type to the
pathetic, as in *Rudin*.

I again return to *Rudin*—and it is impossible not to return to it
when speaking of Turgenev and of that moral process which is
revealed in his works and serves partly, since it is the process of one
of the most remarkable personalities, as a disclosure of the moral
process of the whole age.

This process, which at first offers a striking resemblance to the
process which generated Pushkin's figure of Ivan Petrovich Belkin, is
also distinguished from this latter process by its consequences.

In *Rudin* everything at which Prince Hamlet of Shchigrovo convul-
sively laughed is almost glorified: the "circles," the "sun of the
spirit," and the influence of philosophic ideas—all those trends, in
short, from under whose power the artist dreamed of escaping into
simple actuality. The validity of these trends, their right to citizenship
in the soul, is recognized in *Rudin*.

"Prince Hamlet of Shchigrovo" and *Rudin* are both equally
elucidated by the poetic nature of Turgenev. Too much an artist—
that is, a man fond of the type and a believer in the type—to be
fossilized in the austere and intensely melancholy lyricism of the
author of "Monologues,"[12] and too much a poet—that is, of a
responsive and passionate nature—not constantly and sensitively to
feel those sounds whose

> . . . call
> Is dark or dim,
> But cannot be heard
> Without agitation—

he remained in a kind of strange, irresolute situation in regard to both
the old and new trends, faithful only to his own nature, which, like

[11] From the play *Bednaia nevesta* (1851).
[12] A poem by N. P. Ogarev (1847).

the nature of any genuine poet, is just as frightened of the stern rigidity of logical thought, that is, of theory, as of slavish service to the often blind demands of the present. This is the reason for Turgenev's strong influence on his readers, and the reason for the repetition of the same faults in him. A living soul speaks in his works with a living voice—not logical thought and not only the external strength of talent. What his soul experienced he gave to us—he gave the experience as it was reborn in his soul.

As the negative image of Belkin was composed in the struggle of Pushkin's nature against brilliant but for us illusory types, a new growth of everything simple, sane, and spontaneous appeared, as its distinctive feature, in the soul of our poet protesting against ideals which had taken shape by an external, artificial process in it. Just so did Turgenev's struggle result in a growth of many purely negative images, all more or less resembling one another. One and the same gentleman appears in *The Diary of a Superfluous Man*, in "The Bully," partly in "Two Friends," and, finally, seized in the most ordinary circumstances of life, in "Petushkov." Somewhat different from these persons are the character sketches which he advances in "Kolosov," in "Pasynkov" (in which Turgenev wanted to depict a romantic), and particularly in "A Correspondence."

The first attribute one cannot help noticing in the persons of the first above-mentioned category is their strange nomination to be beaten, or at least to be strangely hounded; the second is to seek an unrequited love. These persons—or at least those like them—are not met only in Turgenev; presented in a sickly fashion, they play the chief role in the works of the so-called natural school; depicted more calmly and easily, they appear in the first novels of Pisemsky, in the persons of "The Simpleton," of Ovtsynin in "Batmanov," and others; they are present in innumerable persons of Ostrovsky's comedies, only with a completely special, purely Russian imprint; finally, Tolstoy nourishes a special sympathy for them. Everywhere— except for Ostrovsky's Khorkov and Borodkin[13] and Pisemsky's "The Simpleton"—they appear in purely negative form, that is, they are given birth not by independent art, but by reflection, by imitation.

[13] Characters in *Bednaia nevesta* and *Ne v svoi sani ne sadis* (1852), respectively.

Everywhere, even in Tolstoy, they express only a protest in the name of the simple, the good, the spontaneous, in contrast with the brilliant but artificially put-together types; everywhere they represent only bare aspirations, with no individual features.

The question of these persons, or, to put it better, of this *negative* type, is extremely important.

The *personality* went to its furthest limit in Lermontov and in the line which proceeded from him. This line expressed the protest of the personality against actuality, a protest in consequence of which there appeared an endless number of satirical sketches and tales inevitably ending with the refrain—either plainly expressed or implied—"This is what may become of a man!" This refrain was Gogolian, but to a Lermontovian tune. The most amazing transformations of the heroes who were suffocated in the mire, in penurious sensations and dull actuality, were achieved in these tales according to the whims and fancies of the authors—and everything that surrounded the hero or heroine was intentionally portrayed as caricature according to a previously set theme. There is no doubt that there was a good side, there was a certain merit in this method of presenting actuality; but the one-sidedness of the method soon became quite obvious.

From another side, "The Overcoat" and several other of Gogol's works engendered another, even more glaring one-sidedness in the works of the so-called natural school, which should more properly be called the school of "sentimental naturalism." The wail of the idealist Gogol for an idea, for "beautiful humanity," here developed into a wail and a protest in the name of enfeebled, morally and physically weak humanity. The bitter laughter of the great humorist at degenerate and degraded humanity, a laughter united with flaming indignation at the lie and the formalism of that way of life in which humanity becomes petty and destroys itself, developed into a sickly protest in the name of degenerate and destroyed humanity, in consequence of which the very protest against the lie and sheer formalism of social reality forfeited its high ethical significance. Only separate the sickly humor of a peevish nature from the aspiration to the ideal in the work of Gogol, and monstrous creations will appear in consequence of the oddities of this sickly humor! Look at Akaky Akakievich from a sentimental point of view, not with the legitimate sympathy due to all mankind, but with an exclusive sympathy; in accordance with the dictates of this sickly sympathy raise the demands of "The Diary of a Madman" to the level of *rights*—and you have works of sentimental naturalism. The transgression of these against art consists in *slavish* naturalism, which does not distinguish the accidental phenomena of actuality from the typical and necessary, and does not control its sickly comic temper by an ideal common to all humanity.

When Gogol says in *Dead Souls* that the virtuous man (that is, the *strong* man) has been vulgarized and that it is time to "harness the rogue," he repudiates, first, the *pseudovirtuous* man, exposing his stilted majesty and flashiness; *second*, he weeps, he is sick at heart because "he nowhere sees a man"; and with the energetic words of another passage in a different work he stigmatizes the feeble man ("Every man has become trash and rags . . .").[14]

The great unmasker of everything that was false in himself, and that he saw false around him, Gogol finally unmasked his unmasking with its inadequacy, its disruption, its want of any vital focus. The unmasking broke the bond with him, and, having broken with him, with its source of life, it strove to live by the force of galvanism. So it has lived until now, and continues to live. The unmasker, in his turn, wanted to rise above himself, wanted to build his world out of materials of the old edifice which he had exposed as unworthy and had himself destroyed. He tried to fit the pieces together and paint them over, but fell down on the job, broken by the consciousness of lifelessness in his creation, burning with a longing for the ideal to which he could give no form.

A dreadful lesson, a dreadful, tragic event! But there is significance in it, a great consoling significance.

Gogol was an artificially *made* man; as a great mind and a great artistic talent, he carried this ulcer within himself and recognized it more clearly than all others who also carried it in themselves; and he persecuted it both in himself and in others mercilessly. A simple great man (one of the simplest Heaven has ever sent to Earth), he wore all shades of alien color without a harmful effect, shed them like "old skin" as the years went by, and retained his own rich nature all the

[14] From "Ob Odissee, perevodimoi Zhukovskim," included in *Vybrannye mesta iz perepiski s druziami* (1847).

way. He defined his own meaning thus: no one knows how to exhibit "the banality of the banal man" better than he.[15] The analysis of everything banal in our soul and the analysis of the life surrounding us through the prism of the analysis of internal banality—that, indeed, is the entire task of Gogolian art. Every writer has his personal word, and it is just this word that he is called to speak to the world, for it is just what the world needs as a new word. This new word is the "matter of the soul" about which Gogol speaks so often in his *Selected Passages from Correspondence with Friends* and in his letters. This word, in its final form, is the last truth of the soul about itself and about its entire understanding of God's world; it is the center of the writer's little world, and in it, bought by suffering and struggle (in one way or another), is an identification with the center of the great world.

Tormented by the artistic question, Gogol was at the same time tormented by the ethical question, and he relentlessly sought in himself the truth that would resolve it. He was inwardly distressed by his calling to present the banality of a banal man, that is, to rip off the mask of a showy exterior from what is essentially trivial and which, unmasked, becomes banal. His distress is exposed in almost all his lyrical pages; but what was in him a striving for the ideal and a justification for his work, as a negative approach to the ideal, was converted by those who were the closest of his followers, the sentimental naturalists, into a blind protest in the name of the feeble man. Gogol said, for example, "In our time the desire to obtain a profitable position and to pay back for insults knots the plot of drama better than does love."[16] Belinsky, with his irascibility, extracted from this a whole diatribe against love (by love should be understood any feeling slightly above staid dryness).[17] The diatribe turned out eloquent, blazing, alarming, so that one may genuinely say that Belinsky wrote an alarming article against alarming feelings on behalf

[15] From the third letter of "Chetyre pisma k raznym litsam po povodu *Mertvykh dush*," ibid. According to Gogol, this definition had been made by Pushkin.

[16] From *Teatralny razezd posle predstavleniia novoi komedii* (1842).

[17] A reference to Belinsky's "Russkaia literatura v 1843 godu," *Otechestvennye zapiski* 1 (1844).

of alarming feelings of another kind—and the naturalists wrote several variations on this theme. I especially remember one of these variations—it belongs to an author who then appeared under the name of Perepelsky, and later became famous for his verses under his real name.[18] A story of his was hidden in *Repertory and Pantheon* in the midst of much rubbish of this literary cesspool; the author has probably forgotten it himself; but small phenomena often throw light on large phenomena. The story (I have forgotten its title) is grown from the seed planted by Gogol.[19] The yearning of a *petty* man to take revenge on a *petty* woman for a *petty* offense was so knotted into this drama that the soul of the author itself became confused. Miserable hypocrisy was here depicted with such sweetness that obviously the writer did not rise above the level of the sentiment he was analyzing, and this lack of ability, here already apparent, to rise above the level of analysis was then reflected in his verses, which, despite the obvious presence of the flame of a broken but still strong and lofty talent, occasionally effect an oppressive and heavy impression on anyone who has not lost the freshness of the aesthetic and ethical sentiment. The poor, truly tormented poet cannot for a moment cease looking through the analytic prism which constantly shows him twisting reptiles. In the simplest, most ordinary fact of daily life, which would lead an equable soul to a calm and peaceful train of thought, for example, in the wedding of a man of the simple people with a woman of the simple people, he is able to see only sin in the past and woe ahead.[20] For the tragic situation of a mother who has no money to bury her child, he sees and can see no other solution than for her to become a street harlot[21]—in a country where, glory to God, alms are still given, and—greater glory to God—they are given without critical distinction of the ethical attributes of the beggar pleading for the sake *of Christ* and without an appraisal of his person; in a country where, when you walk down the street you sometimes see a little wooden

---

[18] Perepelsky was the pseudonym of N. A. Nekrasov.

[19] Grigorev is probably referring to "Pomeshchik dvadtsati trekh dush," published, under the name of N. Perepelsky, in *Literaturnaia gazeta* 12 (1843), rather than in *Repertuar i Panteon.*

[20] Grigorev probably has the poem "Troika" (1846) in mind.

[21] See "Edu li nochiu po ulitse temnoi" (1847).

coffin in a woman's lap and you see how, having taken off his hat and crossed himself, not one passer-by puts a copper penny into the box but more if he can, according to his circumstances and means. But the diseased poet sees in the person of someone collecting to build a temple—however moving the image to him as a poet—only a repentant villain, since he does not know how to deduce such a person's appearance in God's world from the sources whose vital springs are in the people's nature.[22] It is remarkable that even Gogol in the second part of *Dead Souls* looked on this analytical trend as the solution for his Khlobuev—a strange person, one of the few vital ones in this second part who touches the essential strings of our reckless nature and is depicted so broadly and sympathetically—contrary to the intentions of the author. Returning to the poet, who can be called one of the two most brilliant luminaries of the school of sentimental naturalists, I add that he, totally embittered by his weighty thoughts, recognizing the dichotomy between his internal world and the heights of poetic contemplation, full of moving, doleful, genuine groans because

> The heart weary of hate
> Does not learn to love,[23]

appears a melancholy victim of that frightful corrosive principle which only Gogol could hold, restrain. He allowed this principle, which brings out the monsters within man, to weary, to torment, and finally to devour him.

If it is dangerous to let loose in the soul impulses which deviate from a normal psychic order, then it is hardly less dangerous to legitimatize the normal order.

All naturalism is nothing other than the legitimization of such a normal order, the legitimization of the everyday.

Gogol remained correct because he kept himself within the negative limits of naturalism, that is, within the limits of the disclosure of the

---

[22] See "Vlas" (1854).
[23] The last two lines of Nekrasov's poem "Zamolkni, Muza mesti i pechali!" (1855).

false in the human soul and in surrounding actuality. But after disclosing the false, that is, after divesting the real of the envelope that does not belong to it, a positive replacement is demanded by the soul. He did not indicate a positive replacement, or he indicated it in a general ideal which eluded any specificity. He says perpetually to man: you are not a hero, you only pose as a hero; you are no hero in anything; in love you are mostly a Khlestakov, inviting the mayor's wife to "the blue yonder of streams" (a most ingenious absurdity! in it, as in a focal point, is incorporated all the romantic nonsense of the heroes and heroines of Marlinsky, Kukolnik, and Polevoi);[24] in civil relations you are either an Anton Antonovich Skvoznik-Dmukhanovsky or, what is incomparably worse, an Alexander Ivanovich—of *A Businessman's Morning*—tying slips of paper to a dog's tail; you are only ambitious and heedless, and your excessive dreams may lead you, if you are overfervid, to the destiny of the artist Piskarev or to the Spanish throne of Poprishchin. For what will you perish so shamefully, when your comrade Lieutenant Pirogov so prudently suppresses a heroic outburst at an offence and in finest form will prosper and show off at distinguished officials' balls, and when Kochkarev steadily proves that it is extremely easy to get over the misfortune when people spit in your face? You are not Hamlet, you are Podkolesin; neither in yourself nor in the life surrounding you will you find a testimonial to your notion of the heroic, which sometimes arises in you like froth.[25]

Fine! But what will be the logical conclusion of this premise? The first conclusion is a question: which is correct—the notion of the heroic or the contradiction of the heroic, that is, nature? This is the question that gave strength to what was called naturalism. Naturalism decided that if nature does not strengthen the battle for the heroic, if

[24] A. A. Bestuzhev-Marlinsky, a member of the Decembrist movement; N. V. Kukolnik, most famous for his drama *Ruka Vsevyshnego otechestvo spasla;* and N. A. Polevoi, one-time editor of *Moskovsky telegraf.* All were typical representatives of the romantic movement in the 1820s and 1830s.

[25] All the names referred to are characters of Gogol: Khlestakov and Skvoznik-Dmukhanovsky are in *Revizor*, Piskarev and Pirogov in "Nevsky prospekt," Poprishchin in "Zapiski sumasshedshego," Kochkarev and Podkolesin in *Zhenitba.*

it has grown shallow, then there is nothing left to do: things must be taken as they are. This means there is no battle, or the battle is quixotic; it means such impotence must be acknowledged as a law of existence; it means that the sympathy which we had for great ambition must be transferred to Mr. Goliadkin;[26] the sympathy we had for the passion of Romeo and Juliet, for the vengeance of Hamlet, for the preoccupation of various heroes with the common good, for the sublime energy of Verrina (in *Die Verschwörung des Fiesco zu Genua*) must be transferred to the behind-the-corner passions of heroes of various attics or of Petushkov, to the revenge of the hero of Perepelsky's tale, to the preoccupation of Prokharchin with his clothes and underwear, to the savage but feeble frenzy of the hero of the tale "A Tangled Affair."[27]

I repeat: Gogol was not at all guilty in any of this—but the threads of all these sympathies are connected with his works, as with a center, a starting point. All we have enumerated are just those monsters which pursued him in his sickly dreams, and which he did not bring into God's world, controlling them by his consciousness of the ideal.

There is no *heroic* either in the soul or in life: what seems heroic is in essence Khlestakov or Poprishchin! But it is odd that no one has bothered to ask himself just *what* heroic is no longer in the soul and in nature—and *in what* nature it is not. Some preferred to defend the already ridiculed heroic—and it is remarkable that gentlemen more inclined to the practical-juridical doctrine in literature were the ones who did so.[28] Others preferred to defend nature.

They did not turn their attention to an exceedingly simple circumstance. From the time of Peter the Great the national temperament tried on forms of the heroic which were not innate. The caftan turned out to be now narrow, now short; a handful of people was found who pulled it on any which way and began to strut about in it pompously. Gogol told them all that they were parading in a foreign caftan—and this caftan sat on them like a saddle on a cow, and was already so worn out that it was repulsive even to look at. It merely followed from

[26] The hero of Dostoevsky's *Dvoinik* (1846).

[27] A story by M. E. Saltykov-Shchedrin (1848).

[28] A reference to representatives of "official nationality," such as F. V. Bulgarin and N. I. Grech.

this that another caftan, fitted to weight and height is necessary, not at all that one should remain without a caftan or continue to stretch and pull the shabby caftan.

There was still another side to the question. Gogol expressed the failure—as measured against the *heroic* established by centuries—only of that in our souls and in surrounding actuality which tried on the ideal. Meanwhile there was still something in us and around us which lived according to its own special principles (and lived much more strongly than that which tried on foreign ideals), something which remained pure and simple after all the battles with brilliant but foreign ideals.

But these very sympathies, once excited, could not die: the ideals did not lose their fascinating strength and charm.

Why were these sympathies illegitimate in their *bases?*

Let us suppose—or even not suppose but say affirmatively—that it is not good to sympathize with Pechorin, as he appears in Lermontov's novel. But it does not at all follow from this that we should "swear by bell, book, and candle" that we had never sympathized with the character of Pechorin before he appeared in the novel, that is, with the impulses of nature indulged to the point of perversion. It follows still less from this that we should transfer all our sympathy to Maksim Maksimych and elevate him to the hero. Of course, Maksim Maksimych is a very good man, and, of course, more correct and more worthy of sympathy in his actions than Pechorin; but he is really dull and because of his simple nature could not fall into the ugly extremes into which Pechorin fell.

The voice for the simple and good, raised in our souls against the false and bestial, is, of course, a beautiful, sublime voice, but its merit is only negative. Its positive side is a stagnant, sour, moral philistinism.

The process of seeking the simple and spontaneous led us, at first, into unavoidable one-sidedness. For the simple and spontaneous, for the pure type, we at first took those properties of the soul which in themselves are essentially negative, not positive.

In this matter the prime method of our age was purely mechanical.

In western literatures—in consequence of analytical work on

subtle and artificial phenomena in the organization of the human soul, and in consequence of satiety with everything artificial and even everything civilized—there appeared a craving for the spontaneous, the unbegotten, the fresh and organically whole. Essential to the strivings of a great poet of our age, Sand, as well as to some other western writers—among their number quite remarkable people, like Auerbach, the author of *Country Tales*—was just this craving generated by analysis, on the one hand, and satiety, on the other.

Since the Petrine reforms we have been subjected to this same craving, which pushed us, by a law of reverberation, although strenuously still naturally, into the circle of general human life; and this craving appeared in our literature. At least, doubtless of such an origin is that school of writers of the simple, spontaneous way of life of which Grigorovich was the most remarkable representative. Even the most gifted works of his school—"The Village," "Anton the Unfortunate"—were generated not by an internal, but by an external, purely reflective process. They are all no more than mosaics, made-up works. It is as if a gifted but passing traveler from foreign lands should take note in them of the special features of a way of life curious to him, should jot down in a commonplace book words and original turns of speech that are strange to him—and he should then put together his mosaic, his miniature painting, with great care and taste. This little painting would necessarily assume an idyllic character.

But besides this purely mechanical process, an organic process was also achieved in us, a process whose outlines were sketched in our greatest, our only complete artistic phenomenon, in Pushkin, the process of the struggle of Ivan Petrovich Belkin with Silvio, Hermann, Aleko, and so forth—a struggle of a meager, still uncultivated soil with excessively developed vegetable-growing powers.

Turgenev was the representative in our age of this organic Push-kinian process in all its phases—and this is his great historic significance. He did not fully master this process, was not a conjurer of elementary forces, like Pushkin; in short, he did not possess the conscious power of genius which could prophesy the future and define future limits; but, as a highly poetic nature, he did respond to all the trends experienced by him through the various stages of this process, he did candidly transmit to us all his inner world, and spontaneously and boldly—despite the gentleness of his poetic nature—he artistically drove every trend to its furthest extreme. He responded to Lermontovian romanticism with "Three Portraits"; to the depiction of actuality, Lermontovian in principle and Gogolian in form, with a tragically somber or tragically bemired view in the poem *The Landowner*, which is full of a protest of personality and of enmity against *goatish* shoes; to the sentimental romanticism of conservative Hegelianism by his "Jasha Pasynkov"; to sentimental naturalism by his dramas and the magnificent tale "Petushkov"; to the idyllic populist school by the rural Ophelia of *A Huntsman's Sketches*. To the purely organic protest for the simple, the spontaneous, and the typical he responded by a great deal, by all his activity, by all his struggles with the brilliant alien type who falls into contradictions, into extremes, now, as in "Mumu," flattering Slavophilism, now, as in "The Inn," exhaling protest. He obviously acutely experienced all these contradictions and, while he unconsciously, in feminine fashion, submitted to the trends, while serving as their organ, he nevertheless came out himself, thanks again to his lofty poetic nature which did not yield to theory.

An analysis of Turgenev's creative career is therefore an analysis of our entire age with its scores of processes. We have no other representative of it who is so complete. Ostrovsky and Tolstoy, each in his own way, is stronger than Turgenev, but more one-sided.

That is why, when speaking of Turgenev and his last work, a critic is forced to make constant digressions, a consequence of constantly arising questions. These questions are our contemporary *psychic* questions: they are as important as our social ones; perhaps they are profoundly bound up with these latter—and no one arouses these profound questions so strongly in the soul as Turgenev.

In his poetic sincerity, like Lavretsky in his last work,

> He burned everything he had worshiped,
> Worshiped everything he had burned.

We, that is, the public, the readers, were witnesses both of these burnings and of these worships of what was burnt. Still more: we could see how the worship of what had originally been burned, how the craving of Ivan Petrovich Belkin for what had originally been repudiated, for the simple, the typical, passed beyond bounds; how an old type, profoundly absorbed by the spirit, came back with a vengeance in the apotheosis of Rudin; how a false attitude to this type and an enthusiasm for a purely negative type resulted in psychological blunders, in the artistic imperfection of many beautifully conceived creations.

Of all the literary phenomena of either the present or the past year, the profound impression which the latest work of Turgenev, *A Nest of the Gentry*, has produced on all more or less sensitive people in various strata of society has been equaled only by that produced by Ostrovsky's work of a different genre, *A Protégée of the Mistress*. It can be explained only by the overflowing organic life both in *A Nest of the Gentry* and in *A Protégée of the Mistress*, by the organic and nonartificial process of artistic conception, which underlies creation. The sympathy aroused by these two far from perfect but organic works is not at all like the sympathy aroused by others which are much more voluminous, much more full of remarkable details, much more appealing to curiosity.

If you begin to look at *A Nest of the Gentry* coldly and mathematically, then its construction appears hideously unfinished. First of all, an enormous frame with the canvas for a huge picture is revealed; on this canvas only one little corner or perhaps the center is completed; in some places perfectly finished parts, in others outlines and sketches, in others daubed-in backgrounds flash. In that little corner or perhaps center, one thing lives a full life, while another appears as a study, an experiment. But this is not a fragment, not an episode out of the picture; no, this is a drama in which only one relation has been worked out: it is a living, organic whole, almost ruthlessly picked out of the background to which it was bound by all its nerves; and the broken threads, the broken bonds hideously hang before the viewer's eyes.

I think it is impossible to say anything worse than what I am saying about the work of one of my favorite contemporary writers, although it is only just, as just as it is, from another side, to say that the hideously unfinished *A Nest of the Gentry*, like the overboldly and compactly outlined *A Protégée of the Mistress*, is incomparably better than anything that has appeared in literature in the current or past year; for these works, although unfinished or sketchy, are still not manufactured, but living, born of life.

Perhaps you will say that I am going too far both in severity of judgment and in enthusiasm. But I hope to prove my point, that is, in so far as it is possible, to demonstrate it at this time in connection only with *A Nest of the Gentry*.

The enormous canvas which had been stretched for an enormous historical picture remained uninjured, first, in the very title of the novel, second, in the crude and inartistic expression of its idea in the epilogue. It is clear that his creation really appeared to the artist originally as a huge sketch of a whole "nest" of types from the gentry class of a certain geographical region. In the center, interconnected with all the broadly conceived historical picture, there had to be one relationship, the relationship between Lavretsky and Lisa. The center was grasped in the highest degree accurately, with the genuine tact of the poet, as we will see. At the start (in the conception) a novel was shaping up, that is, a creation which was to bind the individual dramatic relationship with a whole special world, with a special region, with the mores of a specific life. The problems presented were genuinely enormous, for the very particularity of this life, the seclusion of this world, had to be comprehended, illuminated, brought into an organic bond with life in general. A "nest of the gentry" should have been woven, like varied verdure, around the central group, and the light which was to fall primarily on this group should have illuminated to a certain degree all the perspectives of the world with which the central group was bound by a physiological identity. That is obviously why the enormous canvas of the picture was prepared. For otherwise why would Turgenev (1) have surrounded his Lavretsky with new offspring of the old nest; (2) have commented on his ancestors; and (3) have placed him in juxtaposition with them through conversations with their portraits? From another side, why would he—if he did not originally have such or a similar broad concept in mind—why would he have *generalized* the private character of the relationship, devising, for instance, a general Russian outcome

for the spiritual drama of his Lisa—the convent? Why otherwise
Lavretsky's meeting with Lisa in the convent? In short, why are all
the features of this work there—all the features that are sketchy and
roughly daubed and yet do not offend as manufactured, made,
because they were clearly extracted from an organically unified life,
so that you will unwillingly say: all this is monstrous, ragged bits
stick out all over it, but it was all given birth to naturally, not com-
piled; it may be aborted, but it is not Wagner's homunculus, it may
be the premature creation of a poet, but it is not the labor of a story-
teller. Why, you might again stipulate, should an etude be drawn in
the form of the old musician Lemm? He is clearly necessary for only
one moment of the psychological drama, a moment when Beethovian
sounds are indispensable to the human soul, and even then he is
obviously a mere shade of Beethoven. Why otherwise, you must
admit the question, is he necessary? Lavretsky could dream about
"the pure stars" without him; it would be possible to send notes to
Lisa without going through him. Is he perhaps there just to set off the
simple and genuinely profound feeling for Beauty, innate to the nature
of Lavretsky, against the false artiness of Panshin? Why, you might
ask with absolute correctness, the superb but purely episodic appearance of the original Mikhalevich and the superb conversations with
him, if Lavretsky, from one side physiologically bound to the "nest
of the gentry," bound to such a degree that he believes in the prophecy
of Aunt Glafira Petrovna ("Remember my words, nephew: you will
not build a nest anywhere, you will wander all your life"), if this very
Lavretsky was not profoundly, spiritually, still bound to the world of
Rudin, Faust, the Hamlet of Shchigrovo District?

The last "why," engendered by all these different ones, the "why"
which a strict reading constantly gives rise to, will be the following.

Why did Turgenev not let his undertaking mature, that is, why
did Turgenev not *believe* in his undertaking, in the possibility of its
realization? Had he believed in it firmly, with that faith which moves
mountains, disseminates the worlds of a *King Lear*, of *A Midsummer
Night's Dream*, or the worlds of a Consuelo, a Teverino, and so forth
—something would have come forth that would outlive our age, as
one of its complete expressions, something genuinely epic.

From this "why" arises a new and last "why," which is concerned
with the whole age of our modern development. For you can propose

the Turgenevan "why" in other connections to Ostrovsky, with respect both to *A Protégée of the Mistress* and to *A Profitable Place*, and above all with respect to his most ambitious work, *Do Not Live as You Fancy*. For Tolstoy it is quite a different matter and another "why" is almost always proposed: why *this waste*, that is, why is so much strength of talent, so many powerful caprices displayed, if there is no content? In connection with Turgenev and Ostrovsky, the question turns into the question of the age, it goes without saying of an age peculiar to us in *Rus*—of an age in which all undertakings only rise like froth, never turning even into a home brew, much less into real beer, and are strewn about like Fata Morgana—of an age of trials of enormous powers, which have not found scope for activity, are strangely aroused, yet are inevitably forced to end their attempts in unbelief, in a distrust of those widely expanding worlds which haunt them in their dreams!

It is a sad age, if you will, when talents with profound content do not find a form in which to trust; they give us only a conscientious struggle instead of artistic worlds, or they vainly and aimlessly display the strengths of their gifts; while strong talents of secondary importance artificially construct entire huge edifices on the bases of almost elementary or at least narrowly practical, but in every case inartistic thoughts. It is a sad age when art has no foresight and does not comprehend the phenomena of life as it speeds ahead!

The center of the drama—which was obviously posed against a broad background in the imagination of the artist according to his concept of the work—is Lavretsky and his relation to Lisa.

As I have already stipulated, I will not only not recount, I will not even remind you in particular or readers in general of the content of *A Nest of the Gentry*. I read it four times, on various occasions; probably you, and most readers, also read it more than once. I repeat, the work made a profound impression: it is more or less known to everyone, save for those who read *The Beauty of Astrakhan*, *The Stormy Ataman*,[29] or *The Count of Monte Cristo* and the novels of Paul Féval. Consequently, I can trace the psychological development

---

[29] Both novels, *Prekrasnaia Astrakhanka, ili Khizhina na beregu reki Oki* (Moscow, 1836) and *Ataman Buria, ili Volnitsa zavolzhskaia* (Moscow, 1835), were published anonymously and ridiculed by Belinsky at the time.

of the characters without resorting to the story (which is almost always dull in critics) of the events, of the persons, or of the situations in which they are placed.

And so, in the foreground is Lavretsky: all the light in the picture is concentrated on him; a number of figures and details set off his person, and what is more, those psychological problems of which he is the representative are set off positively by all the figures and details. This is as it should be; this is how the creation was born—rather than manufactured—in the soul of the artist. The figure of Lavretsky and the psychological problems of which he is the representative are of important significance in the ethical, spiritual process of the poet and of our age. Lavretsky, first of all, is the last (that is, until now) word of Turgenev in his struggle with the type which disturbed him and tormented him by its passions and its extremes, by its overintense development, the type which had provoked him and which he sometimes provoked in himself before the creation of Vasily Luchinov. Lavretsky is the fullest (until now, be it understood) expression of his protest in favor of the good, the simple, the humble, against the predatory, the complexly passionate, the overintensely developed. However, this personality itself turned out to be most extraordinarily complex, perhaps because the poet's very struggle with his antithetical type was still far from over, or he had hitherto terminated it forcibly and it constantly recurs, as it recurred in Rudin.

Lavretsky is partly that person whom Pisemsky, with unusual strength and energy, with all the relentless logic of truth, but without an intelligent artistic illumination, depicted in his hitherto loftiest work—in tone and spiritual problem—"The Simpleton." His *love from behind the corner* for Varvara Pavlovna, his marriage, that drama which beset him in his conjugal relations, presents many similarities with the love, with the wedding, and with the drama of conjugal relations of Pisemsky's hero. But this similarity is only external. Lavretsky only appears a simpleton, a simpleton only so long as he is morally asleep. Pisemsky's Beshmetev is a beast, a beast with our native and our tenderly beloved tail, and the author almost curries it and cherishes it on his hero, really as a jewel, an adornment. An indignant soul finds a terrible truth in that terrible after-dinner scene when the drunken Pavel talks with his footman about his wife in front

of his wife; this and innumerable other details propound an im-
measurable difference between him and Lavretsky. The similarity
between them is only external; however, Lavretsky in the eyes of
Maria Dmitrievna, who calls him a slob, of Panshin, of his wife, of
M. Ernest, and probably of M. Jules, who writes a *feuilleton* on Mme
de Lavretsky, "cette grande dame si distinguée, qui demeure rue de
P."—in their eyes he is a simpleton, or, as M. Ernest expresses it in a
letter to his wife, "gros bonhomme de mari." Still more, even in the
eyes of Marfa Timofeevna, whose nature is completely spontaneous
and uncontaminated by refined taste, he is also a simpleton, although
a very good man. "So he is, I see, quite a fast one . . . Look at the
bashful lad!" she says with surprise when she learns of his relations
with Lisa. Obviously, even she did not suspect that he could fascinate
a woman. This is all because Lavretsky by nature is much more
a simpleton than Pisemsky's hero. Pisemsky's hero is not just a simpleton: on the one hand he is a beast, on the other a cynic, a cynic
stagnating in his cynicism, a cynic for whom there is no way out of
his cynicism. Between his marriage, and consequently between his
first feeling for a woman, or to put it better, womanhood, and the
feelings of Lavretsky there is a great difference. The motives for Pavel
Beshmetev's marriage are entirely animalistic. The environment into
which he was thrown, the environment from which—a strange thing!
—even a university education did not tear him but which was such
as to allow his *progressive* and *honest* sister to indulge his brutal
instincts and happily to arrange an unethical marriage with a girl
who does not love him at all, on the basis of the customary hope that,
quoth she, "they would bear it—they would grow fond of each
other," this environment curried, cherished, and grew his tail. The
potent strength of his work consists in that Pisemsky took his hero
as one with the environment of his life, but along with that went a
psychological-artistic mistake. His nature passionate to the point of
brutality, strong and impressionable, savage and primitive, Pavel
Beshmetev attracts profound sympathy to himself; but a question
cannot help but arise: how is it that the progress of the century passed
this passionate and impressionable nature by, how did it not operate
on him internally? For he was acquainted with its external form, he
read, studied, studied even more thoroughly than the hero of *A Nest*

of the Gentry, who is almost self-taught. Pavel Beshmetev falls in love purely animalistically, does not love anymore subtly than Zador-Manovsky, another of Pisemsky's heroes ("The Boyardom"); Pavel Beshmetev would have been capable of living with his wife even knowing her to be unfaithful, which is impossible for Lavretsky, because he fell in love with an ideal, not with the flesh, and he loved the ideal; once the ideal was smashed his love was smashed.

A comparison of these two persons, *externally alike* in nature and situation, is extraordinarily instructive; but it does not bring any result if you stick to it only within the limits of purely artistic criticism.

An artistic presentation is not engendered by the brain but is an offspring of flesh and blood. In the different presentations of two persons who apparently belong to one type there is a difference of moral and all other kinds of beliefs, a difference between the world views of two ages apparently not far from each other, to the former one of which belongs the author of *A Nest of the Gentry*, and to the latter one of which the author of "The Simpleton" belongs.

One age believed solely in progress, that is, in historical forces and their aspirations.

The other believes solely in nature, that is, in soil and environment.

Among a number of episodic scenes of Turgenev's work, that is, episodic in respect to one separate corner of his picture, not in respect to the whole canvas on which the picture was conceived, there is one which is especially striking by its profound belief in progress, in forces. This is the scene of the meeting between Lavretsky and Mikhalevich, a scene in which a whole age is painted, a whole generation's aspirations, a profoundly distinguished historical scene which supplements the depiction of that world from which Rudin came.

This small episode, taken separately, by itself, is a masterful historical picture, which will survive for a long time, so long as the types of Lavretsky and Mikhalevich live among us; and they will live for a long time yet, thanks to the strong fermentation that bred them. In these two persons both the aspirations and the forms of the aspirations of a whole age of our development were profoundly caught. This is an age of the powerful influence of philosophy, which, in the modern world, put forth such deep, living roots only among us and in the land of its birth, in Germany; with this difference, that in Germany it is constant, and consequently organic, while among us, thanks to reasons independent of it, it is fitful. Because it succeeded in acting only in fits, and because of the peculiarity of the Russian mind, which broadly and boldly seizes the ultimate conclusions of a thought, it quickly passed into practical application, quickly communicated a tone, a special cast to an age of intellectual life. Russian resourcefulness not only prompted such a lofty nature as, for example, the nature of Belinsky, to the ultimate conclusions of Hegelianism—it even placed the self-taught Polevoi higher than Cousin, from whom he had drawn his wisdom.[30] The chief thing is that once a thought was recognized it instantly received a practical application. Every trend was converted, so to speak, into religion, into a united existence of ideal and actuality, of thought and life. In this is our strength, but, I repeat again and again, and probably will many times more, also our weakness. Books are not simply books for us, objects of study or amusement; among us they have been and are converted spontaneously into life, into flesh and blood, they have changed and often do change the entire essence of our moral world. Therefore, every ideal trend, as it is spontaneously converting among us into something real, communicates a special color and smell to an intellectual age of development. Therefore, in every backward area of our fatherland an unconscious aversion to thought developed, a disease of fear of ideas. But blind backwardness, moral and intellectual narrow-mindedness, does not see, because it is hidebound, that, by attempting to interfere with the organic activity of ideas and by compelling them in this way to crash in and act in fits, it is actually causing these ideas to smash and distort facts instead of sorting out and discarding facts with due toleration.

Thought, which always crashes in by fits, operates and has operated in us agonizingly and painfully. In order palpably to present this painful activity of thought at a blow, I again return to the sole

---

[30] Victor Cousin, author of *Du vrai, du beau et du bien*, was widely read among educated Russians in the first half of the nineteenth century, but, in contrast to German idealists, was regarded as something of a low-brow philosopher.

interpreter of the secret of life, to poetry, and I point out to you the wild results of the stormy and blind elemental trends of romanticism in poetry, in Polezhaev's nature, the terrible and coldly ruthless logic of Lermontov, the tormented "Thoughts" of the self-made Koltsov which have had such a ruinous effect on the nature and life of our lofty popular lyric poet, the deep religiosity of Tiutchev's poetry, the woeful groans of the poet of "Monologues." You always and unwittingly call the last to mind when you speak of the effect of thought on life:

> Night and gloom! How weary and deserted!
> Sleepless rain hammers at my window.
> Candlelight flickers, shifting long shadows,
> Mournful and dark in my heart.
> I still hunt ghosts in the distance,
> Desire, unwilled, boils in my breast;
> But life and thought have killed my dreams.
> Thought, thought, how terrible now is your movement to me,
> Terrible your grievous struggle.
> *Inexorable, like fate itself,*
> *You carry destruction more dreadful than heaven's storms.*
> Long ago you broke innocent peace in me,
> Involved me forever in doubt,
> *Destroyed faith after faith in my soul,*
> *Termed yesterday's light dark to me.*

In this profound, sincere, and artless moan is the heartfelt confession of a whole age, the moan of a whole generation. In the blessed days of youth gone by this generation, which was supremely devoted to thought, which conversed, like the circle of the Hamlet of Shchigrovo, about the eternal sun of the spirit, "which developed *ins Unendliche* from Goethe and merged with the life *des absoluten Geistes*, triumphed, exulted childishly, trembled with rapture in the consciousness that life is a great secret." This generation then said with the lips of one of the loftiest of its representatives, referring with angry and obdurate neophytism to the eighteenth century, to its great predecessor, which it did not yet understand, enraptured as it was by the smoke of its symbols and mysteries:

There was a time when everyone thought the ultimate goal of human life is happiness. They stressed the vanity, the instability, and the inconstancy of everything under the moon and hastened after life, so long as life there was, and took pleasure in life, come what may. Naturally, everyone understood and interpreted the happiness of life in his own way, but all were agreed that it consists in pleasure. Laws, conscience, the moral freedom of man, all social relations were considered simply as things indispensable for the cohesion of the body politic, but empty and worthless in themselves. They prayed in temples and blasphemed in talk; they entered into conjugal contracts, accomplished conjugal rites—and abandoned themselves to all the fury of sensuality; they knew, by the experience of centuries, that people are not beasts, that they must be held together by religion and law, they knew this well—and they adjusted their religiosity and civil understanding to their understanding of life, of happiness: the loftiest and best ideal of the public edifice was considered to be that political society whose arrangement and foundation were inclined to the notion that people should not prevent people from enjoying themselves. This was the religion of the eighteenth century. One of the best people of this century said:

> Life is a momentary gift of Heaven:
> Make it ease for yourself,
> And with your pure soul
> Bless fate's blows. . . .
>
> Drink, eat, rejoice, my friend!
> Our time to live in the world is fixed.
> Spotless alone is enjoyment
> That leaves no regrets behind.[31]

This was the loftiest ethic: the best people of that time could not rise to any other lofty ideal. But suddenly it was all changed: they began to call the philosophers who had disseminated this concept of the human race swindlers, to use Baron Brambeus' favorite word.[32] New swindlers appeared, the German philosophers, for whom, in justice, the above-mentioned gentleman has a horrible antipathy, whom Mr. Masalsky

[31] The first quatrain is from G. R. Derzhavin's poem "Na smert kniazia Meshcherskogo" (1779), the second from his "K pervomu sosedu" (1780).

[32] The pseudonym of O. I. Senkovsky. Belinsky is referring to his article "Germanskaia filosofiia," *Biblioteka dlia chteniia* 9 (1835).

once so beautifully polished up in his splendid tale, "A Nineteenth-Century Don Quixote," that genuine *chef d'oeuvre* of Russian Literature, and whom, finally, *The Library for Reading* not long ago killed outright. These new swindlers, with amazing impudence and charlatanism, began to preach the most unethical principles, according to which the goal of a man's life consists not in happiness, not in the enjoyment of earthly goods, but in the full consciousness of his human dignity, in the harmonious development of the treasures of his spirit. But the audacity of the pitiful free-thinkers did not end with this: *they began to maintain that only a life fulfilling disinterested impulses to the good, enduring hardship and suffering, could be called a human life, while any other one is more or less an approximation of animal life.* Several poets began to act as though they were in agreement with these evil-intentioned philosophers and to disseminate various damaging ideas, such as: *that a man must without fail express some human side of his human existence, if not all,* that is, either he must act practically for the benefit of society, if he has an important position in it, without any motive of personal reward; or he must devote himself to knowledge for the sake of knowledge itself, not for money and position; or he must apply himself to an appreciation of art as an amateur, not for the sake of high-society culture as before, but because art (as they claim) is a link connecting earth with Heaven; or he must dedicate himself to it as a practitioner, if he feels a lofty call to this, but not because of the call of the pocketbook; or he must fall in love with another soul, so that every earthly soul would have the right to say:

> I achieved everything earthly:
> I loved and lived on earth—

or, finally, he must simply have a kind of lofty human interest in life, but not in pleasure, not in satiation with earthly goods. Then historians came to the help of these philosophers, and they began to show, by theories and facts, that not only every man privately, but the whole human race aspires to a kind of lofty development and evolution of human perfection; for which the honorable Baron Brambeus makes mincemeat of them, the mischievous ones! I, on my side, honestly do not know who is correct: the earlier French philosophers or the current German ones; which is better, the eighteenth or the nineteenth century; but I do know that there is in many ways a great distinction between the former and the latter.[33]

[33] From Belinsky's review "*Natalia.* Sochinenie gospozhi***," *Molva* 22 (1835). See *Polnoe sobranie sochineniy*, 1: 203–5.

The age was originally full of just such beliefs, an age of which two offshoots, two representatives were depicted by Turgenev in the episode of the historical picture conceived by him. The cited passage from Belinsky, one of the passages most characteristic of the philosophical-lyrical enthusiasm of that time, shows how strong was the ferment communicated to intellectual life by philosophy.

Philosophical belief was genuinely a belief transferred into life, into flesh and blood. Needless to say, the matter ended with the famous image of the serpent biting its own tail—and it is also needless to explain that in the end the idealism of the nineteenth century, which had proudly revolted against the eighteenth century, came to agree with its final results. The point is not the results—the point is in the process which leads to the results, as one of the great teachers of the nineteenth century said in his phenomenology.[34]

Twice, and both times in the highest degree successfully, Turgenev depicted a recapitulation of the great philosophical trends in life: in the cited episode of his latest work and in the epilogue of *Rudin*—an epilogue which is as much above the rest of the tale as the tale is superior to a number of more polished, apparently integrated works of many contemporary writers. The difference between these two depictions is that Mikhalevich-Rudin is a Don Quixote, an honorable Don Quixote, but nevertheless a Don Quixote, while Lavretsky is a poeticized Lezhnev, a Lezhnev given many of the qualities of Rudin.

In Lavretsky and Lezhnev the philosophical tendency ends in humility in the face of actuality, humility in the face of what Lavretsky calls, in another episodic scene of *A Nest of the Gentry*, *the people's truth*. In Mikhalevich and Rudin, although the one speaks about practical activity and the other throws himself into it, the philosophical tendency ends with a protest, an eternal, hopeless protest. The humility of Mikhalevich and Rudin is only a logical demand (a postulate), just like the humility of the author of "Monologues":

> Deep in the soul did we bury
> Many feelings, images, thoughts. And then what?
> Will an arrogant mind speak reproaches to Heaven?

[34] The reference is to Hegel.

Reproaches to what end? We will invest the soul with humility
And enclose ourselves with it—minus bile, if we can.

The humility of Lezhnev and Lavretsky (doubtless more dearly
acquired by the latter than by the former) is actual humility. By
nature they are simpletons, I dare say laggards, as Mikhalevich calls
Lavretsky, or slobs, as Maria Dmitrievna calls him—but not simpletons like the "Simpleton" of Pisemsky.

Their intellectual and ethical process is crowned by humility,
because there is more nature in them, more, if you will, physiological
personality, than in Rudin and Mikhalevich—more internal physiological unity with the soil that produced them, with the environment
that educated their first impressions. Each of their sacrifices is more
dearly obtained than Rudin's and Mikhalevich's—again because
there is more nature in them—in them in particular is accomplished
the ethical process which the lofty poet of our physiognomy expressed
in Ivan Petrovich Belkin.

They are, if you will, Oblomovs (since the word Oblomov has
become a faddish word), but not in any way Stolzes, which does them
great honor, for Stolzes are artificial growths among us. But Turgenev,
as a genuine poet by nature and as one of the last of the Mohicans of
an age created by powerful trends, could never so sharply isolate this
type as Goncharov isolated it in his novel. The traits of Rudin somewhat penetrated Lavretsky as two or three traits of Lavretsky,
inversely, penetrated Rudin—the trait, for instance, which, according
to Pigasov's correct judgment, rendered him *scanty*.

On the other hand, Turgenev, either unable or unwilling to make
Lavretsky a logical focus which would combine the common features
of various persons, could at the same time not make him entirely
dependent on his soil and environment, as Pisemsky had made Pavel
Beshmetev. The difference between these two personalities is too
obvious. As far as physiologically determined personality is concerned, Lavretsky surpasses Rudin and Mikhalevich to the same
degree that Pisemsky's simpleton surpasses him. Compare the scenes
where each becomes convinced of the unfaithfulness of his wife; and
see the difference in all their subsequent relations with the unfaithful
wives, even though in these points Turgenev does not at all yield to

Pisemsky either in psychological truth—which is not at all surprising —or in energy, which he seldom attains to such a degree.

In the scene where Lavretsky discovers his wife's infidelity there is a whole hell of suffering—and what suffering! It is fully, profoundly human; it is connected with the struggle against the elemental, the physiological, with the struggle of *artificial* nature created by ideas, by education, against coarse, bestial nature. It is true that the tides of bestial nature are only froth here and not a real affair. Lavretsky did not just not kill—he could not even beat his wife: one may vouch for this. Even at a later moment, when a long separation had disclosed the whole nature of Varvara Pavlovna to him and when another, more meaningful and profound feeling had filled all his being, at the moment when Varvara Pavlovna's appearance smashes the world of firm and poetic bliss he has created; at the moment, finally, when, in consequence of the contrast, her nature and all the qualities of this nature should be in the highest degree hateful to him—at this moment only a foam forms on the scum, no more.

Of course you understand to what a degree the gentleness, the submissiveness, and the coquetry of his wife—this whole abyss of odious, incurable moral lies—must be alien to Lavretsky. You also understand how terrible for a weak but self-respecting man must be the consciousness that "Varvara Pavlovna was not at all afraid of him but pretended she might at any moment fall into a faint," while he could only "breathe heavily and now and then clench his teeth." In this terrible but profoundly genuine scene Ogarev's groan is heard: "I must laugh at my weakness." It is still more—it is the eternal groan of Hamlet. The truth is carried to the point of cruelty, to recording Lavretsky's purely histrionic action when he "buttons himself all the way up."

However, this same Lavretsky, whose inner psychical activity needs warming up, never once—and this may be boldly certified—will alter the decision he had taken under the influence of ideas, a decision to which Turgenev wanted to allude, and did allude masterfully by the description of the figure and pose of Varvara Pavlovna. In contrast, the simpleton of Pisemsky might have been reconciled with his wife even so far as an intimate relationship with her, and the Volynsky of *antiquated* Lazhechnikov devoted himself supremely (and this is a surprising trait in a typical portrayal of a passionate Russian character) to a passionate enthusiasm for his wife, who had just arrived, barely a day after he had ruined Marioritsa.[35] It is true that Volynsky could not hate his wife, because he had no reason to hate her. Consistency is given Lavretsky not merely by a sluggish nature; for this is still a question: is his nature sluggish, or has it been reworked by the powerful influence of ideas which penetrated it throughout? Let us suppose that a somewhat weak, or rather a reworked, nature would help him in consistency; still the basis of consistency is purely spiritual: he believes in principles, he serves principles, principles have become his life for him. This is the sense in which I say that Turgenev attached somewhat Rudin-like features to him.

The mistake, or, to put it better, tour de force, in Pisemsky's "The Simpleton" is contained in the author's having carried perhaps too far the thought of the inseparability of nature from soil and environment, and having trusted only in physiological features. So the mistake—if it can be called a mistake—of Turgenev's is a logical consistency in the depiction of a simpleton, a laggard, a slob.

I said, if it can be called a mistake. For, like you, I do not know, but I do not like logical consistency in an artistic depiction, for the simple reason that I do not see it anywhere in life. Every difference between the two depictions of this externally similar type is in the difference between the ages under whose influences they were created.

After the philosophic age, that is, after the age of powerful philosophic trends, a purely analytic age came into our intellectual life, an introspective age, an age of testing aspirations against life, an age of doubt in the strength of the trends and the validity of the aspirations engendered by them.

His talent chiefly sensitive, sensitive, as I have already repeated several times, to a degree of femininity, Turgenev clung to the old trend, in spite of his new aspirations; still he was incapable of being hardened in a gloomy although lyrical negation and yielded to the analytic trend of the new age. Humility before the soil, before actuality, rose up in his soul, as in the soul of a poet, not because of a

[35] A reference to I. I. Lazhechnikov's historical novel *Ledianoi dom* (1835).

purely logical Rudin-like or Mikhalevich-like demand, but as an out-growth of the soil itself, of the environment itself, of Pushkin's Belkin.

Since he was only a talent and not a genius, nor a conjurer, he went too far—

> He burned everything he had worshiped,
> Worshiped everything he had burned.

It is clear to an observer how and why the process, whose final word was humility, took place in his creative career in general and in his latest production in particular.

Lavretsky is set off against a foil, even perhaps too much of a foil. The foil is Panshin.

The significance of the figures of Lavretsky and Panshin—as conceived for a large historical picture—is clearly denoted in the strikingly colorful episode of their moral and intellectual skirmish.

Is it not true that the harshly, but in the highest degree surely penciled-in personality of Panshin, a man of theory, extraordinarily sets off the personality of the man of life, as Turgenev's Lavretsky appears throughout?

But to say that Panshin is a man of theory is not enough. Rudin is also a man of theory to a certain extent, and the soul of Lavretsky himself is subjected to theory, at least in some respects. Panshin is an *active* man, a reformer from the heights of a bureaucrat's outlook, a leveler who believes in abstract law, in abstract justice. He is offensive to our Russian soul, whether he appears in Sollogub's pretentious comedy in the person of Nadimov, or in the sick creation of Gogol in the person of Kostanzhoglo, or in the hopeful laureate Lvov's dramatic works, or in the brilliant work of a beloved and honored talent, that of Pisemsky, in the person of Kalinovich.[36]

---

[36] Nadimov is the hero of V. A. Sollogub's *Chinovnik* (1856); Kostanzhoglo is a character in the unfinished second volume of Gogol's *Mertvye dushi;* of N. M. Lvov's comedies Grigorev probably has in mind *Predubezhdenie, ili ne mesto krasit cheloveka, chelovek–mesto* (1858); Kalinovich is the hero of Pisemsky's *Tysiacha dush* (1858).

Turgenev's attitude toward this personality is absolutely correct and valid, but the personality itself was not brought to a conclusion and polished off. Panshin is magnificent when he condescendingly pays compliments to Gedeonovsky, magnificent in the scenes with Lisa, magnificent when he gracefully plays piquet with Maria Dmitrievna, magnificent in his conversations with Lavretsky: in short, the whole outward side of his personality is artistically finished, but internally he should have been caught more broadly, on a larger scale. After all, he is a reformer (albeit one with Ivan Alexandrovich Khlestakov in essence), and as such he should have combined in himself a whole range of similar reformers—the kind of reformers whose actions drive men of life, men with broad dreams and plans, to an attachment to the soil, to a humility before the truth of the people. He should have come into the picture in relief, so that it might be obvious in what way he was developed.

And what do we know about him? Nothing except those features which show a simply empty and simply superficial, vacuous man, and even of these few features some are completely false.

You are left somewhat in a quandary: just what did Turgenev want to say in the figure of his Panshin, and with what sides of his nature does Panshin set off the person of Lavretsky? Is it that his nature is purely superficial, superficially clever, superficially brilliant, and so forth, in contrast to the sincere but in appearance far from brilliant personality of the main hero? Does he set off Lavretsky by being one of those common hackneyed worldly heroes, the kind we find in the tales of Count Sollogub and, in general, in the tales of the forties? Or, finally, is his cold and theoretic nature meant to contrast with the vital nature of Lavretsky?

You will say all three. All right, but why, compared to the figure whom he should set off in a certain way, do some of his qualities stand out in even bolder relief? He is clearly presented this way in the extremely remarkable episode of Lavretsky's intellectual skirmish with him. There he is treated in relief like a man of theory in contrast with a man of life and soil. I do not in the least deny that he could be a superficially clever and worldly modish gentleman; but the artist should have turned more attention to his dry methodicism, to his reformer habits; he should have shown how such methodicism was created and developed in him.

But we do not see this, or this is but touched upon, first superficially, second falsely.

First of all, I raise a problem for which—entirely fairly, although it seemed amusing to many at the time—one of our serious journals took Pisemsky to task in connection with his Kalinovich:[37] Vladimir Nikolaevich Panshin, just like Kalinovich, could not be a graduate of any university. They are both products of specialized institutions.

From our universities graduated either Beltovs and Rudins, that is, generally persons who do not serve their full time in state service before retirement because their ideals do not match practice and they stubbornly and grimly withdraw into their ideals; or Lavretskys and Lezhnevs, who also fail to stay in their jobs until retirement, although they may serve a little longer. Other university graduates may become the Dosuzhevs of *A Profitable Place* who live off the "blockheads," or even live with the blockheads, that is, with the lower merchant class, making use of their knowledge both of the "blockheads," mores and of the law which is abstract and dark for the "blockheads." They know how to cope with the abstract world of law to the benefit of the "blockheads," and for this the latter love, cherish, honor, and pamper them. These are our jurists in the true sense of the word. Finally, university graduates may simply turn into bribees and scriveners. But under no circumstances do they become reformers from grand officialdom's heights.

Such reformers could only be educated under the influence of pedantic theories, not under the influence of philosophy or of university education, since the latter always has a more or less encyclopedic character.

Turgenev did not have enough consistency to carry the idea of theoretical purity and abstraction all the way through the characterization of Panshin. And the reason for this was that he did not have a definitively clear attitude to Lavretsky himself.

1. He certainly wanted to make Lavretsky a simpleton, a slob, a

[37] See P. V. Annenkov's article "O delovom romane v nashei literature," *Atenei* 1, pt. 2 (1859).

laggard, out of a strong liking for the type of the harried man, a liking born of his struggle with the brilliant, somewhat predatory type. Turgenev

> . . . burned everything he had worshiped,
> And worshiped everything he had burned.

But the point is that the artist in him is stronger than the thinker, and in Lavretsky the artist, against the will of the thinker, glory to God, does not at all paint a harried man, but a sketch of someone uniquely alive. The artist's intention to make Lavretsky a simpleton, a laggard, a slob is a sacrifice he yielded to the idea of the harried type, the idea to which his burning of "everything he had worshiped" led him. Lavretsky is a simpleton and a slob for women like Varvara Pavlovna and Maria Dmitrievna; but do we have to look at the world through only one window? Are there no other natures than those of the above-mentioned ladies? It seems to me generally that, since his attitude toward his hero, toward his spiritual type, was somewhat unclear, Turgenev lost sight of certain of his attitudes to people and unclearly set up others. Could it be that, before he met Lisa, no natures could be found capable of valuing and loving Lavretsky? Or that no person apart from Mikhalevich could understand him better than M. Ernest and M. Jules? Judging by his nature, it is possible authentically to conclude the contrary, that is, that there were at any rate women who loved him passionately, but did not perhaps conform to his ideal. There are two kinds of women—two types, and the aspirations of these two types, between whom there are, it goes without saying, innumerable shades, are diametrically opposed. But Turgenev—and this refers not only to Lavretsky but to innumerable figures passing before the reader in his stories and tales—is so intimidated by the brilliant type, by the predatory type, that the other type appears to him in the shape of a harried man vainly looking for sympathy. The most he could manage was a limp, half-hearted sympathy for this type in Lezhnev. In Lavretsky—and this is an enormous step forward in the moral process—the type develops from the harried into one having the right of citizenship, receives a poetic aura of a kind, but there is still a great deal of vagueness, of inconsistency, to be seen in the author's attitudes to him.

2. In consequence of this, Turgenev attaches to Panshin some qualities belonging to Lavretsky, and the other way round.

It is on the whole a false idea to place between them the figure of the old musician Lemm, this touchstone of *feeling* (not only of feeling for beauty but of feeling in general) in the natures of the one and the other. The point is that the cold, superficial giftedness of Panshin, for which every impression is commonplace and artificial, must at first have succeeded in *fooling* the old German. Those Veretev-like artistic features which Turgenev attached to Panshin, features of spontaneous talent, of poetic understanding, do not at all fit him: much more native to such people are a *made-to-order* enthusiasm for Beethoven and a superficial knowledge of music, with adequate interpretation and even tolerable performance. All the Veretev qualities—reduced, of course, to a lesser degree—would suit Lavretsky better than Veretev himself as delineated by Turgenev.

For above all in Lavretsky is nature, above all he is a child of the soil—in consequence of which he ends with moral humility before it.

There is an internal kinship between the idea that begot Stankevich's Levin (in "The Idealist") and the idea that begot Lavretsky. The idea even proceeded by a single process; in "The Idealist" it attained consciousness and only passed into *action* in Lavretsky. The Levin of Mr. Stankevich understood his helplessness in the face of reality: but his humility before it, before the truth of life, is expressed in hardness, in petrification, in isolation. Such an outcome of the spiritual process in Stankevich's "The Idealist" (a creature of the "irritation of imprisoned thoughts," a product harsh and naked) verges on the ludicrous, despite the intention of the author. Turgenev's Lavretsky is just such an idealist, but there is flesh, blood, and nature in him: his consciousness was not constricted by negation alone and it passed into action. There is as much nature and attachment to the soil in him as idealism. Memories of childhood, family traditions, the life of his native land, and even superstitions evoke a profound response in his soul. He is a man of the soil, he is, if you will, an Oblomov, against whom the remarkably clever publicist of *The Contemporary* was filled with such enmity not long ago.[38] In this is

[38] That is, N. A. Dobroliubov, who devoted his article "Chto takoe oblomovshchina?" to Goncharov's novel in *Sovremennik* 5 (1859).

his weakness, but in this also is his strength; weakness, it goes without saying, in the present, strength in the future. He is *ours*, he is native *to us*, to us, the Russian people, such as the reform made us.[39]

Thus far, like the Oblomovs, he does not exactly fit into any action; but he is our defense against the Panshin-reformers, against the Konstanzhoglo-organizers, finally against the aimless activity which Goncharov mathematically harshly but correctly presented in the freak (for I cannot call him a person) of Stolz.

I would be finished with Lavretsky and with this work of Turgenev's if I were a publicist and not a critic.

But for me an artistic work is a revelation of the great secrets of the soul and of life, the sole decider of social and ethical questions. For the first time in our literature, our Ivan Petrovich Belkin in the person of Lavretsky emerged from his frightened, purely negative state. Let him appear in a clearly unfinished work, let the poet's attitude to him be indeterminate; this indeterminate attitude is already evidently not the same as Turgenev's attitude to the type in *The Diary of a Superfluous Man*, in "Two Friends," in *Rudin* when painting Lezhnev. Lavretsky already exists by himself, not as a contrast to Rudin, like Lezhnev, for there are Rudin-like traits in him, he himself needs a contrast in the picture, which the poet fails to provide in Panshin because of the indeterminate attitude to the main hero. As has been said, he is not an "idealist" either, not a man proudly and obdurately sullen.

When, weary of life, half broken by life, he returns to the world of his old attachments, to the natal soil which had nurtured him, he does not return there to die, like Mr. Chulkaturin to "Lambswater." He lives, and for the first time lives a full harmonious life.

This is a lofty poetic idea, which alone makes it possible to forgive Turgenev the unfinished quality of his creation!

From the very minute of Lavretsky's appearance, you know, you feel, that this man will *live*, that he *ought to live*. At his first encounter with Lisa and with the priceless old woman, who constitutes an artistic pearl in *A Nest of the Gentry* and in all our contemporary literature, you know this; because on the first evening of his appear-

---

[39] That is, the reforms of Peter I.

ance in "Marfa Timofeevna's room, in the light of the lamps hung before the dark old icons, Lavretsky sat in an arm chair, his elbows on his knees and his face in his hand: the old woman standing before him occasionally and silently stroked his hair." The ability to sympathize with this old woman has been preserved in his soul as a physiological bond between these two creatures, despite the differences in their years and education; this is the holy bond of Pushkin's nature with Arina Rodionovna,[40] a holy love for the soil, for traditions, for the natal way of life, our defense against dry practicality and grim methodicism!

You know that he will live, that he already lives, this man whose heart is half-broken and whose mind is developed to the highest degree; he has but to breathe the air of his native land.

The rich value of Goncharov's talent was recognized by everyone, without exception, when his first novel, *A Common Story*, appeared. His tale "Ivan Savich Podzhabrin," written, they say, before but printed after *A Common Story*, seemed to many unworthy of a writer who had so brilliantly embarked on a literary career, although, I frankly admit, I never shared this opinion.[41] In "Podzhabrin," exactly in the same manner as in *A Common Story*, all the facets of Goncharov's talent were almost identically disclosed, and both works suffered from equal, although contradictory, faults. In *A Common Story* the bare bones of the psychological problem stick out too sharply from the details: in "Podzhabrin" the particular external details completely engulf a content which was not rich to begin with. Therefore, both these works are not strictly artistic creations, but studies, although, it is true, studies which glitter with lifelike color; they display the indubitable talent of a lofty artist, but an artist in whom analysis gnawed away the whole basis, all the roots of creativity. The dry dogmatism of *A Common Story*'s structure hits everyone in the face. The value of *A Common Story* consists in the separate, artistically cultivated particulars, but not in the whole, which to everyone, even to the most partial reader, is presented as a kind of

---

[40] Pushkin's nurse.

[41] "Podzhabrin" was written in 1842 and published in 1848; *Obyknovennaia istoriia* was written between 1844 and 1846, and published in 1847.

forced development of a theme set beforehand. To whom is it not clear that Petr Ivanovich, with his relentlessly practical outlook, is not an actually existent person, but the embodiment of a certain point of view, something like the Starodums, the Zdravomysls, and the Pravosudovs of the old comedies[42]—with this difference, however: that the Starodums, the Zdravomysls, and the Pravosudovs, for all their absurdity, were representatives of much more honorable and human convictions than the narrow practical theory of Petr Ivanovich Aduev? Is it not clear also that Alexander Aduev is deliberately exhibited by the author as weaker and pettier than his uncle, and that such an antipoetic theme, such a banal thought, which even the brilliant details cannot redeem, overlay everything? It is most remarkable that *A Common Story* pleased even a dying generation, even old men, even, I recall, *The Northern Bee* (forgive me the reference!).[43] This testified not to its special artistic value, but simply that the outlook under whose influence it was written was not above the common level.

The same antipoetic thoughts are revealed in "Oblomov's Dream," that kernel from which all *Oblomov* was born, that focal point to which it is all tied, almost the very reason for which it was written. The antipoeticism of the primitive practical theme affected impartial readers all the more unpleasantly because the external strengths of the author's talent stood out extraordinarily brightly. You remember that before the author leads you to the "heavenly corner of earth" created by Oblomov's dream, with a few touches of his masterful pencil he draws another place, another life, which is completely the opposite of that to which his hero's dream conveys us. In the style of the account you feel the presence of that genuine, calm, creative power which conveys you at will to this or another world and can equally sympathize with each. A way of life you have known from childhood is created before you in its smallest tones, a quiet world, imperturbably calm, in all its immediacy. The author becomes a

---

[42] *Starodum* means "old thought"; *Zdravomysl*, "sensible thought"; and *Pravosudov*, "right judgments." The *raisonneurs* of eighteenth-century didactic comedies bore such names, e.g., Starodum is a character in D. I. Fonvizin's *Nedorosl* (1782).

[43] See Bulgarin's review of the novel in *Severnaia pchela* 81 (1847).

genuine poet—and as a poet he knows how to stand on a level with the world he is creating, how to be comically naïve in the tale of the monster found in the ravine by the inhabitants of Oblomovka, profoundly moving in the creation of Oblomov's mother; how to be a genuine psychologist in the story of the letter which was so direfully opened by the peaceful dwellers of the "heavenly corner of earth"; and finally, how to be an epically objective artist in the depiction of the siesta which embraces all Oblomovka. Do you remember the passage about the tales which are related to Ilia Ilich and, of course, were at one time more or less to all of us, whose motley and broad fanciful design the poet unfolds with such forceful fantasy? Do you remember the remaining details: the domestic talk in the twilight, the indignation of Ilia Ivanovich's wife at his forgetfulness concerning various omens, his preparations to answer the letter which for some time has been the object of uneasy fear? All this is a complete, artistically created world, irresistibly drawing you into its magic circle.

But why *all this waste*? Why evoke all this world, why is it objectively depicted both as it now is and with its traditions? In order to inveigh against it in the name of a practical primitive principle, in the name of the Chinese views of Petr Ivanovich Aduev, or in the name of the Tatar-German views of Stolz? For Stolz, although a German, is a Tatar nevertheless, a Tatar in soul and in business as he disposes of Ilia Ilich's creditor. Why in the "Dream" itself is there an unpleasantly sharp tone of irony concerning what is all the same loftier than Stolzism and Aduevism?

The literary works of our times present strange problems. How, reading the works of Goncharov, can you not say that the talent of their author is immeasurably above the views that gave birth to those works?

But everything has its historic causes.

Gogol's attitude to actuality, expressed for the most part in humor, is one of bitter laughter, scourging like Nemesis, because a moan for the ideal is heard in it; a laughter full of love and sympathy, a laughter elevating the moral essence of man. Such an attitude could appear correct and morally acceptable only in the integrated nature of a genuine artist. This love acting by means of laughter, this fervent aspiration for the ideal, was not then fully apprehended by everyone.

To many, even to most, only the form of Gogol's work was understandable; the only clear thing was that a new mine had been opened by a great poet, the mine of analysis of everyday common actuality; and the very thing at which Gogol looked with a love of the inalterable truth, with a love of the ideal, was perceived by others, even by extremely gifted people, from the point of view of either personal conviction or of prejudice. This is the origin of various satirical sketches and of an endless number of tales of the literature of the forties—all of which ended with the eternal refrain: "This is what can become of man!"—tales in which the most marvelous *metamorphoses* of heroes and heroines choked in *filthy* actuality were accomplished by the will and whim of their authors, in which everything surrounding the hero or heroine was intentionally depicted in caricature. An innumerable quantity of works with such a tendency was written in the past; their lie consisted for the most part in that they entangled readers in details apparently taken from simple everyday actuality, demonstrating their authors' undoubted talent for observation, but leading ignorant people unacquainted with manners and customs into error. It is incontrovertible that there was a good side and merit of a kind in this purely negative style—but its onesidedness and falsehood was soon disclosed exceedingly clearly. Most amusing of all was that romanticism was never so strongly abused as in this age of the most romantic attitudes of authors to actuality.

Such an attitude to actuality could not be continued because of its own basic principles. Reconciliation, that is, a clear cognition of actuality, is indispensable to the human soul, and it had perforce to be sought in that same actuality itself—the more so since many people shook their heads doubtfully when they read the various caricatured depictions of actuality, and they made bold to think that too many somber or too many crude paints were used in the picture, that the painters evidently were in a fit of *melancholy*, that the *kinsmen* of various young ladies were not at all such beasts as they seemed to the writers, even that they appeared especially foul only because some *melancholy* author wanted to exhibit the *cleanliness* of some Natasha as a special virtue. They doubted, in short, that actuality was so foul and black and the romantic personality so correct in its claims as writers chose to depose. As is well known, the Russian is distinguished by a special sagacity: he is prepared to acknowledge all his actual faults—but he does not take to exaggerating them and therefore does not yield to somber mystical despair.

In the public consciousness a protest against the exclusive claims of the romantic personality was organized—a protest in the name of actuality.

But of what actuality?

Among us two actualities are discernible. The one on show is the official one, the other under the bushel is the living one. It is not necessary here to clarify this thought. A confused protest, indistinct in its aims, then arose—even though at first it asked for no more than an external, showy actuality.

In response to this confused, uncertain protest a remarkably bright but purely external gift appeared, lacking a profound content, lacking an aspiration to the ideal—the gift of Goncharov. It responded to the demand as it could, as best it knew how, with *A Common Story*, this epic poem of a petty official's outlook and elementary wisdom, perfectly in accord with the first, superficial beginnings of the protest for actuality against the romantic personality. Goncharov's gift did not walk a new road: it came entirely out of that same category of works and was only its bloom. Reconciliation was expressed in *A Common Story* by the irony of a kind of despair, by a laughter at the protest of personality from one angle and by glorification of the triumph of a dry, lifeless, groundless practicality. Everything was sacrificed to this irony. The author portrayed two figures: one is wishy-washy, slight, weak, with a label on his forehead: "the romanticism of the quasi-young generation"; the other is stern, calm, specific, like mathematics, with a label on his forehead: "the practical mind." The latter, it goes without saying, triumphed in the end, like virtuous love in the old novels and comedies. Such was the idea of Goncharov's work, an idea not in the least hidden, but on the contrary, bursting to the surface, crying out in every figure of the novel. Much talent was necessary to make the readers ignore the obviously artificial structure of the work—but, besides the strength of talent, the idea responded to the demands of the majority, that is, of the moral and social petty bourgeoisie. The novel, I repeat, pleased all so-called practical people who always like it when the younger generation is scolded for various *absurd* and *incongruous* aspirations, it even pleased those gentlemen who had looked askance at *Dead Souls* or berated it. In their naïve joy the protesters for external superficial actuality did not notice that the irony of the novel vanished to no purpose, that the romantic trend did not acknowledge, does not acknowledge, and will not acknowledge its foster child in the wishy-washy Alexander Aduev.

Much time passed before the protest for actuality was bred and strengthened to consciousness. In the course of all this time Goncharov's talent gave evidence of its existence only in the story of the round-the-world voyage of the frigate *Pallas*—and in this book he remained faithful to himself, or, to put it better, to that low level to which he had descended. Strikingly bright descriptions of nature, masterfully trimmed minutiae, acute and pointed observation, and positive absence of ideal in viewpoint—this is what appeared in this book which all the public again read avidly—for our public is rather a lover of the Japanese point of view, especially if an indisputably strong talent has consecrated itself to the service of this point of view.

Finally the long-awaited *Oblomov* appeared. First of all, it did not say anything new. Everything that was new in it had been expressed much earlier in "Oblomov's Dream"[44]—I mean everything substantially new, which provokes talk, which provokes both hostility and sympathy. The success of *Oblomov*—whatever you say—was debatable, completely unlike the success of *A Common Story*. And this had to be so. Another age, another consciousness has been born. *A Common Story* pandered to the demands of the moment, the demands of the majority, of officialdom, of the moral petty bourgeoisie. *Oblomov* pandered to nothing—and came out at least five or six years too late. Goncharov was the same in *Oblomov* as he had been in *A Common Story*, and his *Oblomov* was constructed according to the same dry dogmatic theme as *A Common Story*. In its details it is, if you will, higher than *A Common Story*, in psychological analysis more profound; but our consciousness, the consciousness of the age, has gone forward, while the consciousness of the author of *A Common Story* has been stuck in Japan. *Oblomov* flattered only an extremely

---

[44] "Son Oblomova" had been published in the literary supplement to *Sovremennik* for 1849. The novel as a whole appeared ten years later.

small circle of people who still believe that our enemy in matters of progress is our own nature, our essential living traits—and that all our salvation is comprised in remodeling ourselves according to some kind of narrow theory. The viewpoints of this small circle have also fallen behind the questions of the age.

The hero of our age is not Goncharov's Stolz, nor his Petr Ivanovich Aduev; and the heroine of our age is not his Olga, who in old age, if she remains the same despite the many gracious sides of her nature which her author reveals to us, will become a repulsive dame, with a perpetual and purposeless neurotic anxiety, a genuine persecutor of everyone around her, one of the victims of God knows what. I am almost convinced that she will die like the dame in Tolstoy's "Three Deaths." If one were to choose a definite heroine from among the feminine figures of Goncharov, an impartial mind unclouded by theories would choose, as Oblomov chose, Agafia Fedoseevna—not only because her elbows are seductive and because she makes good pies, but because she is much more a woman than Olga.

The fact is that the heart of the author of *Oblomov*—like his enormous and consequently living talent—inclines much more to Oblomov and Agafia than to Stolz and Olga. For the epitaph to Oblomov and for his appealing traits the violent persecutors of Oblomovism, to whom he had pandered, almost reproached him and—*plus royalistes que le roi*—violently attacked not only Oblomov but, in connection with him, Onegin, Pechorin, Beltov, and Rudin, in the name of Stolz, and made a purifying sacrifice of Stolz himself to Olga.[45] On the latter point, it is impossible not to agree with them: Olga is, precisely, more intelligent that Stolz: on the other hand, he will bore her, he will be henpecked by her and really will be a victim of that spirit of neurotic *self-laceration* which is an imposing trait in her only while she is young but in age will change to pettiness and become an ordinary physiological function.

Turgenev went another way: his works, as I have already said, represent the development of our entire age. He loved with it, trusted, doubted, execrated, hoped anew and trusted anew with it—he did not fear the uttermost limits of thought, or, to put it better, he carried

[45] An allusion to Dobroliubov's review of the novel, in *Sovremennik* 5 (1859).

through to its uttermost limits and lightheartedly gave himself up to every enthusiasm. Therefore, reading his last work, at every step you review the process which was accomplished in the entire age, at each step you encounter images reborn, if you like, in new and better forms, whose seeds, however, and even embryoes are rooted in the distant past. You peel off layer after layer—and most of all you are astonished by the organic unity of the layers.

There is particular evidence of this organic unity in *A Nest of the Gentry* in the story of Lavretsky's father and grandfather, one passage among many others which appeared to one critic, as he expressed it, retrospective. The critic, who had been a powerful pleader for the liberation of art from enslavement, in the enthusiasm of his exclusively aesthetic outlook did not notice the exceedingly obvious and essential fault of *A Nest of the Gentry*, about which I spoke at the beginning of the preceding section.[46] Only to a blind man is it not apparent that the center of the drama alone was drawn on the enormous canvas stretched for an enormous historical picture, while in some passages disjointed episodes, in others mere sketches were scattered.

The type whose last expression in Turgenev is Lavretsky was created by a long process and should have embodied all this process, the process of our post-Pushkin age. But there is a considerable difference between what should be and what is, what was given to us. To judge the type by how he appeared in *A Nest of the Gentry* and on this basis alone to reach conclusions about the artistry or nonartistry of Turgenev's achievement and of the entire work in which the type appears means positively not to understand the affair so far as Turgenev is concerned, not to understand the problem, the inner purport of his poetic creativity.

What is the main thing *revealed* in *A Nest of the Gentry*?

Do you know that it is *more difficult* to answer this question than it is to answer the question of what is *revealed* in *Oblomov*? You will not answer this question by any ethical precept, by any aphorism. What was revealed? A great deal was revealed! The whole age from the death of Pushkin to our days was revealed: the entire Pushkinian process, which I call our psychical Ivan Petrovich Belkin, was

[46] A reference to A. V. Druzhinin, who reviewed the novel in *Biblioteka dlia chteniia* 12 (1859).

revealed; for all this process had to be repeated in Turgenev in order that, for better or worse, a new living type might be created, not just negative, but positive; and in order that such a living, positive figure might be made of the harried, humble, simple man who had hitherto only allowed himself an occasional critical or derisive attitude to the brilliant predatory man, who for the most part had entangled himself in love meant for others and even that at the wrong time, who had laughed at his weakness with the convulsive laughter of "Prince Hamlet of Shchigrovo" or had wailed the bitter wail of "the superfluous man."

What was revealed in *A Nest of the Gentry*? All the intellectual life of the post-Pushkin age, from its hazy beginnings in the Stankevich circle to the shrill questions asked by Belinsky, and from the shrillness of Belinsky to the concessions (quite significant concessions) which contemporary thinking has made to life and soil. The struggle of Slavophiles and Westernizers, and the struggle of life with theory—Slavophile or western, it is all one—ends with the victory of life over theory in the poetic propositions of the Turgenev type.

Again I repeat: Lavretsky came not to die but to live on his native soil—and his natal life immediately welcomes him into its world, and this world is his own world, from which he cannot, indeed, from which he had no need to separate himself.

What an enormous difference there is between the tender attitudes to actuality in *A Nest of the Gentry*, between this sympathetic presentation of it and the negative style of the literature of the forties, that is, Turgenev's original attitude to actuality! How much falsity there was in the poet's original attitudes to life, to actual existence— it was almost ludicrous! There really was a time when he painted the landowner, for example, as follows:

> From childhood he disliked tight belts;
> *He liked leisure, he liked rest*
> *And sloth:* country-like was the style
> Of his fanciful peaked cap;
> He liked fat pancakes, and so forth.

The literature of those past years had an amazing hostility to leisure and, in the main, to health. If an author (I take all examples from Turgenev himself) happened to be at a provincial ball, it became unbearable for him to see a healthy, artless, girlish physiognomy:

> This is a *purely Russian* beauty:
> Badly dressed, *heavy* (?)
> And *clumsy*, but cheerful,
> Genial, talkative as a chatter-box.[47]

Properly speaking, if our violent enemies of "oblomovism" should wish to be, and could be, consistent, they would have to turn in horror from the present Turgenev and prefer the former Turgenev. It is neither more nor less than what they call Oblomovka and oblomovism that he now treats with artistic sympathy. Lavretsky and his Lisa, and the priceless Marfa Timofeevna, all this is oblomovism; they are all Oblomovs, and what Oblomovs, tightly, physiologically bound not only to the present and future, but to the long past of Oblomovka!

[47] Both verses are from the narrative poem *Pomeshchik* (1845). The italics and the question mark are Grigorev's.

Nikolai Strakhov

TOLSTOY'S *WAR AND PEACE*

Strakhov wrote three reviews of Voina i mir. *The first of these is the longest and most significant; it was written after the appearance in print of what were originally the first four books of the novel, and was published in two installments in the journal* Zaria 1–2 *(1869). The second review, published in* Zaria 3 *(1869), is devoted to book five of the novel; and finally the last review, in no. 1 (1870) of the same journal, concludes the critic's remarks on the basis of the whole novel. The present translation is a selection from the first review: it contains sections 1–4 of the first installment and sections 1, 6–8 of the second. The sections omitted are largely a survey of Russian literary criticism, with particular emphasis on Apollor. Grigorev.*

The present essay has been occasioned by an event of such magnitude that we cannot undertake its discussion without questioning our competence.

In 1868 one of the greatest works of our national literature, *War and Peace*, appeared in print. Its success was extraordinary. No one book had been read with such eagerness for a long time. Moreover, its success was of the highest order. *War and Peace* has been intently read not only by artless devotees of the printed page who had theretofore admired Dumas and Féval, but also by the most discriminating readers—by all those who have just or unjust claims to scholarship and erudition. Even those have read it who otherwise despise Russian literature and read nothing in Russian. Since our reading public grows every year, it came to pass that none of our classical works—from among those that not only have but deserve success—sold so fast and in such a great number of copies as *War and Peace*. Let us add that no outstanding product of our literature has had such wide scope as Count L. N. Tolstoy's latest novel.

119

Let us proceed directly to an analysis of the literary event that has occurred. The success of *War and Peace* is a perfectly simple and clear phenomenon which does not involve any complication or confusion. It cannot be attributed to any side issues or causes other than the work itself. Tolstoy did not try to captivate his readers by involved, mysterious adventures, by descriptions of sordid, horrifying scenes, by depictions of dreadful mental torments, nor, finally, by some bold, new-fangled tendency; in short he did not resort to any of those means by which the reader's thought and imagination are titillated, nor to those pictures of unexplored, strange life which morbidly excite curiosity. Nothing could be simpler than the multiplicity of events recorded in *War and Peace*. All the occurrences of ordinary family life—conversations between brother and sister, between mother and daughter, the separation and reunion of relatives, the chase, yuletide, the mazurka, card-playing, and so forth—are made into gems of artistic creation with as much love as the battle of Borodino. Simple objects occupy as much space in *War and Peace* as, for instance, the immortal descriptions of the Larins' life, of winter and spring, of the journey to Moscow, and so forth, in *Eugene Onegin*.

Along with these, it is true, Tolstoy also depicts great events and persons of immense historical significance. But it could not be claimed that the reader's interest is aroused just by the latter. There may have been readers carried away by representations of historical happenings or even by a feeling of patriotism. But without doubt there are quite a few who do not like to seek history in works of fiction, and quite a few others who are dead set against any underhanded appeal to patriotic feelings; yet even these read *War and Peace* with the liveliest interest. We might remark incidentally that *War and Peace* is in no respect a historical novel: that is, its purpose is by no means to make romantic heroes out of historical personalities and, while relating their adventures, to unite the interest of the novel with that of history.

The matter is clear and simple. Whatever the author's aims and intentions may have been, and however lofty and important the subjects treated, the success of his work depends, not on these intentions and subjects, but on what he accomplished with these aims and subjects in mind: that is, it depends on *the excellence of execution*.

If Tolstoy attained his goals, if he compelled all to fix their eyes on what exercised his mind, it was only because he was in full command of his medium, his art. In this respect the example of *War and Peace* is most instructive. It is not likely that many have discerned the ideas guiding and inspiring the author; but all are equally struck by his art. People who approached this book with preconceived notions—expecting to find either contradiction or confirmation of their own bias—were often at a loss, unable to decide whether to be indignant or delighted, but all equally conceded the exceptional mastery of the enigmatic work. Art had not revealed its persuasive, irresistible effect to such an extent for a long time.

But the art of writing is not given in vain. Let no one think that it can exist apart from profound ideas and feelings, that it can be a flighty affair, devoid of serious meaning. In this connection one must distinguish between genuine art and false, misbegotten appearances. Let us attempt to analyze the art manifest in Tolstoy's book, and we will see how deep its foundations are.

What was it that struck everyone in *War and Peace?* Naturally, its objectivity and graphic quality. It is hard to conceive images more distinct or colors more vivid. One sees everything exactly described and hears the sounds of everything happening. The author does not relate anything in his own person: he introduces his characters directly and makes them speak, feel, and act, each word and each movement being true to life with an amazing degree of precision, that is, conveying the character of the person it belongs to. It is as if one dealt with living people and saw them more clearly than in real life. One can perceive not only the form of each character's expression and feelings, but even his mannerisms, gestures, and gait. The pompous Prince Vasily once, under unusual and trying circumstances, had to walk on tiptoe; the author knows perfectly how every one of his characters walks. "Prince Vasily," he says, "did not know how to walk on tiptoe and jerked his whole body awkwardly at each step."[1]

[1] Book 1, part 1, chap. 19 of the standard Russian text, i.e., of the 1886 edition, consisting of four books. Strakhov of course cites the first edition, but we shall refer to the standard one (from which translations have been made), indicating the book, part, and chapter in parentheses within the text. More recent English translations, such as the Penguin edition translated by Rosemary Edmonds

The author knows all the feelings and thoughts of his characters with just such clarity and distinctness. Once he has brought them on stage, he ceases to interfere with their affairs and does not assist them, letting each behave according to his nature.

It follows from these efforts to maintain objectivity that Tolstoy presents no landscapes or other descriptions of his own. Nature appears as it is perceived by the characters. Tolstoy does not describe the oak standing at the edge of the road, nor the moonlit night during which Natasha and Prince Andrei could not sleep: rather, he describes the impression the oak and the night made on Prince Andrei. In the same way, battles and events of all kinds are related, not according to the author's own conceptions, but according to the impressions of the participating characters. The action at Schön Graben is described mostly through the eyes of Prince Andrei; the battle of Austerlitz, according to Nikolai Rostov's impressions; the Emperor Alexander's arrival in Moscow, through Petia's excitement; and the effect of prayer for deliverance from the invasion, in Natasha's feelings. This way the author never steps forward from behind the characters, and he depicts the events not in the abstract but, as it were, in the flesh and blood of people who constituted the very fabric of the events.

In this sense *War and Peace* is truly a wonder of art. What it captures is not separate features but the whole—that atmosphere of life which varies from person to person and in different strata of society. The author himself speaks of a loving and family atmosphere in the Rostov's house. Let us recall some other depictions of the same kind: the atmosphere surrounding Speransky; that prevailing in the presence of the Rostov's *Uncle;* that of the theater where Natasha finds herself; of the military hospital which Rostov visits; and so forth. Anyone who enters into one of these atmospheres or passes from one to another, inescapably feels their effect and we experience the effect with them.

This way the highest degree of objectivity is achieved. Not only do we have the characters' actions, appearance, movements, and speeches

---

(Baltimore, 1957), retain the standard division into books, parts, and chapters. All quotations will be given in Rosemary Edmonds's translation.

right in front of us, but their inner life also opens up before us in just as distinct, clear contours; nothing shields their souls, their hearts from our gaze. Reading *War and Peace*, we literally *contemplate* the objects chosen by the writer.

What kind of objects are these? Objectivity is a common property of poetry which must always be inherent in it, whatever the object of representation. Even the most ideal feelings, the loftiest life of the spirit must be expressed objectively. Pushkin is perfectly objective when he recollects the image of a certain *majestic matron:*

> The shawl over her head I do recall,
> And her fair eyes, as sparkling as the sky.

He hears her voice:

> She would in sweet and soothing accents
> Speak to the children in her charge.[2]

He represents the sensations of "The Prophet" just as objectively:

> I heard the spheres revolving, chiming,
> The angels in their soaring sweep,
> The monsters moving in the deep,
> The green vine in the valley climbing.[3]

Tolstoy's objectivity obviously leans in a different direction: not toward ideal objects but toward that which we contrast with the ideal —toward the so-called reality, which does not attain the ideal, deviates from it, and yet exists as if to testify to its weakness. Tolstoy is a *realist*, that is, he belongs to a long prevalent and extremely potent trend in our literature. He profoundly sympathizes with the striving of our minds and tastes for realism, and his strength lies just in that he can fully satisfy this striving.

He is, indeed, a magnificent realist. One might assume that he not only portrays his characters with incorruptible veracity, but appears

[2] From the lyric "V nachale zhizni shkolu pomniu ia..." (1830), not translated into English.

[3] Babette Deutsch's translation, *The Poems, Prose, and Plays of Pushkin*, ed. Avrahm Yarmolinsky (New York: The Modern Library, 1936), p. 62.

to be deliberately casting them down from the ideal height to which we, obedient to the perennial inclination of our human nature, so readily and easily raise people and events. Tolstoy unmasks his characters' infirmities ruthlessly, cruelly; he conceals nothing; nothing will daunt him; so much so that he even inspires fear and induces sadness over the imperfection of man. Many a sensitive soul cannot, for instance, swallow the idea of Natasha's infatuation with Kuragin. Without this incident, what a wonderful character would have emerged, drawn still with an amazing trueness to life! But the poet of reality is merciless.

Looking at *War and Peace* from this point of view, one could take the book for the most frenzied *indictment* of Alexander's epoch: for an uncompromising exposure of all the ills from which it suffered. Exposed are the selfishness, frivolity, falsity, depravity, and stupidity of the high society of the time; so is the senseless, indolent, gluttonous life of the Moscow gentry and of wealthy landowners such as the Rostovs. Add to this the utter disorder everywhere, especially in the army, during the war. At every step people are shown whose guiding principle is personal gain in the midst of bloodshed and strife, people who sacrifice the common good for selfish interest. The terrible calamities that arise from the leaders' disagreements and petty vanities and from the lack of a firm hand in the government are revealed; a throng of cowards, scoundrels, thieves, profligates, and cardsharps is assembled on stage; even the common people's crudeness and savagery is exhibited (the husband beating his wife in Smolensk, the mutiny in Bogucharovo).

If someone should take it into his head to write an essay on *War and Peace* similar to Dobroliubov's article "The Realm of Darkness,"[4] he would find in Tolstoy's novel ample material for his theme. N. Ogarev—one of the writers belonging to the foreign section of Russian letters—once reduced the whole of our contemporary literature to the formula of unmasking: he said, namely, that Turgenev exposed the landowners, Ostrovsky the merchants, and Nekrasov the

---

[4] N. A. Dobroliubov's article, written on the plays of A. N. Ostrovsky, was published in *Sovremennik* 7 and 9 (1859) and constituted one of the most important pronouncements on literature by the group of radical critics—a frequent target of Strakhov's remarks.

civil servants.[5] If we were to follow such a viewpoint, we would rejoice over the appearance of a new exposer and say: Tolstoy is the exposer of the military, of our heroic deeds, and of the glory of our history.

It is highly significant, however, that this viewpoint has caused only feeble reverberations in our critical literature on Tolstoy—a clear proof that even the most biased eyes could not help but see its unfairness. But such a viewpoint is possible, of which we have precious historical evidence. A participant in the War of 1812 and a veteran of our belles-lettres, A. S. Norov, was carried away by his partiality—a partiality, incidentally, which evokes sincere and profound respect—and mistook Tolstoy for an exposer. Here are Norov's own words:

Reading the first parts of the novel [*War and Peace*], the reader is struck initially by the dismal impression the highest social circle of the capital makes—a circle which is represented as frivolous and almost immoral, yet exercises influence over the government; then he is startled by a lack of a higher sense in the military operations and by an almost total absence of valor in combat, although our army has always prided itself on the latter.

The year 1812, which resounded with glory in military as well as in civilian life, is held up before our eyes like a soap bubble. It is claimed that a whole phalanx of our generals, whose fame in battle is virtually riveted to the pages of military chronicles and whose good names have passed on to new generations in the service by word of mouth, were actually shiftless, blind instruments of fate, only at times operating successfully; and even when success is acknowledged, it is spoken of slightingly, often with irony. Was that indeed what our society was like? Is that a correct representation of our army?

As an eye-witness of the great national events, I could not read this novel, claiming to be historical, without a sense of offended patriotic feelings.[6]

---

[5] Strakhov is referring to N. P. Ogarev's preface to the anthology *Russkaia potaennaia literatura XIX veka* (London, 1861), which Ogarev concluded with general characterizations of Gogol, Nekrasov, Turgenev, and Ostrovsky.

[6] A. S. Norov, *War and Peace (1805–1812) from an Historical Point of View and According to the Reminiscences of a Contemporary. Occasioned by Count L. N. Tolstoy's "War and Peace"* (St. Petersburg, 1868), pp. 1–2. (Author's note.)

As we have said, this aspect of Tolstoy's novel, which affected A. S. Norov so sensitively, has made no noteworthy impression on the majority of readers. And why not? Because it was vastly overshadowed by other aspects of the novel; because other motifs, of a more poetic quality, stood out more noticeably. It is obvious that Tolstoy showed the unseemly features of objects not out of a desire to exhibit them, but because he wanted to represent objects in their totality, with all their features, unseemly ones included. His purpose was *truth* in representation—a faithful adherence to reality—and it was this truthfulness that engaged the reader's attention. Patriotism, the glory of Russia, moral principles—all was forgotten, all receded to the background in face of this realism which stepped forward in full armor. The reader eagerly watches these pictures of life evolve, as though the artist, preaching nothing and exposing no one, carried him, wizardlike, from one place to another and let him see what was happening there.

Everything is vivid, graphic, and at the same time real, true to life, like a daguerreotype or a photograph: this is where Tolstoy's strength lies. One feels that the author did not want to exaggerate either the dark or the bright side of objects; did not wish to lay on a special coloring or to achieve a lighting effect; he strove with all his heart and soul to represent matters in their real, actual shape and color—hence the irresistible charm which captivates even the most resistant readers. Yes, we Russian readers have long been resistant to works of art, have long been powerfully armed against what is called poetry, elevated feelings, and ideas; it is as though we had lost the ability to be carried away by idealism in art and were stubbornly resisting the least temptation in that direction. Either we do not believe in ideals or—which is much more likely since only an individual, not a whole nation, can lose its faith in ideals—we place them so high that we cannot trust the power of art to express them, we cannot see the possibility of their material incarnation. Such a state of affairs leaves only one route open to art, realism. For what can you do, how can you arm yourself against truth, against a representation of life as it is?

But there are different realisms. Art, by its nature, never renounces the ideal; it always strives for it, and the more clearly perceptible this striving in works of realism, the loftier they are, the closer they come to true artistic creation. Many people interpret realism in a crude fashion. They imagine that for the best effect in art they simply have to turn their minds into photographic cameras and take pictures of anything that happens by. Our literature abounds in such pictures; and the simplehearted reader, who fancied he had genuine artists before him, is quite astonished afterwards when he sees that these writers have come to nothing. In fact, their failure is understandable. These authors adhered to reality, not because they could see it clearly in the light of their ideals, but because they could see no further than the object they copied and could not rise above the level of the slice of life they represented.

Tolstoy is neither an exposer of social ills nor a mere photographer in his realism. What makes his novel invaluable, what constitutes its strength and explains its success is that, while he fully satisfied all the requirements of contemporary art, he fulfilled them in their purest form and deepest sense. The essence of Russian realism in art had never before been manifested with such clarity and force; with *War and Peace* it has reached a new stage, has entered a new period in its development.

Let us take one further step in characterizing this novel, and we shall be close to our goal.

What is the most singular, strikingly prominent feature of Tolstoy's talent? His unusually subtle and correct depiction of psychological processes. One could call him an essentially *psychological realist*. He has long been renowned on the basis of his previous works as an astounding master in the analysis of all kinds of psychological changes and conditions. Applied with a certain partiality, this analysis used to fall into pedantry, becoming unduly strained. In the new work all extremes fell away while all his former precision and perspicacity remained; the artist's prowess found its limits and settled into its natural course. All his attention is fixed now on the human psyche. His descriptions of the surroundings, of costumes, in short of all the extraneous attributes of life, are scarce, brief, and incomplete; but for all that he never omits the impression and effect these extraneous attributes make on people's minds. The place of honor is occupied by the characters' inner life, the extraneous serving only as motive or incomplete expression. The slightest nuances of psychic life and its profoundest traumata are depicted with equal distinctness and veracity. The air of indolent boredom in the Rostovs' house in Otradnoe and the feelings of the whole Russian army in the heat of battle at Borodino; the youthful stirrings of Natasha's emotions and the agony of the elder Bolkonsky losing consciousness, close to a stroke of apoplexy: all this is equally clear, vivid, and precise in Tolstoy's narration.

Here is, then, the focal point of the author's interest and, consequently, of the reader's interest. However great and important events are taking place—whether we see the Kremlin, chock-full of people at the time of the emperor's arrival, or the meeting of the two emperors, or a horrendous battle with cannons thundering and thousands dying—nothing diverts the poet, and with him the reader, from an intent scrutiny of the inner world of individuals. It is as though the writer were not at all occupied with the event, but fixed his attention exclusively on how the human psyche reacted to it, how it felt about it, and what it contributed to it.

Ask yourselves now: what is it that the poet seeks? What pertinacious curiosity compels him to research the slightest sensations of all these people, from Napoleon and Kutuzov to those little girls whom Prince Andrei surprised in his ravaged garden?

There is only one answer: the writer is looking for traces of beauty in the human soul; he is looking in each character portrayed for that divine spark which carries the individual's human dignity: in short, he is seeking to discover and define with full precision how and to what extent man's ideal strivings are fulfilled in real life.

It is very difficult to convey, even in no more than its most essential outlines, the idea of a profound work of art, for it is incarnated in the work so completely and so multifariously that an abstract summary of it will always be inaccurate, insufficient, never, as the expression goes, exhausting the subject.

One can formulate the idea of *War and Peace* in different ways.

It could be said, for instance, that the guiding notion of the work is the *idea of the heroic life*. The author himself hints at this when, in the midst of his description of the battle of Borodino, he makes the following remark: "The ancients have passed down to us examples of epic poems in which the *heroes* furnish the whole *interest of the story*, and to this day we are unable to accustom our minds to the idea that history of that kind is meaningless for our epoch" (3. 2. 19).

With these words the artist announces to us that he intends to depict the kind of life we usually call heroic; only he wants to depict it in its real meaning and not in those inaccurate images which we have inherited from the ancients. He wants us *to grow out of the habit* of these false conceptions and, in order to achieve this, he provides us with genuine conceptions. In place of the ideal, we must receive the real.

Where do we look for heroic life? Naturally, in history. We are accustomed to think that the people on whom history depends—those who create history—are heroes. Therefore the artist's attention was fixed on the War of 1812, and on the wars preceding it, as on an essentially heroic epoch. If Napoleon, Kutuzov, and Bagration are not heroes, who is a hero? Tolstoy chose enormous historical events, a horrific struggle, and a straining of national resources in order to capture the highest manifestations of what we call heroism.

But in our human epoch, as Tolstoy writes, the heroes do not of themselves exhaust the interest of history. Whatever our concept of the heroic life, we must define its relationship to ordinary life: this is, indeed, the most important part of the matter. What is an ordinary man in comparison with a hero? What is an individual in relation to history? In its more general form, this is the same question which our artistic realism has so long been attempting to answer, that is: what is ordinary, everyday life in relation to ideal, sublime life?

Tolstoy strives to answer the question as fully as possible. For instance, he presents Bagration and Kutuzov in their incomparable, overwhelming greatness. They seem to have the ability to rise above everything human. This is especially clear in the portrayal of Kutuzov —a man who is weak from old age, absent-minded, lazy, and morally reprehensible, who has retained, in the author's expression, *all the habits of passion although he no longer has the passions themselves.* When it comes to action, everything private disappears from the vision of Bagration and Kutuzov; even the terms *courage, restraint, composure* are not applicable to them, for they do not summon up courage, do not need to strain, restrain, or compose themselves. They perform their tasks naturally and simply, as if they were spirits capable of pure contemplation and able unerringly to follow the dictates of the purest feelings of duty and honor. They look fate straight in the eye; the very thought of fear is impossible for them, and they could not under any circumstances hesitate in action, because they are doing *all they can* within the limits of the course of events and of their own human frailty.

But in addition to these elevated spheres of the utmost limits of valor, the artist has also presented us with a world in which the dictates of duty struggle with the turbulence of human passions. He shows us *all the varieties of both courage and cowardice*. What ground is covered from the original cowardice of the cadet Rostov to the brilliant bravery of Denisov, to the firm manliness of Prince Andrei, and to the unconscious heroism of Captain Tushin! The artist describes all the sensations and aspects of battle from the panic flight at Austerlitz to the invincible steadfastness and the bright glow of *a secret inner fire* at Borodino. The same people appear to us, now *blackguards*, as Kutuzov calls the fleeing soldiers, now fearless, self-sacrificing warriors. In effect, they are all simple people, and the writer shows us with amazing mastery how the spark of valor—to be found in every man—glows, dies out, or flares up with varying intensity.

Most important, however, is the demonstration of what all these souls signify in the course of history, what they contribute to great events, to what extent they participate in the heroic life. It is demonstrated that tsars and military leaders are great only because they constitute focal centers for the heroism that lives in simple, undistinguished people. An understanding of this heroism, an empathy with it, and a faith in it are what make the Bagrations and Kutuzovs great. A lack of such understanding, a neglect or even contempt for this heroism lead to the ill luck and small stature of such leaders as Barclay de Tolly and Speransky.

The war, affairs of state, great cataclysms make up the stage of history, which is dominated by heroism. Having shown with blameless veracity how people behave, what they feel and do on this stage, the artist also wants, for the sake of completeness, to portray the same people in their private lives, where they appear simply as people. He writes:

Meanwhile life—actual everyday life with its essential concerns of health and sickness, work and recreation, and its intellectual preoccupations with philosophy, science, poetry, music, love, friendship, hatred, passion—ran its regular course, independent and heedless of political alliance or enmity with Napoleon Bonaparte and of all potential reforms. (2. 3. 1)

These words are followed by the description of how Prince Andrei travels to Otradnoe and meets Natasha for the first time.

Prince Andrei and his father are real heroes in the sphere of national concerns. When Prince Andrei leaves Brünn to join the army which is in danger, the jestful Bilibin twice gives him the title of a hero, and by no means in jest (1. 2. 12). Bilibin is absolutely right. Review Prince Andrei's actions and thoughts during the war: you will find him without blemish. Remember his conduct during the engagement at Schön Graben: nobody understands Bagration better than he, and he is the only one who sees and values Captain Tushin's heroic deeds. But Bagration does not know Prince Andrei very well; Kutuzov knows him much better, and it is he to whom Kutuzov turns during the battle at Austerlitz when it is necessary to stop the fleeing men and lead them forward. Remember, finally, Borodino, where Prince Andrei and his regiment stand under fire for long hours (he did not wish to stay at headquarters, yet did not get to the front lines): all human sensitivities are alive in his soul, but he does not lose his complete self-control for a second, and he shouts at the adjutant who threw himself on the ground: "For shame, officer!" at the very moment when the grenade explodes and he is about to receive a severe wound. The path such people travel is indeed the *path of glory*, as Kutuzov says. They can without hesitation do everything demanded by the strictest code of courage and self-sacrifice.

The old Bolkonsky is no different. Think of the Spartan admonishment he gives his son who is going off to war and whom he loves with warm fatherly tenderness: "Remember one thing, Prince Andrei: if you get killed, it will be a grief to me in my old age...

But if I were to hear that you had not behaved like the son of Nikolai Bolkonsky, I should be—ashamed!"

His son has every right to answer: "You need not have said that to me, father" (1. 1. 25).

Further, for this old man all Russia's concerns become his own personal concerns and constitute the main part of his life. He follows events eagerly from Bald Hills. His continual mockery of Napoleon and of our military operations is obviously generated by a sense of hurt national pride; he cannot believe that his powerful country has suddenly lost its strength; he would like to attribute this to some accident rather than to the might of the enemy. When the invasion has begun and Napoleon has reached Vitebsk, the weak old man is completely at a loss: at first he cannot even understand what he reads in his son's letter; he refuses to admit the mental image which he cannot bear and which must destroy his life. But at last he has to accept it, has to believe it—and then the old man dies. The mental image of the general calamity kills him more surely than a bullet would.

Yes, these people are real heroes; such people are the mainstays of nations and states. But why, the reader will probably ask, does their heroism appear as though shorn of all its striking features? Why do these heroes look like ordinary people? This is because the artist has depicted them *in full*, not only showing how they act in relation to duty, honor, and national pride, but also showing us their private, personal lives. He describes the old Bolkonsky's home life, his unhealthy relationship with his daughter, and all the failings of a desiccated old man who unwittingly becomes the tormentor of those around him. In Prince Andrei, Tolstoy exposes outbursts of terrible vanity and pride, cold yet jealous attitudes to his wife, and generally a difficult character, in its intransigence resembling that of his father. "I am afraid of him," Natasha says of Prince Andrei just before he proposes to her.

Outsiders are struck by old Bolkonsky's greatness. When he comes to Moscow and becomes a leader of the local opposition, he inspires respect in everyone. "The old-fashioned house with its huge pier-glasses, pre-Revolution furniture, powdered footmen, and the stern shrewd old man (himself a relic of a past century) with his gentle daughter and the pretty Frenchwoman, both so reverently devoted to him, presented a majestic and agreeable spectacle" (2. 5. 2). In the same way, Prince Andrei inspires involuntary respect in everyone and plays something of a majestic role in high society. Kutuzov and Speransky cherish him, the soldiers idolize him.

All this, however, makes a full impact only on outsiders, not on us. For the artist has led us into the innermost life of these people, has initiated us into all their thoughts and anxieties. Their human weaknesses—those moments when they are on the same level as any ordinary mortal, those situations and mental states in which all feel the same way, in which all are equally people—are revealed to us clearly and fully. This is the reason why the heroic features seem to be submerged in the mass of simply human features.

This refers to all the characters in *War and Peace* without exception. Everywhere the same kind of story crops up as that of the innkeeper Ferapontov, who mercilessly beats his wife because she suggested leaving, who bargains with the coachmen in a niggardly fashion just when danger is approaching, yet who later, realizing the state of affairs, shouts "It's decided, Russia!" and sets fire to his own house. It is just in this way that all sides of each character's inner life are depicted—from bestial impulses to that spark of heroism which is often hidden even in the pettiest and most perverted souls.

It would be a mistake, however, to think that the author wishes by this to belittle heroic persons and actions or to debunk their false greatness. On the contrary, his purpose is to show them in their true colors, thereby teaching us to see heroism where we were unable to notice it before. Human weaknesses must not overshadow human virtues in our eyes. In other words, the poet teaches his readers to penetrate to that poetry which is hidden in reality, is deeply buried beneath the triviality, the pettiness, and the dirty and senseless vanity of everyday life, and is impenetrable and inaccessible to our indifference, sleepy laziness, and egotistically preoccupied state of mind. The poet illuminates *all the mire encompassing human life* in order that we may see a spark of the divine flame in its darkest corners, that we may understand those people in whom the flame burns brightly though invisibly to myopic eyes, and that we may sympathize with causes which seemed incomprehensible to our small-mindedness and self-love. He is not a Gogol, illuminating the *banality of the banal man* with the bright light of his ideal; he is an artist who can discern the human dignity of man through the triviality visible to the world. It was with unprecedented daring that he undertook to depict the most heroic period of our history—the period which in fact originated the conscious life of modern Russia. Who will not admit that he has emerged a victor from the struggle with his subject?

Before our eyes arises a picture of that Russia which withstood Napoleon's invasion and dealt a fatal blow to his power. The picture is drawn, not only without embellishments, but even with the harsh colors of all defects, all those ugly and pitiful imperfections which ailed the society of that time in intellectual, moral, and administrative respects. And yet, the strength that saved Russia is plainly shown.

The idea underlying Tolstoy's much-debated *military theory* is that the individual soldier is not a mere material instrument, but a man whose strength lies in his *spirit*, and that in the long run the whole undertaking depends on the soldiers' morale, which can decline to the point of panic fear or rise to the level of heroism. Military leaders are effective when they do not limit themselves to commanding troop movements and operations, but also command the soldiers' morale. In order to achieve this, military leaders must rise in morale *above their whole army*, above chance accidents and misfortunes—in short, they must have sufficient strength to carry on their shoulders the destiny of the army and, if necessary, the destiny of the state. The aged Kutuzov is such a leader at the time of the battle of Borodino. His faith in the might of the Russian army and of the Russian people is obviously loftier and firmer than the faith of each individual soldier; it is as if he concentrated all their fervor in himself. The fate of the battle is in effect decided by his words, spoken to Wolzogen: "You know nothing about it . . . The enemy is defeated and tomorrow we shall drive him from the sacred soil of Russia" (3. 2. 35). It is evident that at this moment Kutuzov stands immeasurably higher than all the Wolzogens and Barclays: he stands on the level of Russia.

Generally, the description of the battle of Borodino is worthy of its subject, which is no small praise. Tolstoy has wrested praise for it even from such partial judges as A. S. Norov. "Count Tolstoy," writes Norov, "has depicted the general phases of the battle of Borodino *beautifully and correctly* in Chapters 33–35."[7] Let us remark in parentheses that if the battle of Borodino is described well, then it is hard not to believe that the author is capable of describing any kind of military event well.

The power of the description of this battle issues from the whole preceding narrative; it is a culminating point, the comprehension of which has been prepared by all that preceded it. By the time we come to this battle, we already know all the varieties of courage and cowardice; we know about the conduct, or potential conduct, of all members of the army from the general to the lowest-ranking soldier. This is why the author is so concise and terse in narrating the battle. There is not just one Captain Tushin, described in detail in the Schön Graben engagement, at work here: there are hundreds like him. A few scenes—on the redoubt where Bezukhov is, in Prince Andrei's regiment, at the dressing station—make us feel the exertion of each soldier's spiritual strength and make us understand that united and unshakable spirit which inspires the whole of this horrendous mass of people. Kutuzov appears as if he were tied with invisible threads to the heart of each soldier. Hardly ever has there been another such battle, and hardly ever has anything like it been narrated in any other language.

Thus, the heroic life is presented in its loftiest manifestations and in its real forms. The question which captured the artist's attention— how war is conducted, how history is made—has been answered with mastery and perspicacity above all praise. In this connection we cannot omit mentioning the author's own explanations with regard to his understanding of history.[8] With a naïveté one can justly call an attribute of genius, he almost directly claims that historians, by the very nature of their methods of inquiry, can depict events only in a false and distorted form, and that the real meaning, the real truth of the matter is accessible only to the artist. What can we say to this? We cannot help saying that Tolstoy has considerable rights to such a bold claim with regard to history, for all the historical descriptions of

[7] Ibid., p. 36. (Author's note.)

[8] See Count L. N. Tolstoy, "A Few Words of Explanation," *Russian Archives* 3 (1868). (Author's note.)

1812 do indeed appear *false* in comparison with the vivid picture of *War and Peace*. There is no doubt that with this work our literature stands incomparably higher than our historical scholarship and consequently has a right to lecture it on the understanding of events. In just this way did Pushkin once wish to expose, in his "History of the Village of Goriukhino," the false features, false tone, and false spirit of the first volumes of Karamzin's *History of the Russian State*.

Heroic life, however, does not constitute the whole theme Tolstoy has set himself. His subject is evidently much wider. The main principle guiding him in depicting historical phenomena is an effort to unveil their *human* foundations, to show heroes as *people*. When Prince Andrei gets acquainted with Speransky, the author remarks: "Had Speransky sprung from the same class in society to which Prince Andrei belonged, had he possessed the same breeding and moral traditions, Bolkonsky would soon have detected the weak and prosaically human side of his character; but as it was, Speransky's strange and logical turn of mind inspired him with respect the more because he did not altogether understand it" (2. 3. 6). What is not given to Bolkonsky in this case is masterfully achieved by the artist with regard to all his characters: he reveals all their human sides to us. Thus his narrative acquires a human rather than heroic character; it is not a history of heroic deeds and great events, but a history of the people who took part in them. The author's wider subject, therefore, is simply *man*; it is evident that people interest him quite independently of their social positions and of the great or small events that befall them.

Let us examine how Tolstoy portrays people.

The human soul is portrayed in *War and Peace* with a realism unprecedented in our literature. What we see before our eyes is not abstract life, but fully defined beings with all the limitations of space, time, and circumstance. We see, for instance, how Tolstoy's characters *grow*. The Natasha who runs into the drawing room in book one and the Natasha who goes to church at the end of book two are really the same person at two different ages—at the ages of childhood and girlhood—rather than two different ages merely attributed to the same person (as often happens in the works of other writers). The author also shows us the intermediate stages of her development. Nikolai Rostov grows up before our eyes in the same way, Pierre Bezukhov turns from a young man into a Moscow nobleman, the old Bolkonsky grows senile, and so forth.

The psychic features of Tolstoy's characters are so clear and bear such a marked stamp of individuality that we can trace *family traits* in persons related by birth. The old Bolkonsky and Prince Andrei obviously have the same nature, only one is old, the other young. The Rostov family, despite the diversity of its members, displays common traits, amazingly captured by the author, the nuances of which we can only sense but not formulate. For some reason we can feel, for instance, that even Vera is a genuine Rostov, although Natasha's soul has obviously different foundations.

One need not go into detail about the foreigners. Just remember the Germans—General Mack, General Pfuel, Adolf Berg—or the Frenchwoman Mlle Bourienne, or Napoleon himself. The psychic peculiarities of nationalities are captured and followed up to the finest details. As regards the Russian characters, it is not only clear that each of them is fully Russian, but we can even discern the classes they belong to and the social positions they occupy. Speransky, who only appears in two brief episodes, proves to be a seminarist from head to toe at the same time as the individual peculiarities of his psyche are expressed with the greatest clarity and without the slightest exaggeration.

Everything that goes on within these well-defined souls—every feeling, passion, movement—is just as distinct and is depicted with the same realism. There is nothing more commonplace than the abstract portrayal of feelings and passions. The hero is usually given *one* state of mind—love, vanity, or a thirst for revenge—and the matter is presented as if this one disposition *constantly* existed in his soul. The manifestations of a certain passion, taken separately, are described and then attributed to a character. Not so in Tolstoy's works.

In Tolstoy's characters each impression and feeling is complicated by the echo it produces in the different dispositions and aspirations of the soul. If we were to compare the soul to a musical instrument that has many strings, we could say that the artist, describing a certain stimulus received by the soul, never limits himself to the dominant sound of the string, but records all the sounds, including even the weakest, hardly audible ones. Remember, for instance, the portrayal of Natasha—this creature whose psychic life is so tense and full. In her soul several voices—vanity, love for her fiancé, gaiety, thirst for life, attachment to family, and so forth—are heard at one and the same time. Remember Prince Andrei as he stands over the smoking grenade:

> "Can this be death?" Prince Andrei wondered, casting a fleeting glance of quite unwonted envy at the grass, the wormwood and the thread of smoke that curled upward from the whistling black ball. "I can't die, I don't want to die. I love life—I love this grass, this earth, this air..." *These were the thoughts in his mind, and at the same time he remembered that people were looking at him.* (3. 2. 36)

Whatever feeling takes hold of a man, Tolstoy describes it with all its variations and fluctuations, not as a constant quantity but as the potential of a certain feeling, as a spark ever smoldering, ever ready to flare up with a bright flame, but sometimes smothered by other feelings. Remember, for instance, the hatred Prince Andrei feels toward Kuragin, or the contradictions and oscillations, reaching eccentric proportions, in the feelings of Princess Mary, who is religious, has an amorous disposition, loves her father boundlessly, and so forth.

What is the author's purpose in doing this? What idea guides him? Depicting the human psyche in its dependence and changeability, in its subjection both to its own peculiarities and to the temporary circumstances enveloping it, he seems to be disparaging psychic life, seems to be depriving it of its unity, of its constant, essential meaning. The inconstancy, triviality, and vanity of human feelings and aspirations seems to be his main theme.

But we shall be wrong once more if we dwell just on the artist's realistic tendencies, so powerfully demonstrated, and forget about the sources from which these tendencies spring. A realism in the representation of the human soul is necessary so that a perhaps weak but still real incarnation of the ideal may rise before us all the more brightly, all the more convincingly and indubitably. In these souls which are agitated and overwhelmed by their own desires as well as by extraneous events, and which bear such indelible marks of individual peculiarities, the author can still find every sign and every trace of genuine spiritual beauty—of genuine human dignity. If we wish to find a new, broader formulation for the problem of Tolstoy's work, we can perhaps say:

What does human dignity consist of? How can we understand the lives of people, from the most powerful and brilliant to the weakest and least significant, in such a fashion that the most essential feature —the human soul in each—would not be missed?

The author himself provides a hint at this formulation. Discussing how small Napoleon's contribution was to the battle of Borodino and how much the spirit of each soldier doubtless contributed, he remarks: "*Human dignity . . . tells me* that each one of us is, if not more, at least *not less a man than the great Napoleon*" (3. 2. 28).

The artist's general purpose is to show what it is that makes each man no smaller than any other, in what sense the simple soldier is equal to Napoleon and the hidebound, obtuse mind to the greatest intellect—in short, what it is we must *respect* in man, what *value* we must attach to him. With this purpose in mind he exhibits not only great people and great events, but also the adventures of the cadet Rostov, the *salons* of high society, the life styles of *Uncle* and Napoleon as well as of the innkeeper Ferapontov. It is for this purpose that he tells us about the family affairs of simple, weak people as well as about the strong passions of brilliant, powerful characters; this is why he depicts transports of nobility and magnanimity as well as examples of the basest human failings.

Human dignity is hidden from us either by the various shortcomings of people or by the circumstance that we place too high a value on other qualities and measure people only by their intellect, power, beauty, and so forth. The poet teaches us to penetrate deeper than this surface. What could be more simple and ordinary, more humble, so to speak, than the figures of Nikolai Rostov and Princess Mary? They do not shine with any special quality, have no special skills, nothing raises them above the lowest level of the most commonplace people; and yet these simple creatures, going along their simple path of life without a struggle, are obviously wonderful beings. The irresistible sympathy with which the artist manages to surround these two characters—apparently so insignificant yet no one's inferior in spiritual beauty—is one of the masterly features of *War and Peace*. Nikolai Rostov is clearly a man of limited intellectual abilities, but, as the author remarks in one place, "He possessed the common sense of the mediocre man which showed him what he ought to do" (2. 4. 1).

Indeed, Nikolai makes a good many stupid mistakes because he has little comprehension of people and circumstances, but he always understands *what he ought to do*. This invaluable wisdom preserves the purity of his simple and mettlesome nature under all circumstances.

Need we speak of Princess Mary? Despite all her weaknesses, her image attains an almost angelic purity and gentleness; it seems at times as if a saintly halo encircled her.

At this point we are forced to stop at a frightening depiction: the relationship between old Bolkonsky and his daughter. If Nikolai Rostov and Princess Mary are manifestly engaging characters, then, it seems, we cannot possibly forgive the old man for all the suffering he causes his daughter. It seems that none of the characters delineated by the artist deserves a stricter censure. Yet, what final conclusion do we come to? The author has described with amazing mastery one of the most frightening human weaknesses—a weakness which neither reason nor will power can overcome and which evokes, above all, a sincere pity. In essence the old man loves his daughter with a boundless love—he literally *could not live without her*—but this love of his has been perverted into a desire to cause pain both to himself and to the loved one. It is as if he were incessantly tugging at the unbreakable cord which bound him to his daughter and were finding morbid pleasure in *such* a sensation of the bond between them. All the nuances of these strange sensations are captured by Tolstoy with inimitable veracity, and the final scene when the old man, felled by sickness and close to death, finally expresses the whole tenderness of his feelings toward his daughter produces a staggering effect.

To what degree can even the strongest and purest feelings be perverted! How much suffering can people cause themselves by their own fault! It is impossible to imagine a picture that shows more clearly how little control people sometimes have over themselves. The majestic old Bolkonsky's relations with his daughter and son, based on a jealous and distorted feeling of love, provide an example of the evil that is often hidden in family nests and prove to us that even the holiest and most natural feelings can acquire an insane and wild character.

It is these feelings, however, that are at the root of the matter, and their perversions must not hide their pure sources from us. Their true, deep essence often surfaces in moments of powerful shocks: when he is dying, his love for his daughter takes hold of Bolkonsky's whole being.

Tolstoy is a great master at discovering what is hidden under the play of passions, under the various forms of self-love, egotism, and animal impulses. The infatuations and exploits of such people as Pierre Bezukhov and Natasha Rostova are very pitiful, very senseless and disgraceful, but the reader can see that underneath it all these characters have *hearts of gold*, and he does not doubt for a moment that if it came to self-sacrifice—if wholehearted devotion to the good and beautiful were called for—a clear response, a full readiness would be found in these hearts. The spiritual beauty of these two characters is striking. Pierre is a grown-up child with a huge body and terrible sensuality; like an impractical and unwise child, he combines in himself a childish purity and gentleness of spirit with a naïve—and for that very reason lofty—mind and a character to which ignoble acts are not only alien, but simply incomprehensible. This man, like a child, fears nothing and has nothing evil on his conscience. Natasha is a girl with such overflowing psychic energy that (in Bezuhkov's words) *she cannot deign to be clever*, that is, she has neither time nor inclination to translate this psychic energy into abstract forms of thought. This infinite exuberance of life (which, as the author says, leads her into *a state of intoxication* at times) involves her in a terrible mistake, in an insane passion for Kuragin, for which she later atones by acute suffering. Both Pierre and Natasha are people who, by their very nature, must err and meet with disappointments in life. As if to set them off by contrast, the author also introduces a happy couple—Vera Rostova and Adolf Berg—who avoid all errors and disappointments and settle into life quite comfortably. One marvels at the restraint of the author who exposes all the meanness and pettiness of these souls, yet never yields to the temptation to ridicule them or to be indignant over them. Here is true realism, genuine veracity! We see the same veracity in the portrayal of the two Kuragins—Helen and Anatole. These heartless creatures are exposed without mercy, yet without the slightest desire to castigate them.

What is the effect of this even, clear, daytime light with which the author illuminates his picture? Neither traditional villains, nor traditional heroes are seen; the human soul appears in a great variety of types; it appears weak and subject to passions and circumstances; but essentially, in the last analysis, it is guided by pure and good aspirations. In the midst of all this diversity of characters and events we feel the presence of some firm and unshakable principles, on which life rests. Familial, social, and marital obligations are clear to all. The concepts of good and evil are distinct and firm. The author depicts the false life of the highest social circles and of the staff surrounding high-ranking persons with great verisimilitude, but he contrasts it with two sound and genuinely vital spheres of existence—with family life and with true military life, that is, with life in the active army. The Bolkonsky and Rostov families represent a life guided by clear, indubitable principles, an adherence to which is regarded by members of these families as a matter of duty and honor, virtue and comfort. In the same way, life in the army (which Tolstoy in one place compares to paradise) offers fully defined concepts of duty and merit; so much so that the simplehearted Nikolai Rostov once even prefers to stay with his regiment rather than go home where he would not be quite sure how to conduct himself.

All in all, the Russia of 1812 is presented to us in its broad, clear outlines as a mass of people who know what their human dignity demands of them—what they have to accomplish for themselves, for other people, and for their fatherland. Tolstoy's narrative amounts to a description of the many varieties of the struggle between this sense of duty and the passions and accidents of life, and also of the struggle in which the sturdiest and most populous class of Russia engages against the false and inconstant upper class. Eighteen twelve was a time when the lower strata of society had the upper hand and, thanks to their firmness, withstood the onslaught of Napoleon. This is beautifully seen, for instance, in the actions and thoughts of Prince

Andrei, who leaves the headquarters for the regiment and who, talking with Pierre on the eve of the battle of Borodino, keeps mentioning his father killed by the news of the invasion. Sentiments similar to those of Prince Andrei saved Russia at that time. "The French have destroyed my home," he says, "and are on their way to destroy Moscow; they have outraged and are outraging me every moment. They are my enemies. In my opinion they are all criminals . . ." (3. 2. 25).

Because of these and similar words Pierre, as the author says, "understood the whole meaning and significance both of this war and of the impending battle."

On the Russian side the war was defensive and consequently had a holy, popular character, while on the French side it was offensive, that is, coercive and unjust. At Borodino all other relations and considerations were leveled off and disappeared; two nations faced each other, one attacking, the other defending itself. Here the power of those two *ideas* which moved the two nations on this occasion and placed them in a mutual relationship emerged with the greatest clarity. The French represented the cosmopolitan idea capable of resorting to violence and genocide in the name of general principles; the Russians represented the national idea, fondly defending the spirit and structure of an original, organically developed civilization. The question of cosmopolitanism versus nationality was raised on the field of Borodino, and the Russians decided it, here for the first time, in favor of nationality.

No wonder, therefore, that Napoleon did not understand, and never could understand, what happened on the battlefield of Borodino; no wonder that he was seized by bewilderment and fright at the sight of the unexpected and mysterious force which rose up against him. But since the matter was really very simple and clear, it is understandable that Tolstoy allows himself the following comment on Napoleon:

And not for that day and hour alone were the mind and conscience of this man darkened, on whom the burden of all that was happening weighed more heavily than on all the others who took part in it. Never to the end of his life had he the least comprehension of goodness, beauty or truth, or of the significance of his actions, which were too contrary to goodness and truth, too remote from everything human for him ever to be able to grasp their import. He could not disavow his deeds, lauded as they were by half the world, and so he was obliged to repudiate truth and beauty and all humanity. (3. 2. 38)

This is one of the final conclusions: in Napoleon, in this hero of heroes, Tolstoy sees a man who has completely lost his genuine human dignity, a man overtaken by a darkening of mind and conscience. The truth of Tolstoy's conclusion is self-evident. As the good name of Barclay de Tolly is forever injured by his failure to understand the state of the battle at Borodino, and as Kutuzov is elevated above all praise by his full comprehension of what was happening during this battle, so is Napoleon condemned by posterity for his lack of recognition of that holy and simple thing which we accomplished at Borodino and which was understood by each of our soldiers. Napoleon failed to grasp that the truth was on our side in this affair whose meaning cried out loudly. Europe wanted to smother Russia, and in its arrogance it imagined that it was acting brilliantly and justly.

It appears that in the character of Napoleon the artist wished to present an entirely insensitive human soul, wanted to demonstrate that the heroic life may contradict genuine human dignity, and that goodness, truth, and beauty may be much more attainable by simple and insignificant men than by some great heroes. The poet elevates the simple man and the simple life above heroism by both merit and power; for simple Russian people, with hearts like those of Nikolai Rostov, Timokhin, and Tushin, were the ones who defeated Napoleon and his huge army.

Up to now we have been speaking as if Tolstoy had completely defined aims and tasks—as if he wished to prove or elucidate certain thoughts and abstract propositions. This has only been an approximate method of expression. We have spoken this way only for the sake of clarity, in order to set our thoughts in relief; we have been deliberately ascribing crude and sharp forms to the matter so that they may meet the eye more vividly. In reality, the artist was not guided by such bare considerations as we have been attributing to him; his creative power performed on a wider scale and at a greater depth, penetrating to the innermost, sublime meaning of phenomena.

Following the same method, we could arrive at several more formulations of the purpose and meaning of *War and Peace*. *Verity* is the essence of every genuinely artistic work, and therefore whatever philosophical heights of contemplation we might rise to, we would still find points of support for our view in *War and Peace*. Much has been said about Tolstoy's *theory of history*.[9] Despite the excessiveness of some of his pronouncements, people of widely differing opinions have agreed that even if he is not entirely right, he is only *one step away* from the truth.

One could generalize his theory and say, for instance, that over and above historical life, any kind of life is guided not by reason and will, that is, not by ideas and aspirations reaching a clear consciousness of form, but by something dark and powerful, by what we call the *nature* of people. The springs of life (of both individuals and whole nations) are much deeper and mightier than those arbitrary ideas which enter awareness and those conscious considerations which people seem to follow. *A faith in life*—an acknowledgment of a greater significance in life than that reason is able to grasp— imbues the whole of Tolstoy's novel; and it would be possible to say that it is based on this idea.

Let us quote a minor example. After his trip to Otradnoe, Prince Andrei decides to leave his village and go to St. Petersburg. Tolstoy writes:

A whole series of sensible, logical reasons showing it to be essential for him to visit Petersburg, and even to re-enter the service, kept springing to his mind. Indeed, it now passed his comprehension how he could ever have doubted the necessity of taking an active share in life, just as a month before he could not have believed that the idea of leaving the country could enter his head. It seemed clear to him that all he had experienced would be wasted and pointless unless he applied it to work of some kind and again played an active part. He could not understand

9 See reviews of the novel, among others, by P. V. Annenkov in *Vestnik Evropy* 2 (1868), and by D. I. Pisarev in *Otechestvennye zapiski* 2 (1868).

how formerly he could have let such wretched arguments convince him that he would be lowering himself if after the lessons he had received from life he were to believe in the possibility of being useful or look forward to happiness and love. (2. 3. 3)

Reason plays a similarly subordinate role in the conduct of Tolstoy's other characters. Everywhere life proves to be broader than the realm of scanty logical considerations, and the poet shows us magnificently how it reveals its power against the will of people. Napoleon rushes toward what must destroy him. The state of confusion in which he catches our army and government is to save Russia because it entices him to Moscow, lets our patriotic feelings ripen, makes Kutuzov's appointment necessary, and generally alters the whole course of events. The genuine, deep forces governing events have the upper hand over all calculations.

Thus the idea of *War and Peace* is the mysterious depth of life.

We would have every right, however, to take some other high-principled interpretation of phenomena and ascribe it to the novel. It is possible, for instance, to claim that the highest point of view reached by the author is a religious view of the world. When Prince Andrei—a nonbeliever, like his father—having gravely and painfully experienced all the vicissitudes of life, lies mortally wounded and catches sight of his enemy Anatole Kuragin, he suddenly feels that a new view of life is revealed to him:

"Sympathy, love of our brothers, for those who love us and for those who hate us, love of our enemies—yes, the love that God preached on earth, that Princess Maria tried to teach me and I did not understand— that is what made me sorry to part with life, that is what remained for me had I lived." (3. 2. 37)

This sublime understanding of life is revealed in varying degrees not only to Prince Andrei, but to many characters in *War and Peace*— for example to Princess Mary, who has suffered much and loved much, to Pierre after the infidelity of his wife, to Natasha after her betrayal of her fiancé, and so forth. The poet shows with amazing clarity and power that a religious view is an ever-available refuge for the soul wearied by life and that it is the only support for the mind struck by the mutability of all the good things of human existence. The soul, renouncing the world, rises above the world and discovers a new beauty—forgiveness and love.

In one place the author remarks in parentheses that people of limited intellect "speak of 'these days' . . . imagining that they have discovered and appraised the peculiarities of 'these days' and that *human nature changes with the times*" (2. 3. 21). Tolstoy clearly repudiates this gross fallacy. On the basis of all the foregoing we have a right to say that he is faithful to the *unchanging, eternal qualities of the human soul* all through *War and Peace*. In the same way as he sees the human side of a hero, he sees first of all the human being in a man of a certain time, social milieu, and education, and the unchanging laws of human nature in actions determined by time and circumstance. Hence originates the *universally human* interest of this astonishing work, which combines artistic realism with artistic idealism, historical veracity with general psychological truth, poignant national distinctiveness with all-human breadth.

These are some of the general points of view from which *War and Peace* can be approached. But our definitions have not yet referred to the *particular* character of Tolstoy's work—to those peculiarities in it which constitute, over and above the general meaning, its particular significance for our life and literature.

There is a classical work in our literature with which *War and Peace* has more in common than with any other work. This is *The Captain's Daughter* by Pushkin. There is a similarity between these two works in the outward manner, in the very tone and subject of narration; but the main similarity is in the inner spirit. *The Captain's Daughter* is not a historical novel either, that is, its purpose is by no means to depict in the form of a novel life and mores which have already become alien to us, or persons who at one time played an important role in history. Historical personalities, such as Pugachev and Catherine, appear in Pushkin's work fleetingly and only in a few scenes, in exactly the same way that Kutuzov, Napoleon, and others appear in *War and Peace*. The main interest is focused on the events of the Grinevs' and Mironovs' private lives, while historical events are related only in so far as they touch upon the lives of these simple people. *The Captain's Daughter*, properly speaking, is *a chronicle of the Grinev family;* it is the very narrative of which Pushkin dreamed as early as chapter three of *Onegin*, the narrative which would depict "Old Russia's family tradition . . . ."[10]

Subsequently, quite a few similar narratives appeared in Russia; the most prominent place among them is occupied by S. T. Aksakov's *Family Chronicle*. Critics have noted the similarity between this chronicle and Pushkin's work. Khomiakov says: "S. T. was influenced by the simplicity of form in the *narratives* of Pushkin, and particularly of Gogol, with whom he was friendly."[11]

A close look at *War and Peace* will convince one that it is also a kind of *family chronicle*. To be precise, it is a chronicle of two families: of the Rostovs and the Bolkonskys. It consists of recollections and accounts of all the important happenings in the lives of these two families, and also of how their lives were affected by contemporary historical events. It differs from a simple chronicle only in this, that the narrative is given more sharply outlined form, more of the quality of a painting, in order better to incarnate the artist's ideas. There is no bare narration in it; everything is expressed in tableaux, in clear and distinct colors. This is the reason why the narrative, although in fact extremely well connected, appears to be abrupt, and why the artist has had to limit himself to a few years of the life represented rather than relate it step by step, from the very birth of a particular hero. Is it not true, however, that even in such a narrative— one condensed for greater artistic clarity—all the "family traditions" of the Bolkonskys and Rostovs arise before the reader's eyes?

By way of comparison, we have finally come upon the *genre* of literary creation to which *War and Peace* properly belongs. It is not a novel in general, not a historical novel in particular, nor even a historical chronicle: it is a *family chronicle*. If we add that by this genre we certainly mean an artistic creation, then our definition will be complete. This original genre, which does not exist in other literatures, and the idea of which caused much worry to Pushkin until finally he created it, can be characterized by the two particulars its name denotes. First, it is a *chronicle*, that is, a simple, artless

---

[10] Chap. 3, stanza 13; Pushkin, *Eugene Onegin*, trans. Arndt, p. 67.
[11] *The Works of Khomiakov*, 1: 665. (Author's note.)

narrative, without an elaborate plot or involved adventures, without formal unity and coherence. This form is obviously simpler than the novel, closer to actuality and verity; it has pretensions to be taken for a real-life occurrence rather than for mere possibility. Secondly, it is a *family* narrative, that is, not the adventures of a separate person on whom the reader's whole attention must be focused, but a series of events important for the whole family in one way or another. It is as if all members of the family, whose chronicle he is writing, were equally dear, equally heroic to the artist. The work's center of gravity is always in family relations rather than elsewhere. *The Captain's Daughter* is the story of how Petr Grinev married Captain Mironov's daughter. The interest is by no means in curious sensations; the adventures of the betrothed have nothing to do with changes in their feelings, which are simple and clear from the beginning, but consist of obstacles hindering the simple denouement; these obstacles are not hindrances to passion, but hindrances to marriage. Hence the natural diversity of colors in the narrative which, properly speaking, has no fictional story line.

One cannot help but marvel at Pushkin's genius as manifested in this case. *The Captain's Daughter* has the external attributes of Walter Scott's novels: it has the epigraphs, the same kind of division into chapters, and so forth. (In the same way, the external form of *A History of the Russian State* was borrowed from Hume.) But Pushkin, with imitation in mind, wrote a work original in the highest degree. Pugachev, for instance, is brought onto the stage with such an amazing delicacy as one can find only in Tolstoy when he introduces Alexander I, Speransky, and others. Pushkin obviously considered the slightest deviation from historical verity to be an irresponsible act, unworthy of poetic creation. Following the same principle, he reduces the romantic story of two loving hearts to such simplicity that the romanticism disappears.

Although Pushkin thought it necessary to build his plot on love and to introduce a historical personality into the plot, his unswerving poetic truthfulness led him to write, not a historical novel, but a chronicle of the Grinev family.

Russian artistic realism originated with Pushkin. Russian realism emerged, not as a consequence of the impoverishment of our artists' ideals, as has happened in other literatures, but, on the contrary, as a result of an intensive search for a purely Russian ideal. All the strivings for naturalism, for the strictest truth; all the depictions of small, weak, sickly men; all the careful shunning of a premature and unsuccessful creation of heroic characters; all the executions and dethronings of types with pretensions to heroism—all these efforts, all this hard work have one purpose and one hope: eventually to behold the Russian ideal in all its truth and undeceptive greatness. A struggle has been going on up to the present time between our sympathy for the simple good man, on the one hand, and an inescapable demand for something loftier, a dream about a powerful and passionate type, on the other. Indeed, what is Turgenev's *Smoke* if not the writer's new desperate effort to grapple with the predatory type, which he so clearly wishes to brand and abase in the character of Irina? What is Litvinov, if not the meek, simple type who obviously has all the author's sympathy but, in effect, shamefully gives up the struggle when faced with the predatory type?

Finally, is it not clear that Tolstoy strives to elevate the simple man, rather than any other, to the level of the ideal? What is *War and Peace*—this vast and multicolored epic—if not the apotheosis of the meek Russian type? Are we not here told, contrary to Turgenev's narrative, how the predatory type lost out to the meek type, how the simple Russian people defeated on the battlefield of Borodino all that can be thought of as heroic, brilliant, passionate, strong, and predatory—that is, Napoleon and his army?

The story of L. N. Tolstoy's creative career, which our one and only critic, Apollon Grigorev, lived to see and evaluate up to the appearance of *War and Peace*,[12] is remarkable to the highest degree. Now, when we can see that this career has led to the creation of *War and Peace*, we can understand its importance and character even more clearly and can appreciate even more the correctness of Apollon Grigorev's observations. Conversely, Tolstoy's earlier works

---

[12] This and subsequent references are to Grigorev's essay "Iavleniia sovremennoi literatury, propushchennye nashei kritikoi: Graf L. N. Tolstoy i ego sochineniia," *Vremia* 1 and 9 (1862).

lead us, more directly than any other considerations, to a comprehension of the individual character of *War and Peace.*

The same can be said about any writer in general: in the works of each there is a connection between past and present, one elucidating the other. But it turns out that the works of no other Russian writer of fiction have such a profound and tight connection, no one else's career displays such symmetry and integrity as do the works and career of Tolstoy. He began his literary pursuits together with Ostrovsky and Pisemsky; his works started coming out just a little later than those of Turgenev, Goncharov, and Dostoevsky. Yet all his literary contemporaries had already revealed themselves, had already displayed the greatest strengths of their talents, making it possible to judge their volume and direction in full, when Tolstoy was still persistently cultivating his gift, not disclosing its full power until the appearance of *War and Peace.* This was a slow and difficult process of ripening, but the fruit it has yielded is all the more succulent and prodigious.

Tolstoy's previous works are no more than *études,* sketches, experiments; the artist did not intend to offer integrated creations, to express his ideas in full, or to draw complete pictures of life as he understood it. His purpose was simply an exploration of specific questions, separate personalities, particular characters, or even only of particular mental states. Take the short story "The Snow Storm," for example: it is obvious that the whole attention of the artist and the whole interest of the story are focused on those strange and hardly noticeable sensations which are experienced by a man benumbed by snow, now falling asleep, now awakening. This is a simple *étude* from nature, similar to those studies in which painters depict a corner of a field, a bush, a section of a stream in a particular light or with an effect of water difficult to convey, and so forth. All of Tolstoy's earlier works—including even those which show a certain external wholeness—have a similar character to a lesser or greater degree. For instance, *The Cossacks* apparently presents a full and masterly picture of the life of a Cossack village, but the harmony of this picture is obviously disturbed by the vast space given to the feelings and anxieties of Olenin. The author's attention is all too tangentially drawn in this direction; and instead of a well-proportioned picture, *a study in the inner life* of a young man from Moscow emerges. For this reason Apollon Grigorev accepted as "completely organic, living creations" only Tolstoy's *Family Happiness* and *Army Tales*. Now, after the appearance of *War and Peace*, we must modify this opinion. The *Army Tales*, which appeared as *completely organic* works to the critic, also turn out, in comparison with *War and Peace*, to be no more than *études*, preliminary sketches. There remains, consequently, only *Family Happiness*—a novel which does indeed constitute a fully living whole, because of the simplicity of its theme and the clarity and distinctness of its execution. "This work," wrote Apollon Grigorev, "is serene, profound, simple, and highly poetic, without showy effects, and with a straightforward and even presentation of the question of how a feeling of passion can change into another kind of feeling."

If this is correct, if with one exception Tolstoy did indeed produce only *études* before the appearance of *War and Peace*, then the question arises: what was the cause of this struggle, what problem held him up along the path of creative work? It is easy to see that there was some conflict within him all this time, some difficult inner process was taking place. Grigorev was well aware of this and insisted in his essay that the process had not yet been completed. We see now how correct this opinion was: only with the creation of *War and Peace* has the artist's inner development reached completion, or at least considerable maturity.

What was this process? Grigorev thought that an essential factor of Tolstoy's inner labors was *negation*, and he related these labors to that *negative process* which had begun with Pushkin. What dominated Tolstoy's creative work right up to the writing of *War and Peace* was precisely a negation of *everything borrowed and unnatural in our development*.

The inner struggle which took place within our poetry has acquired a partially new aspect, absent in Pushkin's time. A critical attitude is no longer limited to "high-flown dreams," to those mental states in which "it seemed essential" to the poet to sing about

> Deserts, the pearl-white foam of waves,
> The murmur of the sea, high cliffs,

A proud maiden as an ideal,
And nameless torments.[13]

Nowadays the searching glance of poetry is directed at our society itself, at the actual phenomena which arise in it. In essence, however, it is still the same process. People never have lived and never will live in any other way than under the power and guidance of ideas. We may imagine a society whose substance is entirely trivial: yet the life of even such a society will always be guided by some concepts which, perverted and dim as they may be, will never be able to lose their ideal nature. Thus a critical attitude to society is in essence a struggle with the ideas of that society.

No other Russian writer has given such a deeply sincere and truthful account of the process of this struggle as Tolstoy. The heroes of his earlier works are usually tormented by this struggle, and relating the struggle is the essential content of these works. For an example let us quote what one of his early heroes, Nikolai Irtenev, writes in a chapter bearing the French title "Comme Il Faut":

My favorite and chief division of people at the time of which I am writing, was into the *comme il faut* and the *comme il ne faut pas*. The latter I subdivided into those inherently not *comme il faut*, and the common people. The *comme il faut* people I respected and considered worthy of being on terms of equality with me; the *comme il ne faut pas* I pretended to despise but in reality hated, nourishing a feeling of personal offense against them; the lower classes did not exist for me—I despised them completely.[14]

I even fancy that had I had a brother, a mother, or a father, who was not *comme il faut*, I should have said it was a misfortune, but that it being so there could be nothing in common between them and me.

Here is a demonstration of the power of French and other

---

[13] From a fragment of "Puteshestvie Onegina."

[14] From *Youth*, chap. 31. See Leo Tolstoy, *Childhood, Boyhood, and Youth*, trans. Louise and Aylmer Maude (London: Oxford University Press, 1930), pp. 338–39. The subsequent two quotations are from p. 341 of this edition.

concepts; here is a brilliant example of that social falsity in the midst of which Tolstoy's heroes grew up. Nikolai Irtenev concludes:

> I have known and still know many, very many people, old, proud, self-confident and sharp in their judgments, who if the question were put to them in the next world: "Who are you, and what have you done down there?" would only be able to say: "*Je fus un homme très comme il faut.*" That fate awaited me.

Irtenev's eventual development, however, was quite different; and that inner conversion, that painful rebirth which these young men accomplish in themselves has great significance. Apollon Grigorev wrote about this:

> The spiritual process revealed to us in *Childhood, Boyhood*, and even in the first half of *Youth* is *unusually original.* The hero of these remarkable psychological studies was born and raised in a social environment so artificially created, so exceptional that in effect it has no real existence —this is the so-called aristocratic sphere, the sphere of high society. It is not surprising that the same sphere molded Pechorin—its biggest product—as well as some minor creatures such as the heroes of various society tales. *What is surprising and noteworthy is that the hero of Tolstoy's narrative leaves this narrow sphere, that is, rejects it through analysis.* After all, Pechorin did not leave this sphere, despite his intellect; nor did the heroes of Count Sollogub or Miss Evgeniia Tur! On the other hand, as one reads Tolstoy's *études* it becomes understandable how *Pushkin's nature, despite the same exceptional sphere, managed to preserve in itself a fresh stream of broad, common, popular life* and an ability to comprehend this vital life, deeply sympathizing with it, and at times even identifying with it.

The artist's inner labors displayed extraordinary strength and depth, and led to incomparably higher results than do the labors of many other writers. But how hard and prolonged were his efforts! Let us point out at least their main aspects.

Tolstoy's earlier heroes usually harbored a strong but totally undetermined idealism, that is, a striving for something lofty, sublime, virtuous, without exact shape or clear outlines. These were, as Grigorev says, "ideals up in the air, creations from above, rather than from below—the same kind which destroyed Gogol both morally and physically." Tolstoy's heroes, however, are not content with these airy ideals, do not come to rest on them as on something indubitable. On the contrary, a twofold effort begins: first, an analysis of existing phenomena and a demonstration of their incompatibility with ideals; and secondly, *a persistent, untiring search for such phenomena of actuality which incarnate the ideal.*

The artist's keen analysis, aimed at exposing all kinds of spiritual falsity, is so striking that it is the first thing to capture the reader's attention. Grigorev wrote:

> An analytical acumen develops early in the hero of *Childhood, Boyhood, and Youth* and deeply undermines the foundations of those conventional values which surround him and which dwell inside him.
>
> He patiently and ruthlessly searches through every one of his feelings, including even those which at first sight seem to be perfectly pious (see the chapter "Confession"); he exposes everything *manufactured* in each feeling; he even foresees the final results of every thought, of every childish or adolescent dream. Remember, for instance, the dreams the hero of *Boyhood* has when he is locked in a dark room for disobeying his tutor. The ruthlessness of the analysis forces the soul to admit what the hero finds too shameful to admit even to himself.
>
> A ruthless analysis also guides the hero of *Youth*. He submits to his conventional environment, even accepts its prejudices, but constantly *judges himself* and emerges victorious from the judgment.

The essence of this process is

> a judgment of everything false and ready-made in the feelings of contemporary man—of everything that Lermontov superstitiously idolized in his Pechorin.
>
> Tolstoy's analysis led to a profound distrust of all the *elevated, unusual* sensations of the human soul within a certain sphere. He destroyed ready-made, manufactured, partially alien ideals, forces, passions, energies.

Grigorev further remarks that in relation to such clearly false phenomena Tolstoy's analysis is

> entirely correct, more correct than Turgenev's analysis, for Turgenev sometimes, or even quite frequently, bows down to the false aspects of

our life. Tolstoy's analysis is also more correct than Goncharov's because Tolstoy makes his judgments in the name of a profound love for truth and for the sincerity of emotions, rather than in the name of a narrow, bureaucratic practicality.

These are the aspects of Tolstoy's purely negative work. But the essence of his talent is much more clearly manifest in the positive aspects of his work. His idealism engenders in him neither contempt for, nor hostility to reality. On the contrary, he humbly trusts that reality contains genuinely beautiful phenomena. He is not content with a contemplation of airy ideals existent only in his soul: he persistently searches for incarnations of ideals which—although possibly partial and incomplete—exist in fact, visible to the eye. This path, which he treads with unfailing truthfulness and vigilance, leads him to two possible conclusions: either he meets with weak and insignificant phenomena which have only a faint spark but which he is willing to accept as incarnations of his cherished ideas; or else he is not content with such phenomena, grows weary of his fruitless search, and falls into despair.

Tolstoy's heroes are sometimes presented directly as if they were roaming the world, the Cossack villages and the ballrooms of Petersburg, in search of an answer to the question: Is there genuine virtue on this earth, is there genuine love, genuine beauty in the human soul? Beginning with childhood, they sometimes involuntarily fix their attention on some phenomena which they accidentally come across and which seem to reveal a different, simple, clear life, free of the waverings and divarications experienced by them. They think they have found what they have been looking for in these phenomena. Grigorev says:

Analysis stops when it comes upon phenomena it cannot handle. Highly significant in this context are the chapters about the *nurse*, about *Masha's love for Vasily*, and especially the one about the *holy idiot* in which the analysis comes up against a phenomenon representing a rarity, an exception, an eccentricity even in the life of the simple people. The analysis contrasts all these phenomena with the conventional features of the hero's own environment.

The work of analysis is continued in the *Army Tales*, in the short story "A Meeting in the Detachment,"[15] and in "Two Hussars." It stops when it comes up against phenomena that do not yield to analysis, and in such cases transitions occur, now to pathos evoked by the colossal and the grandiose, such as the epic of Sevastopol, now to wonderment at the humbly great, such as the death of Velenchuk or the character of Captain Khlopov.[16] But the analysis is merciless with everything artificial and manufactured, whether it appears in the bourgeois Captain Mikhailov, or in the Caucasian hero à la Marlinsky,[17] or in the totally warped personality of the cadet in the story "A Meeting in the Detachment."

The artist's hard, time-consuming work, his persistent search for genuinely bright spots in the all-encompassing twilight of gray reality does not, however, yield lasting results for a long time; it gives only hints and fragmentary indications, rather than an integrated, clear view. The artist often becomes weary, often despairs, losing faith in what he is searching for, often submits to apathy. Concluding one of his Sevastopol stories, in which he eagerly searched for but apparently did not find *genuine valor* in people, he writes with deep sincerity:

A painful doubt overwhelms me. It would have been better, perhaps, to have kept silent, for possibly what I have uttered is among those pernicious truths obscurely hidden away in every one's soul, and which, in order to remain harmless, must not be expressed; just as old wine must not be disturbed lest the sediment rise and make the liquid turbid. Where, then, in my tale do we see the evil we must avoid, and the good towards which we must strive to go? *Where is the traitor? Where is the hero? All are good and all are bad.*[18]

[15] The full original title of this story, as published in *Biblioteka dlia chteniia* (December, 1856), was "Vstrecha v otriade s moskovskim znakomym. Iz Kavkazskikh zapisok kniazia Nekhliuɑova." The story is better known under the title Tolstoy gave its later version: "Iz Kavkazskikh vospominaniy. Razzhalovanny."

[16] From the stories "Rubka lesa" and "Nabeg," respectively.

[17] Captain Mikhailov is a character in "Sevastopol v mae"; the Caucasian hero à la Marlinsky is Lieutenant Rosenkranz, a character in "Nabeg."

[18] From the last chapter of "Sebastopol in May, 1855"; Leo Tolstoy, *Sebastopol*, trans. Frank D. Millet (Ann Arbor: University of Michigan Press, 1961), p. 109. The italics are Strakhov's.

The poet has often expressed his despair with amazing profundity, even though the readers, generally little inclined to such problems and feelings, have not noticed this. One can sense the despair, for instance, in "Lucerne," in "Albert," and in the earlier "A Billiard-Marker's Notes." "Lucerne," as Grigorev remarks, "is an obvious expression of a *pantheistic grief over life and its ideals, over everything that is even slightly unnatural and artificial in the human soul.*" The idea is expressed even more clearly and sharply in "Three Deaths." Here the death of the tree seems the most normal death to the artist. "The tree," says Grigorev, "displays a higher consciousness in death than do either the educated lady or the simple man." Finally, even *Family Happiness* expresses, in the opinion of the same critic, "a grim resignation to fate, which has not spared the flowers of human feelings."

These are the characteristics of the hard struggle which went on in the poet's soul; these are the phases of his long, untiring search for the ideal in reality. It is no wonder that in the midst of this struggle he was unable to produce harmonious artistic works, and that his analysis at times became strained to the point of morbidity. The great power of his art was the only reason why even these *études*, engendered by such deep inner toil, preserved their unfailingly high artistic value. The artist was supported and strengthened by his lofty aspirations, powerfully voiced at the end of the same story from which we cited his *painful doubts:*

> The hero of my tale, *the one I love with all the power of my soul*, the one I have tried to reproduce in all his beauty, just as he has been, is, and always will be beautiful, is *Truth.*[19]

Truth is the slogan of our literature; truth guides it in its critical attitude to alien ideals and in its search for its own ideals.

What is the final conclusion we can draw from this history of the development of Tolstoy's talent—a highly instructive history laid out in front of us in the brilliant and true-to-life forms of his works? What did the artist come to, where did he stop?

At the time Grigorev was writing his article Tolstoy had been silent for some time, and the critic attributed this silence to that

[19] Ibid., p. 110.

apathy about which we have spoken. "Apathy," wrote Grigorev, "was inevitably waiting midway along this deep and sincere process, but nobody who has faith in the strength of Tolstoy's talent *can doubt that it is not the end of the process.*" His faith did not deceive the critic; his prediction has proven true. Tolstoy's talent has evolved with all its might and has given us *War and Peace*.

In what direction did this talent lean in the earlier works? What sympathies arose and gathered force in the course of the inner struggle?

As early as 1859 Grigorev noted that Tolstoy was *trying to poetize Belkin's type out of proportion and forcibly.* In 1862 he wrote:

> Tolstoy's analysis has destroyed ready-made, manufactured, *partially* alien ideals, forces, passions, and energies. *In Russian life he sees only the negative type of the simple and meek man*, and he has grown attached to this type with all his heart. He looks for the ideal of simplicity of emotions everywhere: in the nurse's grief over the death of the hero's mother, which is contrasted with the somewhat histrionic, although still deep, sorrow of the old Countess (*Childhood* and *Boyhood*); in the death of the soldier Velenchuk; in the honest and simple courage of Captain Khlopov which in his eyes is obviously superior to the unquestionable but extremely showy bravery of one of the Caucasian heroes à la Marlinsky; and in the humble death of a simple man, contrasted with the death of a suffering, but capriciously suffering lady.

Here is the most essential feature, the most important aspect of Tolstoy's artistic view of the world. It is understandable that this aspect entails a certain one-sidedness. Grigorev finds that Tolstoy arrived at his love for the meek type mainly out of a distrust of the brilliant and predatory type, and that he is sometimes overzealous in his severity with "elevated" feelings. "Few will believe with him, for instance," writes the critic, "that the nurse's sorrow was deeper than the sorrow of the old Countess."

Incidentally, a partiality for the simple type is a common feature of our belles-lettres. Therefore the critic's general conclusion has vast importance and deserves the greatest attention in relation both to Tolstoy and to the whole of our art:

> Tolstoy's analysis is incorrect in that it does not acknowledge the significance of the *really* brilliant, *really* passionate, and *really* predatory

type, which has been justified—that is, the possibility and reality of which has been proven—by both nature and history.

We would be a nation very meagerly endowed by nature if we saw our ideal in the meek type alone, be it a Maksim Maksimych, a Captain Khlopov, or the humble characters of Ostrovsky. Moreover, the types we have experienced from the time of Pushkin and Lermontov were alien to us only partially, perhaps only by their form, by their, so to speak, veneer. We experienced them precisely because our nature is just as capable of assimilating them as any European nature. Not only have there been *predatory types in our history*, and not only would it be *impossible to eliminate Stenka Razin from the epic tradition of our people,* but the very types which have been produced by foreign life are not foreign to us: they have assumed original forms in the works of our poets. Turgenev's Vasily Luchinov represents the eighteenth century; and his passionate Veretev, who carelessly burns the candle at both ends, is even more Russian.[20]

These are the various points of view from which we can judge the *particular* character of *War and Peace*. The late critic clearly defined these points of view; all we have to do is to apply them to the new work of the writer, whom the critic understood so correctly and profoundly.

Grigorev foresaw that the apathy and the feverish tension of analysis must pass. These are, indeed, entirely over. In *War and Peace* Tolstoy's talent is in full command of its strengths; it calmly sets the acquisitions of a long and hard labor in their proper places. What firmness of hand, what freedom, what assurance, what simple and distinct clarity in the depictions! It seems that nothing is difficult for the artist. Wherever he casts his glance—whether at Napoleon's tent or at the top floor of the Rostov's house—everything is revealed to him down to the smallest details, as if he had the power to behold at will both what there is and what there was in all places. He does not hesitate to take on any task; when he comes to difficult scenes, in which contradictory feelings clash or hardly perceptible sensations flit by, he completes his depiction to the very end, to the finest stroke, as if doing it simply for fun. He is not satisfied, for instance, to have presented Captain Tushin's unconsciously heroic actions; he also has

[20] Characters in "Tri portreta" and "Zatishe," respectively.

to peek into the man's soul and eavesdrop on what the man unconsciously whispers. The account of all this is as simple and free as if it were about the most ordinary thing possible:

> A fantastic world took possession of his brain and at this moment afforded him sheer delight. The enemy's guns were in his imagination not guns but *pipes from which an invisible smoker occasionally puffed out wreaths of smoke.*
>
> "There, he is having another puff," *muttered Tushin to himself* as a curling cloud of smoke leaped from the hill and was borne off to the left in a ribbon by the wind. "Now look out for the ball—we'll toss it back!" . . . The noise of musketry at the foot of the hill, now dying away and quickening again, *seemed like someone's breathing.* He listened intently to the ebb and flow of these sounds.
>
> "*Ah, she's taking another breath again!*" he soliloquized.
>
> *He imagined himself as a powerful giant of monstrous stature hurling cannon balls at the French with both hands.* (1. 2. 20)

This is the same keen, penetrating analysis as before, but it has acquired full freedom and assurance. We have seen its results. The artist has adopted a calm, serene attitude to his characters and to the feelings of his characters. There is no struggle going on in him any more; he neither strains to contest "elevated" feelings, nor stops in wonderment when facing simple feelings. He can depict them both in all their *truth* and illuminate them with an even, daytime light.

In "Lucerne," in one of those moments of *painful doubt* we have spoken of, the artist asked himself in despair: "Whose soul possesses so absolute a *standard of good and evil* that he can measure all the confused and fleeting facts?"[21]

In *War and Peace* this standard has obviously been found; it is in the artist's full possession, and he confidently measures with it whatever facts he wishes to choose.

It is clear from the foregoing discussion what the results of such a measurement must be. Everything shining with a false veneer is mercilessly exposed by the artist. Under the artificial, outwardly

[21] Leo Tolstoy, *Nine Stories, 1855–1863*, trans. Louise and Aylmer Maude (London: Oxford University Press, 1934), p. 250. The italics are Strakhov's.

graceful manners of high society he reveals an abyss of emptiness, base passions, and sheer animal inclinations. On the other hand, everything simple and genuine, in whatever base and crude form it may appear, evokes deep sympathy in the artist. How insignificant, how trivial are the drawing rooms of Anna Pavlovna Scherer and Helen Bezukhova! What poetry surrounds the humble existence of *Uncle!*

We must not forget that the family of the Rostovs, even though they are titled counts, is a simple Russian landowning family, tightly bound to the country, maintaining the forms and traditions of Russian life, and coming into contact with high society only accidentally. High society is a sphere entirely apart from the Rostovs; a corrupt sphere, the mere touch of which has a disastrous effect on Natasha. As is his wont, the author describes this sphere through the impressions Natasha receives from it. Natasha is keenly struck by the falsity and lack of naturalness which characterize Helen's attire, the Italians' singing, Duport's dancing, and the declamation of Mlle George; but at the same time the eager young girl is involuntarily carried away by the atmosphere of artificial life, in which lies and affectations provide a lustrous cover for any passions, any cravings for pleasure. In high society one inevitably comes across Italian and French art; and the ideals of French and Italian ardency, so alien to the Russian character, on this occasion exercise a corrupting influence on Natasha.

The other family chronicled in *War and Peace*, the family of the Bolkonskys, does not belong to high society either. One could say that it is *higher* than high society; but in any case it is outside it. Remember Princess Mary, who totally lacks the accomplishments of a society girl; or remember the hostile attitude the old man and his son display toward Princess Lisa, a most charming society lady.

Although one family is that of counts, and the other a princely family, *War and Peace* does not even have a shade of high society character. The beau monde used to have great attraction for our literature, giving rise to a whole series of false creations. Lermontov never managed to free himself of that enthusiasm for it which Grigorev called "the sickness of moral servility." In *War and Peace* Russian art appears entirely free of all symptoms of this illness; and this freedom is all the more significant because art here entered the very sphere which is supposed to be dominated by high society.

The Rostov and Bolkonsky families, by their inner life and the relations of their members, are Russian families, just like any other. Family relations have an essential, overriding importance for the members of both. Pechorin and Onegin had no families, or at least their families played no important role in their lives. They were occupied and swallowed up by their personal, individual existences. Even Tatiana, who stayed entirely faithful to family life, never betraying it in any way, was a little estranged from it:

> Born in their midst, she seemed to be
> A stranger to her family.[22]

But as soon as Pushkin started to depict simple Russian life, as, for instance, in *The Captain's Daughter*, the family immediately came into its rights. The Grinevs and Mironovs enter the stage as two families, as people having close family relations. But Russian family life has nowhere come to the fore in such splendor and might as it has in *War and Peace*. The young men, such as Nikolai Rostov and Andrei Bolkonsky, lead their own special, personal lives, carried away by vanity, carousing, love, and so forth; they are often and for prolonged periods torn away from their homes by service and other occupations; but their homes, their fathers, their families remain sacred for them, absorbing the better half of their thoughts and feelings. As regards the women, Princess Mary and Natasha, they are entirely submerged in the family sphere. The description of the Rostovs' happy family life and of the Bolkonskys' unhappy one, with all the varieties of relations and events, constitutes the most essential, classically perfect aspects of *War and Peace*.

Let us draw one more parallel. A collision between private and public lives is presented both in *The Captain's Daughter* and in *War and Peace*. Evidently both artists felt a desire to explore and delineate the attitude of the Russian to the life of the state. We seem to have the right to draw the conclusion from this fact that a double bond—a bond to the family and a bond to the state—is among the most essential factors of our life.

The kind of life that is depicted in *War and Peace* is not an egotistical personal life, nor a compilation of individual strivings and

[22] Chap. 2, stanza 25; *Eugene Onegin*, trans. Arndt, p. 49.

sufferings, but a communal life, bound on all sides by living ties. It seems to us that this feature manifests the truly Russian, truly original character of Tolstoy's work.

What can we say about passions? What role is played by personalities, characters in *War and Peace?* It is clear that passions cannot under any circumstances be given a prominent place here, and that the individual characters must not stand out of the picture disproportionately.

Passions do not have a sparkling, picturesque quality in *War and Peace.* Let us take love as an example. It is either sheer sensuality, like Pierre's relations with his wife and her relations with her admirers, or, to the contrary, a perfectly calm, deeply human attachment, like Sonia's devotion to Nikolai and like the ever-reviving relationship between Pierre and Natasha. Passion, in its pure form, develops only between Natasha and Kuragin; but even here it represents some kind of insane intoxication on the part of Natasha, and only on the part of Kuragin does it prove to be what the French call *passion*—a concept entirely un-Russian yet, as is well known, effectively grafted into our society. Remember how Kuragin raves about his *goddess* and how "he described to Dolokhov, in the manner of a connoisseur, the attractions of her arms, shoulders, feet, and hair" (2. 5. 11). The genuinely loving Pierre feels and expresses himself quite differently about Natasha: "She is fascinating. But what makes her so, I can't tell you. That is all one can say about her" (2. 5. 4).

In the same way all other passions—anger, vanity, vengeance, and everything else revealing the separate personality of a man—either flare up only momentarily or change into constant, calmer attitudes. Remember Pierre's relations with his wife, with Drubetskoi, and others. In general, *War and Peace* does not elevate passions to the level of ideals. What dominates this chronicle is obviously a *faith in the family* and, just as obviously, a *distrust of passions*, that is, a disbelief in their duration and durability, a conviction that, however strong and beautiful these personal cravings may be, they will fade and disappear with time.

With regard to the characters, it is perfectly clear that the simple and meek types—these reflections of one of the fondest ideals of our national spirit—have remained as close to the artist's heart as they were before. Goodhearted and humble heroes, such as Timokhin and Tushin, as well as goodhearted and simple people, such as Princess Mary and Count Ilia Rostov, are portrayed; and they are portrayed with the same understanding, with the same deep sympathy which is familiar to us from Tolstoy's earlier works. But anybody who has followed the artist's earlier career will be struck by that boldness and freedom with which he has now begun to portray strong and passionate types as well. It seems that in *War and Peace* the artist has for the first time gained a knowledge of the secret of those strong feelings and characters which earlier he always treated with such distrust. The Bolkonskys—father and son—do not belong to the meek types by any stretch of the imagination. Natasha is a charming representation of a passionate feminine type, at once strong, ardent, and gentle.

The artist has of course displayed his dislike of the predatory type by portraying a whole host of such people, like Helen, Anatole, Dolokhov, the coachman Balaga, and others. All these are predominantly predatory natures: in them the artist has created representatives of the evil and corruption which bring suffering to the main characters of his family chronicle.

The most interesting, original, and masterly type created by Tolstoy is, however, Pierre Bezukhov. He is evidently a combination of the two types, the meek and the passionate; he is a purely Russian nature, equally full of both goodness and strength. Although soft, shy, girlishly naïve, and well-meaning, Pierre at times discovers in himself (as the author says) the nature of his father. This father of his, this wealthy and handsome man of Catherine's time, who appears only to die and does not utter a single word in *War and Peace*, is one of the most striking images in the book. He is truly a dying lion, mighty and magnificent to his last breath. The nature of this lion is echoed in Pierre at times. Remember how he shakes Anatole by the scruff of the neck—the rowdy Anatole, the leader of rakes engaged in such pranks "which would long ago have condemned any ordinary man to Siberia" (2. 5. 16).

Whatever the strong types portrayed by Tolstoy are like, however, it is still obvious that there is little of a brilliant and active quality in all these people put together, and that the power of the Russia of that time rested much more on the endurance of the meek type than on the actions of the strong. There are no brilliant aspects to Kutuzov himself—the greatest force depicted in *War and Peace*. He is a sluggish old man whose greatest power is manifested in the ease and freedom with which he carries the heavy burden of his experience. His slogan is *"patience and time"* (3. 2. 16).

The two battles in which the proportions reached by the power of Russian souls are shown most clearly—the engagement at Schön Graben and the battle of Borodino—obviously have a defensive, and not an offensive, character. In Prince Andrei's opinion, the success at Schön Graben was due first of all to "the heroic endurance of Captain Tushin" (1. 2. 21). And the essence of the battle of Borodino was that the attacking French army was panic-stricken in the face of an enemy who, "after losing *one half* of his men, *still stood as formidable* at the end as at the beginning of the battle" (3. 2. 39). The old maxim of historians, that Russians are not strong in attack but unmatched in *defense*, was once more proven here.

We can see that all the heroism of the Russians was contained in the power of the self-sacrificing and fearless, but at the same time meek and simple type. On the other hand, the genuinely brilliant type, full of active force, passion, and rapacity, is represented—and must be represented by the very nature of the affair—by the French and their leader Napoleon. In active force and brilliance the Russians could under no circumstances equal this type. As we have already observed, the whole narrative of *War and Peace* is a representation of the collision of these two vastly different types, and of the victory of the simple type over the brilliant type.

Since we know about Tolstoy's deep-rooted and profound dislike of the brilliant type, we should look for biased and incorrect depictions precisely in relation to this type. But a bias springing from such deep wells may lead to invaluable discoveries; it may unveil the truth hidden from an indifferent and cold vision. In the person of Napoleon the artist wanted, as it were, to unmask and dethrone the brilliant type—to debunk it through its greatest representative. The author has a positively hostile attitude to Napoleon, as if he were fully sharing the feelings experienced by Russia and the Russian army at that time. Compare Kutuzov's conduct with that of Napoleon on the field of Borodino. What purely Russian simplicity in the one, and how much affectation, clowning, falsity in the other!

Faced with such a representation, we are involuntarily gripped by doubt. Tolstoy's Napoleon is not sufficiently clever and wise, not even sufficiently frightening. In his person the artist captured everything that is so repugnant to Russian nature, everything that makes its simple instincts revolt. But it must be assumed that his features do not seem quite so unnatural and harsh in Napoleon's native French world as they are to Russian eyes. That world must also have had its own beauty and greatness.

Yet, since that other greatness gave way to the greatness of the Russian spirit, since the crime of violence and oppression lay on the conscience of Napoleon, and since the valor of the French was really outshone by the glitter of Russian valor—one cannot help but conclude that the artist was right when he cast a shadow on the brilliant figure of the emperor. Also, one cannot help but sympathize with the purity and righteousness of the instincts which guided the author. His depiction of Napoleon is still astonishingly truthful, even though we cannot say that the inner life of Napoleon and his army is described as deeply and fully as is the Russian life of that epoch.

These are some of the *particular* characteristics of *War and Peace*. We hope they will at least show how much of a purely Russian heart is put into the work. We can witness once more that real, true works of art are closely bound to the life, soul, and whole nature of the artist; they represent his confession and the incarnation of his spiritual history. As a creation fully living, entirely sincere, and saturated by the best, innermost aspirations of our national character, *War and Peace* is an incomparable work: it is one of the greatest and most original monuments of our art. The significance of this work for our literature can be best expressed by Apollon Grigorev's words, which were uttered ten years ago and which could not have been more splendidly corroborated than they have been by the appearance of *War and Peace:*

Nature has not given a fair share of vision and other faculties to him who cannot see the mighty growths of the typical, the indigenous, the national.

Vladimir Solovev

IN MEMORY OF DOSTOEVSKY

The first of three discourses on Dostoevsky (1881–83) collected under the title Tri rechi v pamiat Dostoevskogo *in the collected edition of Solovev's works (V. S. Solovev,* Sobranie sochineniy, *ed. M. S. Solovev and G. Rachinsky [St. Petersburg: Obshchestvennaia Polza, 1901–7], vol. 3). The full text of Discourse One is given in translation. The subsequent two discourses are less specifically devoted to Dostoevsky: Discourse Two elucidates the Christianity of the future as prophesied by Dostoevsky, while Discourse Three outlines its historical development.*

In primitive times poets were prophets and priests, the religious idea dominated poetry, art served the gods. Later, as life became complicated, as a civilization based on the division of labor appeared, art, like other human activities, was dissociated and separated from religion. If the earlier artists were servants of the gods, now art itself became their deity and idol. Priests of pure art appeared, for whom perfect artistic form became the main thing, regardless of any religious content. The two springtimes of this freed art (the classic world and modern Europe) were splendid, but not lasting. The bloom of modern European art has come to an end before our eyes. The flowers are dropping, but the fruits are only beginning to nucleate. It would be unjust to demand the qualities of ripe fruit from the ovary: one can only foresee its future qualities. It is precisely in this way that we should treat the present state of art and letters. Today's artists neither can nor want to serve pure beauty, to produce perfect form; they are seeking content. But, as aliens to the former religious content of art, they are turning wholly to current actuality and treating it with a *twofold* servile attitude; first, they are trying to copy the phenomena of this actuality slavishly; and second, they are trying just as slavishly to attend to the concerns of the day, to satisfy the public mood of a given moment, to advocate current morality, thinking that in this way they will make art useful. Of course, neither the one nor the other of these aims is being achieved. In the vain pursuit of imaginarily real[1] details the genuine reality of the whole only gets lost, and the aspiration to unite external didacticism and usefulness with art to the detriment of art's inner beauty turns art into the most useless and unnecessary thing in the world, for it is clear that a bad artistic product, even with the best purposes, teaches nothing and can be of no benefit whatsoever.

Unconditionally to censure the contemporary state of art and its predominant direction is very easy. The general decline of creative power and specific infringements on the idea of beauty are all too obvious—but unconditional censure of all this would be unjust. In this crude and base contemporary art, beneath this twofold slavish aspect, are hidden the guarantees of divine greatness. The demands of contemporary reality and direct usefulness in art, although senseless in their present base and obscure application, hint at an elevated and profoundly genuine idea of art which neither the representatives nor interpreters of pure art have thus far achieved. Dissatisfied with formal beauty, contemporary artists more or less consciously want art to be a *real force*, illuminating and regenerating all the human world. Earlier art *diverted* man from the darkness and evil that dominated the world, it led him to its serene heights and *delighted* him with its sparkling images; today's art, on the other hand, *draws* man to darkness and worldly evil with the sometimes vague desire to light up this darkness, to appease this evil. But whence does art derive this illuminative and regenerative power? If art should not be content with diverting man's attention from the evil of life but should improve this same evil life, then this great goal cannot be attained by the simple reproduction of actuality. To portray does not mean to transform, and accusation is not reformation. Pure art raised man above earth, led him to the Olympian heights; the new art returns him to earth with love and compassion, not to plunge him into the darkness of earthly life (art is not necessary for this), but rather to

[1] Every detail, taken separately, is not real in itself, for only a *totality* is real. Moreover, the realist artist looks at reality *out of himself*, he understands it in his own way. Consequently, it is already not *objective* reality. (Author's note.)

heal and restore this life. For this it is necessary to be concerned with and close to earth, it is necessary to have love and compassion for it, but something more is also necessary. For powerful action on earth, in order to turn it round and re-create it, it is necessary to attract and apply an *unearthly power* to earth. Art, isolated, separated from religion, must enter into a new, free union with it. Artists and poets must again become priests and prophets, but in another, more important, more elevated sense: not only will the religious idea possess them, but they will possess it and consciously govern its earthly incarnations. The art of the future, which will *itself* return to religion after prolonged ordeals, will by no means be that primitive art that was still indistinguishable from religion.

Despite the apparently antireligious character of contemporary art, a perspicacious glance will be able to discern in it the vague contours of future religious art, precisely in its twofold aspiration: fully to incarnate ideas in their minutest material details to the point of an almost perfect confluence with current actuality; and to strive *to have an effect* on real life, improving and bettering it in accordance with certain ideal demands. It is true, these demands themselves are still rather base and the efforts they call for are rather vain. Unconscious of the religious character of its problem, realistic art denies itself the only solid support and powerful lever for moral action in the world.

But all this crude realism of contemporary art is only a hard cocoon in which the winged poetry of the future temporarily hides. This is not only a personal hope—positive facts point to it. Artists have already appeared who, issuing from the domain of realism and still largely remaining on its base soil, nevertheless reach religious truth, bind the problems of their works to it, draw their social ideal from it, consecrate all their social service to it. If there is a kind of prophecy of a new religious art in contemporary realism, then this prophecy is already beginning to come to pass. There are still no representatives of this new religious art, but its precursors are already appearing. Dostoevsky was one of these precursors.

By the genre he cultivated Dostoevsky belonged among the novelists and yielded to some of them in this or that respect, but Dostoevsky had one main advantage over them all—he saw not only his immediate surroundings but far ahead.

Other than Dostoevsky, all our best novelists treat the life surrounding them as they find it, as it has been composed and expressed —in its ready-made, solid, and clear forms. Such in particular are the novels of Goncharov and Lev Tolstoy. They both reproduce Russian society (landowners, petty officials, sometimes peasants) as it has been shaped by centuries, with mores long existent, partly decayed and partly decaying. The novels of these two writers are decidedly similar in artistic subject, despite the distinctive features of their talents. The distinctive peculiarity of Goncharov is that strength of artistic generalization, thanks to which he could create such an all-Russian type as Oblomov, whose like *in breadth* we do not find in any other Russian writer.[2] As for Tolstoy, all his works are distinguished not so much by broad types (not one of his heroes has become a household name) as by masterly pictorial minuteness, by clear depiction of every kind of detail in the life of man and nature, his chief strength being in the sharpest reproduction of *the mechanics of spiritual phenomena.* But this picturing of external details and this psychological analysis appear against the immutable background of a ready-made, already established life, the life of the Russian noble family, accompanied by the still more static figures of the simple people. The soldier Karataev is too humble to overshadow the gentry, and even the world-wide historical figure of Napoleon cannot extend this narrow horizon: the master of Europe is shown only so far as his life corresponds to the life of the Russian nobleman. This correspondence can be limited to very little, for instance, to the famous washing scene in which the Napoleon of Count Tolstoy worthily competes with the Gogolian General Betrishchev.[3] In this immutable world everything is clear and definite, everything is established; if there is a desire for something else, a striving to get out of this framework, then this striving is turned not forward but backward, to a still more simple and immutable life—to the life of nature (*The Cossacks*, "Three Deaths").

The artistic world of Dostoevsky presents a completely antithetical

[2] In comparison with Oblomov, all the Famusovs and Molchalins, Onegins and Pechorins, Manilovs and Sobakeviches, not to mention the heroes of Ostrovsky, have only a *special* significance. (Author's note.)

[3] A character in the second volume of *Mertvye dushi.*

character. Here everything is in ferment, nothing is established, everything is just becoming. Here the subject of the novel is not social *being* but social *movement*. Of all our noted novelists, only Dostoevsky took social movement as the main subject of his work. He is usually compared in this connection with Turgenev, but on no sufficient basis. To characterize the general significance of a writer one should take his best, not his worst works. The best works of Turgenev, in particular *A Huntsman's Sketches* and *A Nest of the Gentry*, present a wonderful picture not of social movement, but only of a social *state*— that of the same old noble world which we found in Goncharov and Lev Tolstoy. Although Turgenev later diligently followed our social movement and partly submitted to its influence, still he did not divine the sense of this movement and the novel especially devoted to this subject (*Virgin Soil*) was a total failure.[4]

Dostoevsky did not submit to the influence of the trends dominant around him, he did not obediently follow the phases of social movement; he foresaw the windings of this movement—and he *judged* them beforehand. He could judge them rightfully, for he had a standard of judgment in his faith, which placed him above the dominant currents, allowed him to see much further than these currents and not be carried along by them. Thanks to his faith, Dostoevsky correctly foresaw the highest far-off goal of the whole movement, clearly saw its deviations from this goal, rightly judged and justly condemned these deviations. This just condemnation referred only to the wrong ways and improper means of the social movement, not to the movement itself, which was necessary and desirable. The condemnation referred to a shallow understanding of social truth, to a false social ideal, but not to the search for social truth, not to the striving to realize a social ideal. This last was still ahead for Dostoevsky: he had faith not only in the past but in the future kingdom of God, and he understood the indispensability of labor and deeds for its accomplishment. He who knows the genuine goal of the movement can and must judge deviations from it. Dostoev-

---

[4] Although the word "nihilism" in its commonly used meaning belongs to Turgenev, the practical sense of the nihilist movement was not divined by him, and its later manifestations, far removed from Bazarov's conversation, were a terrible surprise to the author of *Fathers and Sons*. (Author's note.)

sky had all the more right to this because he had himself initially experienced those deviations, he had himself stood on the wrong road. The positive religious ideal, which raised Dostoevsky so high over the dominant currents of social thought, was not given to him straightaway, it was achieved by him through suffering in a serious and prolonged struggle. He judged what he knew, and his judgment was righteous. The clearer the lofty theoretical truth became for him, the more decisively did he have to condemn the false ways of social action.

The general sense of all Dostoevsky's work, or the significance of Dostoevsky as a social agent, consists in the resolution of this twofold question: of the lofty ideal of society and the genuine way to its achievement.

The lawful cause of social movement is contained in the contradiction between the moral claims of the person and the established social order. That is where Dostoevsky began as a chronicler and interpreter of, and at the same time an active participant in, the new social movement. A deep feeling of social injustice, although in a most inoffensive form, was evoked in his first tale, *Poor People*. The social sense of this tale (which his later novel *The Insulted and Injured* comes close to) amounts to that ancient and eternally new axiom, that in the existent order of things the (ethically) *best* people are at the same time essentially the *worst* for society, for which reason they are destined to be poor people, insulted and injured.[5]

If social injustice had remained for Dostoevsky only a theme for a tale or a novel, then he would have remained only a literary man and would not have attained his particular significance in the life of Russian society. But for Dostoevsky the content of his tales was a vital problem. He at once put the question on an ethical and practical ground. Having seen and censured what is done in the world, he asked, "What must be done?"

---

[5] This is the same theme as that of Victor Hugo's *Les Miserables*—the contrast between the inner ethical merit of man and his particular situation. Dostoevsky valued this novel very highly and was somewhat, although rather superficially, under the influence of Victor Hugo (the propensity for antithesis). Dickens and George Sand, apart from Pushkin and Gogol, influenced him more. (Author's note.)

First of all, a simple and clear solution presented itself: the best people, seeing in others and in themselves a susceptibility to social injustice, united must rise against it and re-create society in their own way.

When his first naïve attempt[6] to carry out this solution led Dostoevsky to the firing squad and to a forced labor camp, he, like his comrades, could at first see in such a conclusion of his schemes only that he had failed and that brute force had been used against him. The sentence which befell him was hard, but a sense of injury did not prevent Dostoevsky from understanding that he was wrong in his schemes for a radical social change which was necessary only to him and to his comrades.

It was in the midst of the horrors in the house of the dead that Dostoevsky first consciously met with the truth of the people's feelings and in its light clearly saw the wrongness of his revolutionary strivings. The enormous majority of Dostoevsky's fellow convicts were from the simple folk and, with a few striking exceptions, were the worst people of the folk. But the worst people of the simple folk usually preserve what the people of the intelligentsia lose: faith in God and a recognition of their own sinfulness. Simple criminals, while standing out from the national mass by their wicked deeds, are not at all separated from it in their feelings and opinions, in their religious world view. In the house of the dead Dostoevsky found actual "poor" (or, to use the folk expression, unfortunate) "people." These former poor people, whom he had left behind, still could have a refuge from social injuries in the feeling of their own dignity, in their personal excellence. The convicts had none of *that*, but they did have something greater. The worst people of the house of the dead returned to Dostoevsky what the best people of the intelligentsia had taken away from him. If there, among the representatives of enlightenment, the remnants of religious feeling compelled him to pale at the blasphemy of a progressive literary man,[7] then here, in the house of the dead, this sentiment had to revive and be renewed under the

[6] Naïve strictly on Dostoevsky's side; the ways of social revolution were extremely vague to him. (Author's note.)

[7] An allusion to Belinsky. Dostoevsky's recollection of Belinsky's blasphemous statements was known to his friends; see, e.g., his letter to Strakhov, May 30, 1871, or the chapter "Starye liudi" in *Dnevnik pisatelia* (1873).

impressions of the humble and pious faith of the convicts. While these people seemed forgotten by the Church and oppressed by the state, they had faith in the Church and did not repudiate the state. At the most distressful moment, behind the fierce and violent mob of convicts, there arose in Dostoevsky's memory the majestic and gentle image of the peasant serf Marei comforting his frightened young master with love.[8] He felt and understood that in the face of this lofty divine truth all his homemade truth was a lie, and the attempt to press this lie on others was a crime.

Instead of the malice of an unsuccessful revolutionary, Dostoevsky took away from the prison camp the luminous view of an ethically reborn man. "The more faith there is, the more unity, and if there is love, too, then everything is done," he wrote. This ethical strength, renewed by contact with the folk, gave Dostoevsky a right to a lofty place ahead of our social movement, not as a servitor of the concerns of the day, but as a genuine mover of social thought.

The positive social ideal was still not fully clarified in Dostoevsky's mind upon his return from Siberia. But three verities regarding it were absolutely clear to him: he understood, first of all, that isolated persons, although the best people, do not have the right to coerce society in the name of their personal superiority; he also understood that social truth is not devised by isolated minds but rooted in the feeling of the whole people; and finally, he understood that this truth has religious significance and is necessarily tied to faith in Christ, to the ideal of Christ.

Dostoevsky's awareness of these verities far outstripped the then prevailing trend of social thought, and thanks to this, he could *foresee* and point out where this trend leads. We all know that the novel *Crime and Punishment* was written just before the crime of Danilov[9] and Karakozov, and the novel *The Devils* before the trial of the Nechaevists.[10] The sense of the first of these novels, despite

---

[8] Marei, a serf on the Dostoevskys' estate, Darovoe, comforted the child Dostoevsky on an occasion described in *Dnevnik pisatelia* (February, 1876).

[9] Danilov was a student at Moscow University who killed and robbed a pawn-broker in accord with some particular plan he had. (Author's note.)

[10] The student D. Karakozov made an attempt to assassinate Alexander II in 1866. With regard to the Nechaev affair, Solovev's claim is wrong: S. G. Nechaev

all the depth of the details, is very simple and clear, although many have not understood it. The central character is a representative of the view that every strong man is his own master and everything is permitted him. In the name of his personal superiority, in the name of his *power*, he thinks he has the right to commit murder, and he really does commit it. But suddenly this deed, which he considered only a transgression of external, senseless law and a bold defiance of social prejudice, suddenly this deed turns out for his conscience to be something much larger, turns out to be a sin, a transgression of internal ethical truth. The transgression of the external law receives legal retribution from without in exile and prison camp, but the internal sin of pride, which separated the strong man from humanity and led him to the murder of a human being—this internal sin of self-idolatry can be expiated only by an internal ethical act of renunciation. Limitless self-reliance must vanish before faith in what is more than *self*, and fabricated self-justification must be humbled before the lofty truth of God which lives in those very simple and puny people whom the strong man regarded as insignificant insects.

In *The Devils*, if the same theme is not deepened, still it is significantly expanded and complicated. A whole society of people, overcome by a dream of a violent revolution in order to remake the world in their own way, commit brutal crimes and perish in a shameful way, and Russia, healed by faith, accedes to its savior.

The social significance of these novels is great; important social phenomena, which were soon to be laid bare, were prophesied in them; what is more, these phenomena were censured in the name of a lofty religious theoretical truth, and the best way out for the social movement was pointed out in the acceptance of this theoretical truth.

Condemning the quest for an arbitrary, abstract truth which produces only crime, Dostoevsky opposes to it the people's religious ideal based on faith in Christ. A return to this faith is the general solution both for Raskolnikov and for the whole society possessed by

murdered I. Ivanov in November, 1869, and Dostoevsky wrote *Besy* (1871–72) using the material of the trial rather than anticipating it.

devils. Only faith in Christ, living in the people, contains that positive social ideal in which the isolated person becomes one with all. It is demanded of the person who has lost this solidarity, first of all, that he should give up his prideful seclusion, and by this ethical act of self-renunciation be reunited with the entire people. But in the name of what? In the name only that it is a people, that sixty million is more than a single unit, or than a thousand? There probably are people who understand it precisely this way. But such a simple understanding would be completely alien to Dostoevsky. Demanding from the secluded person a return to the people, he first of all had in view a return to that genuine faith which is still preserved among the people. The main thing in this social ideal of brotherhood or general solidarity in which Dostoevsky had faith was its religious-ethical, not its national meaning. Already in *The Devils* there is a cutting mockery of those people who worship the folk only because it is a folk and value Orthodoxy as an attribute of the Russian nation.

If we wished to use one word to denote that social ideal to which Dostoevsky came, the word would be not the people, but the *Church*.

We have faith in the Church as the mystical body of Christ; we also know the Church as the collection of believers of a confession. But what is the Church as a social ideal? Dostoevsky had no theological pretensions, and therefore we do not have the right to look for any logical definitions of the Church's essence in him. But, preaching the Church as a social ideal, he expressed a completely clear and definite claim, as clear and definite as the claims professed by European socialism (although directly contradictory to them). (Therefore in his last diary Dostoevsky called the people's faith in the Church our Russian socialism.) European socialists demand that everything be violently brought down to the purely material level of well-fed, contented workers, they demand that state and society be brought down to the rank of simple economic association. The "Russian socialism" about which Dostoevsky spoke, on the other hand, *elevates* all to the ethical level of the Church as a spiritual brotherhood, although with the preservation of the external inequality of social conditions. It demands the spiritualization of the whole state and social structure by the incarnation in it of the verity and life of Christ.

The Church as the positive social ideal was to be manifested in the central idea of a new novel or new series of novels, of which only the first was written—*The Brothers Karamazov*.[11]

If this social idea of Dostoevsky is directly contradictory to the ideal of those contemporary activists who are portrayed in *The Devils*, just as alien to them are the ways of its achievement. Their way is that of violence and murder, Dostoevsky's way is that of *ethical deed*, and furthermore, a twofold deed, a twofold act of ethical self-renunciation. First of all, it is demanded of the person that he repudiate his arbitrary opinions, his homemade truths, in the name of the general faith and truth of all the people. The person must bow before the people's faith, not because it is the people's, but because it is genuine. If this is so, it means that the people itself, in the name of that verity in which it has faith, must renounce and give up everything in its own life which is not in agreement with religious verity.

The possession of this verity cannot be the privilege of a nation, just as it cannot be the privilege of an isolated person. Verity can only be *universal*, and the deed of service to this universal verity is demanded of a people, even, indeed *indispensably*, at the sacrifice of its national egoism. The people must justify itself before the universal truth, and must offer up its soul, if it wants to save it.

Universal truth is incarnated in the Church. The final ideal and goal is not in nationality, which of itself is only a subordinate power, but in the Church, which is the loftiest object of service, which demands the ethical deed not only from the person, but from the whole nation.

And so the Church as the positive social ideal, as the foundation and goal of all our thoughts and actions, as a deed of the whole nation, as the direct way for the realization of this ideal—this is the last word to which Dostoevsky came and which illuminated all his work with a prophetic light.

[11] Dostoevsky communicated to me the main idea, and partially even the plot, of his new work in a brief outline in the summer of 1878. It was at this time that we traveled to Optina Pustyn (and not in 1879, as is mistakenly stated in N. N. Strakhov's memoirs). (Author's note.)

ACKNOWLEDGMENTS

Thanks are due to the American Philosophical Society and to the University of North Carolina at Chapel Hill for their support of the work which has led to the present publication.

The editors also wish to express their gratitude to Washington Square Press, Inc., and Penguin Books, Ltd., for their permission to quote from their editions of *Dead Souls* and *War and Peace*, respectively.

Index

183